SECONDARY SOCIAL STUDIES CURRICULUM, ACTIVITIES, AND MATERIALS

James L. Barth
Purdue University

UNIVERSITY
PRESS OF
AMERICA

LANHAM • NEW YORK • LONDON

Copyright © 1984 by

University Press of America,™ **Inc.**

4720 Boston Way
Lanham. MD 20706

3 Henrietta Street
London WC2E 8LU England

Library of Congress Cataloging in Publication Data

Barth, James L., 1931-
    Secondary social studies curriculum, activities, and
materials.

    1. Social sciences—Study and teaching (Secondary)—
United States. I. Title.
H62.5U5B34   1984   300'.7'1273   83-26103
ISBN 0-8191-3797-9 (pbk. : alk. paper)

All University Press of America books are produced on acid-free
paper which exceeds the minimum standards set by the National
Historical Publications and Records Commission.

Public opportunities for expressions of appreciation come so seldomly that

such opportunities must be treasured and applied to special persons.

Barbara Sue Bauhof Barth is one of those special persons,

and it is to Barbara that this book is dedicated.

PREFACE

In 1971 and again in 1978 the National Council for the Social Studies published The Social Studies Curriculum Guidelines. These guidelines were significant because they set forth for the first time since the creation of the field what classroom teachers ought to be doing when they teach social studies. Simply, according to the guidelines, the social studies curriculum would encourage teachers of kindergarten through twelfth grade to emphasize four objectives: gaining knowledge, processing, valuing, and participating. The guidelines offer the opportunity for teachers in all school systems to coordinate their social studies programs. Those who were looking for some way to integrate a school social studies curriculum found the national guidelines most helpful. The effort to fulfill those guidelines by suggesting an integrated set of activities for kindergarten through twelfth grade started in 1975. The first set of activities for kindergarten through eighth grade was published in Elementary and Junior High/Middle School Social Studies Curriculum, Activities, and Materials in 1979. A revised edition was published in 1983. The companion book, Secondary Social Studies Curriculum, Activities, and Materials, completes the curriculum for ninth through twelfth grades.

The activities in Secondary Social Studies Curriculum have been tested in college classrooms and secondary schools for the past eight years. And though in most cases the activities have passed the test of time, teachers, and students, the text still must be viewed as the creation of one social studies educator. It is not likely that a single author could identify just the right activities for the 36 different required and elective social studies courses that could be offered in a school. Having noted the limitations, it is also appropriate to note that this activities book needed to be written, for there are no other books that illustrate the national curriculum guidelines or offer

v

an integrated, synchronized set of materials for each grade level. Simply, no other works have tried to apply the Council's guidelines to grade level activities.

Undergraduates in teacher education, experienced teachers in graduate programs, curriculum coordinators, university professors, and workshop coordinators, all of whom are concerned with social studies, have been asking for illustrations of an integrated social studies curriculum. They will find that curriculum here. Those social studies educators who are looking for activities that emphasize a multicultural approach, differentiated instruction, and materials for special students--including the gifted and talented--will also find those materials here. The more than 300 pages of activities illustrate the National Council objectives and should stimulate the reader to think creatively about teaching social studies.

The almost decade it took to complete this text should suggest the problems of gathering, compiling, evaluating, and editing the activities. No one person does this alone. Faithful teachers were involved in the teaching and evaluation of the activities in the United States and in other countries. Mary Ellen Thrall, the editor and final draft typist of this text, measurably improved the manuscript through her imaginative layout of the activities. I am in debt to Barbara Sue Bauhof Barth for not only reviewing and typing the first and second copies of the manuscript but also for offering editorial judgment. Without her support this book would not have been completed.

Purdue University   J.L.B.
1984

TABLE OF CONTENTS

INTRODUCTION TO THE THEORY AND PRACTICE OF SOCIAL STUDIES

Social studies, as an organized subject field, has traditionally been a requirement of the elementary, junior high/middle, and high school curriculum. Yet many teachers do not know that there is a social studies curriculum, nor are they aware of how the social studies curriculum is to be integrated and taught. In some states elementary social studies is required to be taught no less than one half-hour a day, and in junior high/middle school no less than one period per day.

Some states mandate, that is, require, that specific topics and, in some cases, certain content be covered at specified grade levels. For example, most states require a number of semesters of social studies for high school graduation. An illustration of this would be a state which requires four semesters of social studies for graduation including two semesters of American History, one semester of American Government, and one semester of any other social studies citizenship course. Some states mandate specific content which should be treated in social studies courses. The following is an example of a state law applied to the teaching of social studies:

> (a) Each public and non-public school shall provide within the two (2) weeks preceding each general election for all students in each of grades six (6) through twelve (12) five (5) full recitation periods of class discussion concerning the system of government . . ., methods of voting, party structures, election laws, and the responsibilities of citizen participation in government and in elections.

> (b) No one may receive a high school diploma unless he has completed a two (2) semester course in American history.[1]

The fact remains, even though states have legislation on the teaching of social studies and citizenship courses, that the social studies curriculum appears to many teachers as unrelated fragments of history and geography. One's remembrances of social studies are bits and pieces of historical events, an odd pile of geographic trivia, and an assortment of government offices, titles, and personalities once memorized for a final examination. The odd lot of memories does not call forth a curriculum. No consistent themes, interesting activities, or developmental and integrative materials come forth to remind one that in the end students were being prepared to be fully functioning, responsible citizens in a complex, interdependent, democratic society. Elementary and secondary schools require students to take the social studies curriculum, though, in fact, the separate courses at the secondary level may be called Global/International Studies, Problems of Democracy, Values and Issues, Senior Problems, etc., whereas in higher education the curriculum name becomes social science and the courses are called Microeconomics, Political Science, Urban Sociology, Child Psychology, or Cultural Anthropology. The notion of social studies is very confusing to some, for not only is it difficult to remember a social studies curriculum which students undoubtedly followed to graduate from high school, but now in college even the name of the curriculum is changed to social science. The proper assumption that one should make is that social studies as a curriculum does not reach beyond high school years. It is, then, an area of study unique and initially created for the school years.

Why Social Studies?

Before there was a social studies field, there was history and geography. One hundred years ago your great-great-grandparents would have studied history and geography, not social studies. There was no social studies. The field of social studies was dimly perceived at the end of the 19th Century. Building on early foundations, social studies was conceived as a curriculum for the schools in the early 20th Century.[2] Clearly, an examination of the texts used in the one-room schoolhouses at the turn of the century would show that responsibility for citizenship training was borne by the entire school curriculum. After the turn of the century, and the adoption of social studies as a collegiate field of study, the mission of citizenship education became the goal. Other subject areas gravitated to purposes other than citizenship, leaving social studies courses and curriculum with the primary responsibility for the training of future citizens.

Why the change from the traditional subjects of history and geography to a social studies curriculum? That change occurred, in part, because some of the educators at the turn of the century identified what they thought to be a crisis. By 1900 America had become an industrialized, interdependent, urban society. That society was in crisis, for the quality of urban life, including the conditions of the factories, was condemning generations of American citizens to lives that were not consistent with a democratic heritage. Educators believed that public schools should be places where future citizens would learn to improve the quality of their lives. The social studies curriculum in those schools was intended to provide an organized, integrative citizenship education aimed at training decision-makers who could use a democratic foundation to earn their dream of the good life.

In summary, the change from traditional subject areas to a social studies school curriculum occurred because some educators believed that public school education should offer practice in democracy, including decision-making. Citizens could not participate in the control of their own lives unless they had training in the skills of reasoning, valuing, and participating. Traditional subject matter of history and geography and traditional teaching as practiced at the turn of the century could not offer a proper training for contemporary citizenship. To illustrate this point, history courses offered in the secondary schools at the turn of the century concentrated on early and medieval western European history. Discussions of modern or contemporary problems that actually faced citizens in 1900 were not part of the curriculum. Geography was conceived as land forms and imports and government was taught as structure and function without reference to the actual practices of the political system. Social studies was to be "something different"--it was to be designed to appeal to the needs and interests of those youth who were not normally served by the secondary school. That is, social studies was to become general education for all students.

What is Social Studies?

Because social studies was conceived and applied some seventy years ago, it does not follow that all schools or teachers have necessarily adopted the notion of a social studies curriculum. It was probably true that social studies was conceived as a citizenship training curriculum for those who attended the public schools. Many of the private academies and more well-to-do public school systems have never accepted social studies in place of the traditional subject content areas, choosing instead to allow the community or the atmosphere of the prep school to instruct students in a proper citizen's conduct. Some have even claimed that social studies is general education for the poor, the immigrant, and the lower-middle class who need an organized introduction to the traditions, the geography, the values, and the problems and processes of the "American way." Others have argued that social studies ought to be a curriculum of general education designed to promote the development of citizens who think for themselves and who are decision-makers. It should be no surprise that different interpretations of the goal of social studies have arisen over the years, for there are those who believe that "the right values and right answers" should be indoctrinated. Alternatively, other educators believe that the goal of social studies should be citizenship based on a process of decision-making. To this day, authorities within the field

debate the meaning of social studies, and though there has emerged some agreement, the field is still evolving. The meaning of social studies you should
find for yourself in such books as The Nature of the Social Studies or Defining
the Social Studies.[3] However, in brief:

> Social Studies is an integration of social
> science and humanities for the purpose of
> instruction in citizenship education.[4]

One part of that definition is particularly significant, for the definition
tells us that the reason for teaching social studies is instruction in citizenship education.

The Goal of Social Studies

Simply put, the goal of teaching social studies is citizenship. If we
agree the goal is citizenship, then what must a teacher do to achieve that
goal? This is a point on which some social studies educators have agreed.

The Four Objectives for Teaching Social Studies to Achieve the Goal of Citizenship[5]

Social studies educators agree that to achieve the goal of citizenship
the teacher should teach social studies to achieve the following four objectives:

1. Gain knowledge about the human condition which includes past,
    present, and future perspectives.

2. Acquire skills necessary to process information.

3. Develop the skills to examine values and beliefs.

4. Encourage the application of knowledge through active partici-
    pation in society.

For use in this book, the four objectives are shortened to:

1. Gaining knowledge (work, roles, services, define, identify)

2. Processing information (interpreting symbols, map skills, fact from fiction, inquiry, propaganda, questioning, stereotyping, bias)

3. Valuing (evaluate, divergent, clarify, rank)

4. Participating (find and solve, social action, establish rules)

Perhaps it is sufficient to know that the social studies field is young and changing. What I do want teachers to know are the four objectives for teaching social studies. In principle, social studies teachers generally accept the four objectives. Just what does this mean? It means that a teacher will plan to practice all four objectives when teaching social studies, whether in kindergarten or twelfth grade. In short, teachers should help students gain knowledge, process information, develop the skill to examine values, and, finally, apply knowledge through active civic participation. The argument is that if students practice the four objectives throughout a K-12 curriculum, then that social studies curriculum is aimed at the goal of citizenship education.

The Meaning of Citizenship

The four objectives define the meaning of citizenship in a social studies program. Given the conflicting meanings of citizenship in pluralistic American society, no one definition has captured the allegiance of all citizens. In such a pluralistic society, the social studies program, rather than offering a definitive definition of citizenship, offers the four objectives (as authored by the social studies teachers' professional organization, the National Council for the Social Studies [NCSS]). One might conclude that the good citizen gains knowledge, processes, and values, and participates in, practices, and perfects these skills in a social studies program, leading to citizens capable of defining the meaning of citizenship for themselves. In practice, then, the four objectives identify the skills necessary for citizens to define their meaning of citizenship.

Is Knowing the Objectives Important?

Why is it important that secondary teachers know the four objectives before reading this book? Because all activities and materials found in this book are categorized under one of the four objectives. In other words, for each subject area all activities and materials are organized to provide instruction in the four objectives. In each subject area (grades 9 through 12) there are activities designed to gain knowledge, process information, develop valuing skills, and encourage participation.

One might ask, "Even if activities are identified for each of the four objectives in the subject areas, why is this different or unique?" This book is one of the first attempts, along with its companion volume, Elementary and Junior High/Middle School Social Studies Curriculum, Activities, and Materials, to organize a kindergarten-twelfth grade social studies curriculum that says to teachers, "The goal and objectives for which you teach kindergarten are the same as those used in each of the succeeding grades right up through the twelfth grade." For the first time teachers can see that their instruction is part of a developmental social studies curriculum; that each teacher, though the courses and topics differ, is following the same general objectives. No longer need teachers feel isolated, alone, separated from others, all teaching bits and pieces of social studies, not knowing they are part of an overall curriculum.

Teaching social studies that is part of an organized school curriculum should be encouraged. In some states social studies seems to have been included in primary education almost as an afterthought--after reading, language arts, math--and in secondary school as a list of unrelated courses. Hopefully teachers will be more likely to use social studies content if they know that the lessons taught in their classes are to be followed the next year by lessons that build developmentally upon their lessons. In summary, if teachers know that the social studies curriculum has continuity and is developmental, they might be more inclined to teach the curriculum, and the students might be more inclined to remember a program that emphasized the development of their skills as citizens.

Some Activities and Materials Include All Four Objectives

One could argue that the best type of social studies activities should be organized to provide knowledge, process information, value, and participate. As the activities become more complex in grades 4, 5, 6, junior high/middle school, and high school, distinctions between the four objectives tend to blur. It is not unusual for a simulation, game, or project to include all four objectives. One needs to know: that all four objectives should be part of a social studies program; that all four objectives be part of each activity is not important; that activities and materials incorporate at least one of the four objectives is important; that all four objectives be part of a K-12 social studies curriculum is essential.

Social Studies Integrated With Other Fields

Social studies is a distinct subject field, but that does not mean social studies should not be integrated with subject fields which offer opportunities for integration. Many of the activities suggested in this book could be and should be found in methods and activities books in other fields, e.g., English, science, foreign languages, health. Some of the social studies activities and materials in this book will look familiar, and while reading through activities in each subject area teachers might say, "I saw that in science methods," or "That's talked about in health. I didn't know that activity could be used in social studies." It is no accident that activities are designed to be integrated with lessons in other fields. Common sense alone tells a teacher who has limited time to teach a course that they should look for opportunities to integrate their topics with content taught by other teachers. Given that social studies is by definition an integration of man's knowledge (humanities, the social sciences, science), it remains the responsibility of the social studies teachers to seek collaboration with their colleagues in other subject fields.

Social Studies Asks the Important Questions

It is natural to suppose that one's field is the most important. Surely without math, science, reading, and music the world would be different. But for the moment consider the social studies educator's point of view. In other fields questions are asked that have to do with why and how things work. In social studies the really important questions have to do with the quality of life. Social studies questions are: "Who am I?" "Who are you?" "How are we related?" "How did we get this way?" "What was the past?" "What is the future?" "Shall we live for the present?" Trying to find answers to these questions takes a lifetime. The task of elementary, junior high/middle, and high school teachers is to use social studies to start the search for answers following the skills of helping students gain information, evaluate that information through processing, test values and beliefs, and make decisions as the basis of participation. The important questions of life (i.e., "Who am I?"

"What do I want?" "What do I think?") are the essence of social studies content, and as one is better able to respond to those questions the goal of social studies citizenship is achieved.

Materials for Differentiated Instruction, Multicultural and Exceptional Students[6]

One would not anticipate that teachers will read straight through this book, any more than one would read straight through a dictionary or encyclopedia. Teachers will identify their subject area and start by reading those parts that are particularly pertinent to them. This is consistent with the author's intention that teachers should be concerned with improving that which they already do. Also, it is important to note that the materials and activities are designed to account for a multicultural approach in each subject area. It is entirely possible that the classroom teacher will find materials and activities that will be appropriate for the differentiated instructional program that is now mandated for many school districts.

Having anticipated how teachers might read this book, the author has designed each chapter to be self-contained. Chapter I is called "Civics and U.S. Government." The activities reflect these two courses, and though related they are usually offered at the ninth and twelfth grade levels. Chapter II is called "Global/International Studies, World History, and Geography," reflecting the tenth grade emphasis on electives offering area studies outside North America. Chapter III is called "U.S. History." Chapter IV is called "Senior Problems, Values/Issues, Futures, and Careers," which reflects courses normally taught at the twelfth grade level.

The subject area courses chosen for these chapters are based upon surveys on social studies courses offered in high schools throughout the U.S. over the past twenty years. Though most subject areas are, in part, found in the activities and materials, there was no attempt to cover all of the different subject areas possible. The topic Future Studies is treated in each of the subject areas rather than appearing in its own separate chapter. Each subject area includes materials and activities for exceptional students, including gifted and talented.

Each chapter is purposely written following the same pattern, so that to know the pattern of one will be to know the pattern of all chapters. Use this book as a dictionary, use it as a text, use it to coordinate a consistent social studies program, because it is a guide to the integration of skills, topics, themes, activities, and materials which should be part of any citizenship program.

Notes

1 Miller, C. W., & Davis, H. D. Indiana law as applied to social studies (1976 Indiana Code: 20-10, 1-4-3, Sec. 3). In J. L. Barth & C. Keener (Eds.), Teaching social studies in Indiana. Indianapolis: Indiana Council for the Social Studies, 1978, p. 7. (This bulletin originally appeared as a special section of the Indiana Social Studies Quarterly, 1977-78, 30(3).)

2 Barth, J. L., & Shermis, S. S. Social studies goals: The historical perspective. In C. Berryman (Ed.), Goals for the social studies: Toward the twenty-first century. Journal of Research and Development in Education, 1980, 13, 2.

3 Barr, R. D., Barth, J. L., & Shermis, S. S. The nature of the social studies (Palm Springs, CA: ETC Publications, 1978), and Defining the social studies, Bulletin 51 (Washington, DC: National Council for the Social Studies, 1977).

4 Barr, Barth, & Shermis, The nature of the social studies, p. 19.

5 The four objectives were originally identified in Social studies guidelines (Washington, DC: National Council for the Social Studies, 1971). The four objectives were also used as the rationale for organizing a social studies teachers' guide--Indiana Department of Public Instruction, Social studies: A guide for curriculum development (Indianapolis, IN: Author, 1978), p. B-1.

6 Some parts of this introduction were originally developed for Elementary and Junior High/Middle School Social Studies Curriculum, Activities, and Materials and have been revised here with the intention of preserving continuity between the two texts.

A SOCIAL STUDIES KINDERGARTEN THROUGH TWELFTH GRADE CURRICULUM

Though the focus is on secondary school social studies, teachers would agree that conceiving social studies as a field in high school only would be a narrow perspective. As in any other field, knowing the whole program is undoubtedly necessary so that one can more easily spot one's part in that total program. What is a social studies kindergarten through twelfth grade curriculum supposed to do for a student? One answer is that the curriculum should help students integrate their life experiences including knowledge gained from a study of the social sciences, history, and humanities for the purpose of performing as effective citizens. Fine, teachers say, "So the goal is to train effective citizens. But just what specifically should an effective citizen be able to do? I, as a teacher, have to know this; otherwise I cannot very well prepare the student for a task without knowing what knowledge and skills are needed." The reader surely can answer this question, having read the preceding Introduction. Of course the answer is that the goal of preparing effective citizens is best accomplished by preparing the student to practice the four objectives of gaining knowledge, processing information, examining values, and knowing how to participate.

A Systematic Curriculum

At each grade level in elementary and junior high/middle school and in each subject area in high school, social studies should be taught so as to emphasize those four objectives. Yes, absolutely. Those four objectives, plus some common activities and materials, offer the best chance for a systematic kindergarten-twelfth grade social studies curriculum. If one agrees that a systematic curriculum should be built primarily upon the teaching of the four objectives at each grade level and in each subject area, then each of the four objectives must be carefully planned. Conceive of a funnel as it <u>spirals</u> and broadens upward from the spout, then imagine how the four objectives are passed from one grade to another, deepening and broadening the child's ability to understand the world. The "deepening and broadening" at each succeeding level is called <u>expanding</u> <u>horizons</u>.

Fragmented Bits and Pieces

Now, be honest when asking yourself this question, "What pattern of social studies topics and courses did I, the reader, follow elementary through high school?" Think about this question for a minute. Odds are that you cannot recall the course topics or whether there was a pattern. If your experience was similar to most high school graduates', you remember social studies as history (with emphasis on events and dates) and geography (with emphasis on land forms and exports), all a bit jumbled together and remembered as fragmented bits and pieces disconnected from time, place, and theme.

Believe it or not, there were supposed to be skills, courses, topics, and patterns taught in a sequential pattern throughout your scholastic years, and together they were to be called the social studies curriculum. Every school system has a social studies curriculum. The fact that you probably do not know this, and also that you do not remember the skills, courses, topics, and patterns practiced on you for twelve years, suggests that the school system was not particularly interested in having you know that a curricular social studies pattern existed. If you are curious at all, you must be wondering why you do not know much about a curriculum that you spent considerable time in school completing.

There are many reasons why you do not know. One reason among many is that teachers--both elementary and secondary--do not know that there might be a state-prescribed social studies curriculum. It is true that nearly all school systems have a kindergarten through twelfth grade social studies curriculum, a part of which may be mandated by the state. That curriculum often is designed by a local school system curriculum committee which has produced a study guide that each social studies teacher in the system is supposed to follow. The practice for many teachers is to ignore the study guide, then proceed to teach whatever course, topic, or pattern fits their individual interests. Of course, the consequences of such liberties have been that little or no continuity exists between courses or topics, and almost no coordination between elementary and secondary levels. Patterns do not emerge, giving the social studies program the appearance of being disjointed, fragmented bits and pieces of government, history, and geography. If math and reading were taught based upon a personal whim of the teacher without planning for continuity, one might guess the consequences. Of course, the same reasoning applies to teaching social studies. Social studies, just as math and reading, requires continuity based upon a developmental system.

Social studies, according to authorities in the field, was never meant to be fragmented bits and pieces. The intent was for a carefully planned curriculum that set forth a pattern of skills, courses, and topics. This chapter introduces a rationale for and the demonstration of a kindergarten through twelfth grade social studies curriculum. Teachers ought to become convinced, based on research on the effect of social studies instruction, that disjointed fragmented bits and pieces of a program are ineffective. A total social studies curriculum aimed at the goal of preparing citizens requires all teachers to know their part in the program. What follows is one illustration of a total curriculum.

Social Studies Curriculum Chart[1]

The following chart is a representation of a curricular pattern that exists throughout the United States. However, this suggested national curricular pattern may not exactly fit any one state pattern.

Instructions: Examine the suggested national curricular pattern in Column 1, then in Column 2 try your hand at identifying the approved (mandated) pattern in your state, then try to identify your school's approved kindergarten-twelfth grade pattern in Column 3.

Column 1 National K-12 Social Studies Curriculum	Column 2 Fill in your state's approved curriculum	Column 3 Fill in your school system's approved K-12 Social Studies Curriculum
Grade/Basic Theme	Grade/Basic Theme	Grade/Basic Theme

K-2   Individuals and Families
 K & Individuals and Families
 1   Locally and in the USA
 2   Individuals and Families
      in Selected Parts of the
      World
	K
	
	1
	2
		K
		
		1
		2

3-4   Communities
 3   The Local Community and
      Selected Communities in
      the USA
 4   Selected Communities of
      the World
	3
	
	4
		3
		
		4

5-6   Countries
 5   The USA Today and Yester-
      day (Postholing certain
      periods in our history
      in the second half of
      the year)
 6   Selected Countries of the
      World (to be studied in
      depth)
	5
	
	6
		5
		
		6

7-8   Basic Problems & Decisions
      in the USA
 7   Problems and Decisions in
      the USA Today
 8   Problems and Decisions in
      the USA Yesterday
	7
	
	8
		7
		
		8

9-10 Cultures
 9   Studies in Depth of the 8
      Major Cultural Areas of
 10   the World "Today and
      Yesterday," Western and
      Non-Western
	9
	
	10
		9
		
		10

11-12 The United States and the
      Emerging International
      Community
 11   United States History
 12   Contemporary Problems in
      the USA and in Other
      Parts of the World
	11
	12
		11
		12

Comment

Some states do not have a suggested kindergarten-twelfth grade social studies curriculum, though there probably are social studies requirements for graduation. The probability is that even if the state does have a mandated curriculum, teachers will not know either their state's or their school system's social studies curriculum. Why is it that school administrators, curriculum directors, social studies teachers, and the students, who obviously are required to pass through a mandated social studies curriculum do not know what their state's or their school's kindergarten-twelfth grade curriculum is? Teachers prepare materials and teach classes and students graduate, not knowing that they are or ought to be part of a systematic program.

Social Studies Course Content, A Brief Overview

Just what content is included in a total K-12 social studies curriculum? The above chart lists, under the suggested national curricular pattern, course titles. Though the titles are suggestive, they give only a hint as to content. Remember, there is no one prescribed national social studies curricular pattern. Each state establishes its own pattern. There are literally fifty different patterns, but, as suggested in the chart, there are similar state patterns. What follows is only a suggestion of a particular pattern of course offerings and content, but the courses do illustrate what a systematic developmental curriculum might be like if planned according to the goal of social studies and the four objectives.[2]

KINDERGARTEN

The child and his investigation of himself, his family, home, school, and neighborhood, and the accompanying living and working functions of each in which the child learns to work in groups, to use classroom tools, to share materials, to use simple inquiry skills, and to engage in social participation.

GRADE 1

Individuals, families, schools, and social institutions of the neighborhood; ways of living and working together using available resources at
home, and in other parts of the world (in other environments); yesterday
and today, with extension of, or introduction of, cooperative and problem-
solving skills.

GRADE 2

Local school neighborhoods, neighborhoods in other countries; how local
communities meet common interests and needs of individuals and institutions through human interaction and through services basic to mankind;
the introduction of valuing skills and simple map reading skills; the
development of the value of responsibility.

GRADE 3

Development of the local community, other communities, states, and regions
in other parts of the world; ways communities adjust to the environments,
develop and use technology and human and natural resources, and adapt
from other cultures while extending student interests; knowledge of
occupations, values and value systems, map skills, organization, and
inquiry processing skills.

GRADE 4

State (history), region, nation, and world communities influenced by the
past; present use of environment, distribution of human and natural
resources, use of societal controls, ever-present problems, and the influence of geography on development with extension of research skills,
problem-solving and valuing activities.

GRADE 5

The United States, Canada (North American Continent), and regions of the
world; the growth and development of nations and regions of the world

with special emphasis on geography, history, physical and cultural environments, and the roles and relationships which develop and exist among them while comparative study, problem-solving, and awareness of how to effect change as an individual are emphasized. Note that study of North America should emphasize historical events between 1400 and the 1850s including the following topics: discovery, colonization, revolution, and geographical development of the United States up to the Civil War.

GRADE 6

Western Europe, Latin America (South and Central American Continent), and other regions of the world, with comparative studies on the growth and development of nations and regions of the world influenced by geography, history, physical and cultural environments, and the roles and relationships which develop and exist among them; also stressing pupil-teacher planning and decision-making.

GRADE 7

Area studies of World Civilization (global studies) including the Middle East, Asia, and Africa.

GRADE 8

United States history (including instruction in the Constitution of the United States of America), with special emphasis on 19th Century, pre- and post-Civil War, industrialization, and internationalism.

GRADES 9, 10, 11, 12

Course offerings of grades 9-12 are allowable at any level but must provide: United States History (2 semesters required, with emphasis on the 20th Century, wars, and social, political, and economic international events; United States Government (2 semesters required or 1 semester of U.S. government or civil government and 1 semester of an acceptable citizenship course). The classes must deal with the historical, political, civic, sociological, economic, and philosophical aspects of the Constitution of the United States. In addition to the required courses, each commissioned high school shall include in the curriculum: ancient, medieval, or modern history, and economic or physical geography. Courses approved for the foregoing additional elective offerings and for other electives are: African Studies, Early World Civilizations, Psychology, Sociology, Urban Affairs, Western Civilization, Anthropology, Asian Studies, Economics, Ethnic Studies (U.S.), Latin America, Area Studies, Modern World Civilization, World Civilization, World Geography, Current Problems, Introduction to Social Science, and Values and Issues.

Expanding Horizons

There are several ideas about the organization of social studies courses and basic themes which you should note from the above kindergarten through twelfth grade curriculum. Notice that social studies starts with individuals, families, and school the first years, and ends twelve years later with contemporary problems of the social system with special interest in the emerging international/global world. This approach is called expanding horizons-- starting with oneself and expanding through the school years to an understanding of the social, political, and economic problems of family, neighborhood, community, state, nation, and the world. The notion of expanding horizons in organizing social studies (skills, courses, and topics) into a consistent developmental curriculum is only one way to visualize the organization of social studies. It is probably true that expanding horizons is the most popular organizing idea, but there are good alternatives such as organization by "basic" concepts and generalizations or by separate social science disciplines.

Spiral

American history is taught three different times throughout the curriculum at grade levels 5, 8, and 11. Also, content about other cultures, that is global studies, is taught at grade levels 2, 4, 6 or 7, 10, and 12. This repeating of topics at ever greater levels of complexity, kindergarten through twelfth grade, is called a spiral. That is, at specific grade levels certain topics and themes are repeated but at a more complex level each time. Imagine what the funnel of a tornado looks like; the small end of the tornado on the ground is kindergarten, with an increase in the size of the funnel as it reaches for the sky representing the higher grades. In practice, when teaching about Latin American, Asian, or African societies in sixth or seventh grade, teachers would be building on topics and themes developed in grades 2 and 4 and preparing students for further study in grades 10 and 12.

Current Events and Comparative Studies

Social studies educators for the past seventy years have strongly recommended that current events and comparative studies be a supplementary part of all social studies instruction. Readiness for current events should originate in first grade and current events is recommended for second grade and each succeeding grade. Each year students should gain additional experience and skill in learning how to inquire into contemporary events and into processing the information about those events. A common thread throughout the entire first through twelfth grade curriculum is current events along with comparative studies. Teachers are encouraged to recall the notion of expanding horizons and the spiral, both of which help to keep social studies content from being seen as fragmented bits and pieces. Both the spiral which holds the bits and pieces together and expanding horizons provide the depth in subject matter and continuity from one grade level to another.

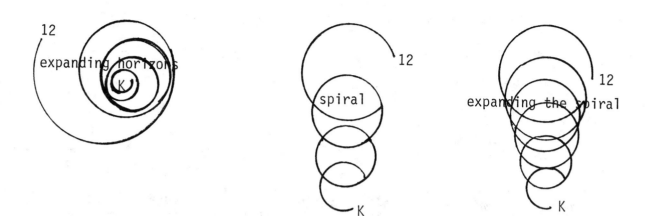

Summary: A Guide to Social Studies Curriculum Construction

Yes, there is a social studies goal, four objectives, themes and concepts, with current ev nts and comparative studies that should be taught in a common kindergarten through twelfth grade social studies curriculum. The goal of social studies is citizenship education. What is citizenship education? It is the four objectives: gaining knowledge, processing information, identifying values and beliefs, and participating through decision-making. What curriculum could account for the four objectives and yet offer opportunities for a differentiated instruction using multicultural materials and yet be for special students including the gifted and talented? The following is an illustration of one response:

spiraling themes and concepts

expanding personal horizons

comparative studies

current events

Teachers might think that practicing the above goals, objectives, and organizational ideas in a social studies curriculum is nothing less than impossible, at the least improbable. One can hear a teacher say, "No way! It's too complex!" There is a way, a way to make the "complex" work. The following chapters on activities and materials in each subject area offer, in part, a practical response that should help social studies teachers achieve the goal of preparing effective citizens.

Notes

[1] The first column on the National Curriculum Pattern was suggested by Leonard S. Kenworthy, Changing the social studies curriculum: Some guidelines and a proposal. Social Education, May 1968, p. 485.

[2] Indiana Department of Public Instruction. Social studies: A guide for curriculum development. Indianapolis: Author, 1978, p. A-4.

NOTES

CHAPTER I

CIVICS AND U.S. GOVERNMENT

ACTIVITIES AND MATERIALS FOR CIVICS AND U.S. GOVERNMENT

CHAPTER I
CIVICS AND U.S. GOVERNMENT

Organization of the Chapter

Each chapter represents a particular subject area, in this case civics and U.S. government. Each chapter consists of three parts: the first part is a brief discussion on courses, topics, and national trends in teaching civics and U.S. government throughout the United States; the second part is an example of a state civics and U.S. government program; the third part has activities and materials for the subject area categorized by the four objectives of teaching social studies--gaining knowledge, processing, valuing, and participating.

I. Topics Taught and National Trends in Teaching Civics and U.S. Government

Many school districts offer both civics at the ninth grade level and U.S. government at the twelfth grade level. Usually civics is an elective course whereas in many states U.S. government is at least a one-semester required course offered in combination with problems of democracy, economics, or sociology.

Course, Topics, and Themes Frequently Covered in Civics and U.S. Government

Objectives of the Civics Course

The traditional civics course will provide students with the structure and function of government which includes governmental processes and institutions at the local, state, national, and international levels, with the objective of encouraging a commitment to democratic institutions. Emphasis is on developing attitudes and skills that will contribute to active and responsible citizenship; expanding the pupil's growth in social studies skills, including critical thinking and problem solving skills; and encouraging rational consideration of current societal problems.

Objectives of the U.S. Government Course

The objective of the traditional U.S. government course is to encourage students to identify the structure and function of national, state, and local governments with the intent of developing a commitment to democratic institutions. In recent years an alternative objective has received popular support from political scientists which encourages critical analysis of the real behavior of political systems, an examination of how the political system actually works at national, state, and local levels with the intent of developing an attitude of critical thinking. This latter objective would have Social Studies Taught as Social Science, whereas the traditional structure-function objective would have Social Studies Taught as Citizenship Transmission.

Basic Content of the Civics Course

The course usually centers on local, state, and national governments: their structure, services they provide, how they operate; how officials are selected, responsibilities of citizens; political parties and elections; and origins of democratic representative government. Sometimes units include attention to Western European origins of democratic institutions and international organizations, especially the United Nations. Some courses include a unit or units on the American economic system and the individual as a consumer and a worker. Some include attention to authoritarian (usually communist) political and economic systems. Other units which are recommended in one or more curriculum guides are: study of a selected current social problem; propaganda analysis; education; juvenile social problems, the family; prejudice; science and race.

Basic Content of the U.S. Government Course

The following are units and topics usually covered in a government course. Emphasis is upon historical documents and theories of government as an historical context for the development of government in the United States. Special emphasis is upon the Constitution with a companion unit on the structure and function of the federal government. There is usually a unit on the citizen's role in government including study of political parties and state and local government. Culminating units are usually over U.S. foreign relations and the role of the U.N. with a comparative study of communism and democracy as they influence world affairs.

Trends in Teaching Civics

Increased attention to international relations and organizations seems to be a trend. Information about communist governmental and economic systems has been introduced into some civics courses. For example, one school system devotes the second semester to "Comparative Political and Economic Systems." Some school systems seem to be combining some "junior" problems units with study of the U.S. political and economic system. However, the traditional civics course predominates in many school systems, where the major focus remains on local, state, and federal government structure. Where schools are seriously revising their total social studies programs, they are moving to a study of culture areas of the world and are putting some of the civics content into the earlier junior high/middle school years.

Trends in Teaching U.S. Government

There seems to be increased attention to the role of the U.S. government in world affairs, international organizations and international relations, and the conflict with the communist block nations. Some courses include a unit on comparative government, sometimes labeled "Democracy vs. Totalitarianism" or "Democracy vs. Communism." The unit on comparative government customarily compares governments of the U.S., Great Britain, and the U.S.S.R. The trend, however, is to include other nations in Europe, Africa, and Asia in the comparisons. Under pressure from social scientists, some teachers and text materials are emphasizing behavioral political approaches replacing the traditional structure and function approach.

II.   Illustration of a State Civics and U.S. Government Course

There is no one prescribed social studies program throughout the United States. However, one state's description of its civics and U.S. government program will illustrate the content which the state expects to be taught. This illustration identifies a state's suggested social studies curriculum for civics and U.S. government.

> This course provides an opportunity to explore the political and governing processes, to study in depth the elements of political theory and government structures that they will soon, if not already, be participating in, politics of the American People, and the various forms of political behavior. The eighteen-year-old vote has added new impetus to this course and demands that we give the student opportunities to examine, to evaluate, and to make decisions concerning the workings of the system in which he lives. The content should include topics such as the constitutional basis of government, the legislative, judicial, and executive processes, government, finance and personnel, civil rights and responsibilities, and the politics of American government.[1]

III. Activities and Materials Categorized by
Gaining Knowledge, Processing, Valuing, and Participating

A. General Objective: To gain knowledge about the human condition which includes past, present, and future

   SPECIFIC OBJECTIVE: Investigate the extent to which the Declaration of Independence and the Constitution of the United States have an impact on the following concepts: human dignity, government by consent of the governed, government of laws.

1. <u>Petitioning for the Declaration of Independence</u>

    when: depends on which of the alternative activities are used

    what: attached petition (next page)

    how: (1) Copy the petition below onto a large poster or display of
                some kind and put into a prominent place where it can be
                displayed for several days. Make sure students under-
                stand they can sign the petition if they agree with what
                it states. Do not tell them it is from the Declaration
                of Independence.

                NOTE: This activity could well be used with many of the
                foundational documents, for example: Preamble to the
                Constitution, Bill of Rights, First Amendment. In other
                words, this activity has application to any fundamental
                documents in which people profess belief. But when asked
                to support that belief in writing, they are reluctant to
                respond. The question, of course, is why are people
                reluctant to support what they profess to believe?

            (2) Have students individually or in small groups identify a
                list of rights which they think they should be able to
                practice, OR through class discussion make a list on the
                blackboard of all rights students think they should have.

            (3) Have students classify the rights in some manner and pick
                out the three which they think are the most basic.

            (4) Hold a class discussion on the theory of natural rights:
                (a) Are there human rights? What are they?
                (b) What is the difference between civil, inalienable,
                    and natural rights?

        <u>Alternative:</u>
        Have students take petition out at lunch hour and see if
        fellow students will sign it.

        <u>Alternative:</u>
        Solicit petition signers at shopping centers. This is a
        rather popular activity which has achieved national attention.
        Some students have taken the Declaration of Independence to
        shopping centers to ask people to sign the petition without
        telling the general public that it is the Declaration of
        Independence. The results of such activities are quite well
        known--that is, most of the citizens who were approached
        refused to sign.

    We have suggested that data can be collected from three different
    sources: the class, the school, or the general public. The impor-
    tance of the activity is the analysis of the reasons people give for
    signing or not signing what has come to be a fundamental statement
    on the relationship of citizens to their state.

We hold these Truths to be self-evident, that all Men are created equal, that they are endowed by their Creator with certain unalienable Rights, that among these are Life, Liberty, and the Pursuit of Happiness-- That to secure these Rights, Governments are instituted among Men deriving their just Powers from the Consent of the Governed, that whenever any Form of Government becomes destructive of these Ends, it is the Right of the People to alter or to abolish it, and to institute new Government, laying its Foundation on such Principles, and organizing its Powers in such Form as to them all seem most likely to effect their Safety and Happiness.

I, the undersigned, subscribe to these sentiments.

2.   Is the Declaration of Independence a Guide to Behavior?

when: one class period

what: copy of the Declaration of Independence for each student

how: Pass out a copy of the Declaration to each student. Have them read it and underline the points they feel are most significant.

Hold a class discussion using the following questions:

(1) According to the Declaration of Independence, why are governments formed?

(2) How would you express the basic rights identified by the Declaration in terms of contemporary usage (i.e., all citizens should have an equal opportunity)?

(3) Suppose you are Thomas Jefferson and have lived to the present. How might you now, if invited, rewrite the Declaration? Would you use different language? Would you include some citizens who are not included in the original document? Knowing the history of the United States and its involvement with other countries, would you continue to be as critical of George III?

(4) Do you believe the Declaration of Independence continues to be an effective guide to America's behavior?

3. Rights and Responsibilities of Citizens

    when: depends on how activity is used

    what: checklist and statements

    how: (1) Use as a pretest before unit study on Bill of Rights and
                general rights and responsibilities of citizenship.
            (2) Use statements and checklist as reference when studying
                the Bill of Rights, etc.
            (3) Have students collect clippings that illustrate rights
                and responsibilities (this can be done from newspapers
                and magazines at home or from a collection of newspapers
                and magazines at school). Students could also collect
                examples of rights and/or responsibilities denied. Use
                as displays for class discussion.

CHECKLIST

Rights of citizens	strongly agree	agree	neutral	disagree	strongly disagree
1. The right to vote without restriction because of race, color, class, or sex.					
2. The right to life and liberty.					
3. The right to free choice of religion.					
4. The right to freedom of speech, writing (press).					
5. The right to meet peaceably and to petition.					
6. The right to be free of having one's property searched or seized unless a warrant has been issued that states a specific cause and where to look.					
7. The right, when accused of a crime, to know what the accusation is, face hostile witnesses, have counsel, have a trial by jury that is swift and public.					
8. Protection against excessive bail or fines and cruel and unusual punishment.					
9. The right of protection by armed militia.					
10. The right to an education.					
11. The right to move freely from state to state.					

cont.

Rights of citizens	strongly agree	agree	neutral	disagree	strongly disagree
12. The right to a government working for the good of its citizens.					
13. The responsibility to vote and thus take part in and influence the decision-making of the government.					
14. The responsibility to abide by laws passed that protect the rights of all citizens.					
15. The responsibility of paying taxes so that government can function and carry out pro-grams for its citizens.					
16. The responsibility to uphold and serve the government in times of need.					
17. The responsibility not to discriminate against others because of sex, race, re-ligion, or color.					
18. The responsibility to protect natural re-sources and environment.					
19. The responsibility to provide for the needy.					
20. The responsibility to work through the government to make changes and avoid vio-lence as a means of change.					

4.   Creating a Data Bank

when: one week

what: newspapers and magazines collected and brought to school by students

how: This activity should follow a study of the Bill of Rights.

(1) Have students identify and collect articles that represent each of the rights listed in the Bill of Rights, using the magazines collected in school.

(2) Students will use their articles to produce a "newspaper." Just as magazines sometimes come out with issues on a single topic, the student newspaper will be a single topic--Rights.

(3) While students are searching for articles that represent the Bill of Rights, they may come across articles that seem to conflict with or deny a right. These articles could be used for class discussion.

(4) This activity can be done by students individually or by groups. The newspapers should be shared with the class and then evaluated by the teacher.

In some schools, the classroom can be a resource center. One resource that students can supply is the weekly news magazine which can be the source of data for many visual projects including posters, collages, and mobiles, along with written and oral reports.

SPECIFIC OBJECTIVE: Identify and examine the idea of separation of powers, democracy, republic, federalism.

5. Federalism II[2] (identifying the structure of government)

when: one class period

what: list of topics and checklist of government responsibilities

how: (1) Using the checklist below, have students establish which are functions of the federal government, which are functions of the state government, and which are functions of local government.

(2) Discuss students' findings:
(a) Are any of the functions shared?
(b) What does the checklist say about the relationship between levels of government? Does one level seem to control the other levels or are the three levels independent of each other?

CHECKLIST OF GOVERNMENT RESPONSIBILITIES

	Federal	State	Local
1. The regulation of production and distribution of new drugs and medicines.	___	___	___
2. Income taxes	___	___	___
3. Issuing license plates	___	___	___
4. New highway construction	___	___	___
5. School construction and renovation	___	___	___
6. Automobile inspection	___	___	___
7. Regulation of health care services and facilities	___	___	___
8. Unemployment insurance benefits	___	___	___
9. Aid to dependent children	___	___	___
10. Welfare	___	___	___

6. <u>Republic or Democracy II</u>[3] (identifying the structure of government)

    when: one class period

    what: no materials necessary

    how: (1) Have students agree on a definition of republic and a definition of democracy. For example: "Republic is a system where representatives of the people make decisions; democracy is a system where people make decisions."

           (2) Draw a scale and place on the scale where certain government activities fit. Is the activity characteristic of a republic or democracy or somewhere in between? For example:

```
republic_____|_____|_____|_____|_____democracy
              Supreme    War is    Local    Senators
              Court     declared   school   are elected
              (Pres. and (Pres. and taxes    (by the
              Congress) Congress) (Voted by  people)
                                  the people)
```

Examples of what to place on scale:

    (a) School taxes go up (as voted by the people)

    (b) Supreme Court judge is appointed by the President

    (c) War is declared by Congress and President

    (d) Senators are elected (by the people)

    (e) Treaty is negotiated between nations by the President

    (f) 55 mile speed limit (set by Congress)

    (g) Car inspection (set by state)

    (h) House of Representatives elected (by the people)

    (i) President is elected (by the Electoral College)

7. <u>Separation of Powers II</u>[4] (identifying the structure of government)

    when: one class period

    what: newspapers, TV news

    how: (1) Discuss separation of powers with class. Have students bring in newspaper stories (or use old newspapers at school) or TV news stories of separation of powers in action, such as Supreme Court declaring law unconstitutional, Presidential veto, or Congress overriding the veto.

(2) Have a student or group adopt a branch of government. Have them list powers granted it by the Constitution. Discuss and list what additional powers that branch has acquired over the years.

(3) Post the powers and acquired powers in different parts of the room around which the students who adopted that branch can post newspaper stories as "living" everyday illustrations of that branch's power.

SPECIFIC OBJECTIVE: Compare and contrast parties, governments, and political leaders.

8. Contrasting Forms of Government

when: four class periods

what: large outline map of world. The easiest way to do this activity is by continents, projected by opaque projector onto large sheets of paper (butcher paper), then outlined and cut out.

how: (1) Divide the class into groups. Give or have each group select a continent or section (West Africa, Central America, Southeast Asia, etc.). The groups should outline the countries in their sections of the map and briefly research the countries to identify the forms of government each has.

Students may want to establish some sort of color coding system for the different types of governments (democracy, oligarchy, dictatorship, republic, monarchy, etc.). If they do so, then all groups should use the same color code.

(2) Bring groups and maps together and discuss findings:

(a) What do the map markings suggest is the most popular form of government around the world? (convergent question)

(b) Are the same forms of government clustered together? For example: North America, Central America, South America, East Africa, etc. (convergent question)

(c) Should there be a strong world government? (evaluative question)

(d) Would you prefer all countries have the same form of government? (evaluative question)

9. Comparative Study: Minor Parties--Many, Few, None?

   when: three class periods

   what: teacher-identified list of minor political parties

   how: Throughout American history minor or "third" political parties have emerged or developed to challenge the American two-party system.

      (1) Separate students into groups and give each group the name of one of the minor political parties.
      (2) Have groups research the history of their parties:
          What brought it into being?
          What were its goals?
          How successful was it?
          Did it influence either of the two major parties (did the major parties adopt any of the third party's ideals)?
          Did a minor party ever become major--that is, win a presidential election?
      (3) Construct a time line of minor party names and dates; include major parties for comparison.
      (4) Hold a class discussion on group's findings. Why are these minor parties generally unable to be successful in becoming a strong political force?

   Alternative: (or extension of above activity)
   Comparative study of the role of minor parties in other countries would be appropriate: Italy and France are the easiest on which to gather information since their politics are reported on TV news and in newspapers and magazines. What is the role of minor parties in a one-party system, i.e., Russia, China?

10. Historically Have Americans Always Agreed?

    when: four-five periods, in the fall before the national elections

    what: short research paper; poster size strength of feeling chart (next page)

    how: (1) Have each student pick a past president. After researching the past presidents, the students should compare where those presidents stood on issues with where each of the present political candidates stands. Does the past president compare more closely with one of the present candidates than with the others? How do you think he would stand on some of the current problems and why?

         (2) Construct a large strength of feeling chart. Students can briefly share findings by noting their chosen president's position on the chart. Chart can be basis of class discussion.

PAST PRESIDENTS STRENGTH OF FEELING CHART

How your President would have thought on the following:	strongly agree	agree	neutral	disagree	strongly disagree
Free public education for all citizens					
Graduated income tax					
Equal rights for all citizens					
Separation of church and state					
Equal opportunities for all citizens					
ETC. (identify those contemporary issues which would be most relevant to class)					

SPECIFIC OBJECTIVE: Identify the role of leaders who reflect their times or times that reflect the leaders.

11. <u>Justices Who Reflect Their Times vs. Times That Reflect the Justices</u>

   when: five class periods

   what: list of Supreme Court Chief Justices

   how: Have each student choose one Chief Justice; students may have to work in pairs if class is large. It would be best if each Chief Justice had someone researching him. Have students make a time line of the Court decisions during Justice's time, then pick out two or three of the most important decisions and explain how they affected the rights of citizens.

   Which Chief Justice would the student like to have at the present time and why?

JOHN JAY	Oct. 1789 - June 1795
JOHN RUTLEDGE	Aug. 1795 - Dec. 1795
OLIVER ELLSWORTH	Mar. 1796 - Dec. 1800
JOHN MARSHALL	Feb. 1801 - July 1835
ROGER TANEY	Mar. 1836 - Oct. 1864
SALMON CHASE	Dec. 1864 - May 1873
MORRISON WAITE	Mar. 1874 - Mar. 1888
MELVILLE FULLER	Oct. 1888 - July 1910

cont.

EDWARD WHITE	Dec. 1910 - May 1921
WILLIAM HOWARD TAFT	July 1921 - Feb. 1930
CHARLES EVANS HUGHES	Feb. 1930 - June 1941
HARLAN STONE	July 1941 - Apr. 1946
FREDERICK VINSON	June 1946 - Sep. 1953
EARL WARREN	Oct. 1953 - June 1969
WARREN BURGER	June 1969 -

Is there evidence to support the argument that the Justices reflect the times in which they lived? Might, for example, Chief Justice Burger have had a different point of view if he had been a Justice during the Court of Chief Justice Jay? Do citizens make their own times or do the times make the citizen?

12. People Who Reflect Their Times vs. Times That Reflect the People

when: three class periods

what: sample list below. Teacher should add to list with current names in the news.

how: Have each student pick one name from the list below. Students should research to establish backgrounds and how the individuals have influenced human rights and laws in their time.

MARTIN LUTHER KING	PHYLLIS SCHAFLEY
SANDRA DAY O'CONNOR	RICHARD NIXON
GERALD FORD	HENRY KISSINGER
RONALD REAGAN	JOSEPH STALIN
LECH WALESA	JOHN F. KENNEDY
POPE JOHN PAUL II	FERDINAND MARCOS

Perhaps the students would prefer to present their findings visually as in a poster, collage, mobile, etc.

SPECIFIC OBJECTIVE: Identify the ideas of control and freedom as they are applied to people in the past and present.

13. Government Controls

when: one week

what: list of questions to ask about other countries

how: (1) Have each student pick a country to study. Suggest countries that are "in the news." Newspaper accounts, TV programs, and other sources of information will make gathering information a bit easier. Remember that it is not the country selected at issue but a comparison and contrast between another country and one's own on the theme of freedom and control. Students should concentrate on their chosen country's government and the amount of control in the country.

Questions for consideration:

> (a) Does the country have one set of beliefs that must be followed?
> (b) Are people free to contradict beliefs of the country?
> (c) Are people jailed for holding contradictory beliefs?
> (d) Are people free to hold whatever job they want?
> (e) Are people free to criticize government or political leaders?
> (f) Must people join workers' organizations?
> (g) Is education compulsory?
> (h) Can people own property?

(2) After doing research on the above questions, student should report on the contrast between the U.S. government and the chosen country's government on the theme of freedom and control.

> (a) What does freedom and control mean in your country as contrasted to the country you selected to research? (convergent question)
> (b) Suppose you lived in the country you selected to research; what changes if any would you suggest on freedom and control for that country? (divergent question)
> (c) What do you think is good or bad about freedom and control in your own country? (evaluative question)

14. Are We Controlled?

when: one period

what: chart (example below)

Time	Activity	Control
_____	_____	_____
_____	_____	_____
_____	_____	_____

how: (1) Give a chart to each student (or have them make their own). Have them record all activities during one 24-hour period. Next to each activity have them state any rules, laws, social controls connected with the activity; for example:

3:30-5:00	basketball practice	rules of game
8:00-9:30	watch TV	FCC regulations
8:00-8:10	ate apple from own tree	no controls

(2) Class discussion:

Are we more controlled than we realize?
How much local, state, and national government control is there in American citizens' lives? Do you "feel" or "sense" being controlled by the government?

Are there any activities that are controlled that could
not be done satisfactorily without those controls?
(Basketball would be difficult to play without rules.)
What controls do you feel are unnecessary and why?

Alternative:

Have students set up chart of different areas of their lives
and have them fill in activities in their everyday lives that
have rules or controls that affect how we live.

SCHOOL	HOME	COMMUNITY	LEISURE	ETC
Dress code	building	traffic light	watch TV	money
tardy bell	regulation	speed limits	sports game	cars
walking in	restrictive	taxes		marriage
hall	use of			
	property			

Class discussion as above.

SPECIFIC OBJECTIVE: Compare lifestyles between generations: past, present, and future

15. Measuring Change Through the Generation Gap[5]

when: one class period

what: list of items identified by students (see below)

how: (1) Have students: list 20 items that you know, see, can do,
or experience which were unknown, impossible, or un-
imaginable for your parents when they were your present
age.

NOTE: This activity can take one back into history or forward in
time (future) by changing parents to grandparents or great-grandparents (about year 1900), or to your children or your children's
children (about year 2020).
The concept change is recognized as a basic theme in most social
studies curriculums. Not only do teachers note change between
generations, but they try to measure the speed with which change is
happening. And even though change is all about us, happening as we
sit in the classroom, that concept is often hard for students to
grasp. This activity is a simple technique that will help students
identify and compare the meaning of change in their lives and the
lives of their families. Not only do students note change between
contemporary generations, but they also learn about the "generation
gap" by reflecting upon the differences that appear to exist between
generations. By reflecting on the changes between generations,
students can identify the values and customs of past generations and
reflect on what changes might mean in the future.

(2) Gather data (perhaps the first five items from each student). List those and categorize them, i.e., medical, technical, space, education, customs, etc. Having noted the difference between parents and students as a measure of change, ask students if they can explain why their view of the world might be different from their parents.

16. <u>Measuring Change Through Group Consensus</u>

   when: three class periods

   what: Group Consensus form and list of identified items from previous activity

   how: (1) Group students and give each group a Group Consensus form. Assign one person in each group to fill out the form as the group makes its decisions.

   (2) When forms are completed, hold a class discussion comparing the lists from all the groups. If there is wide variety, have groups defend the items they have chosen for various categories.

   (3) Have each group create one item of the future. What effect will it have on your children's lives and how would the item have changed your life if your parents had used it? Have each group make a presentation of their future item to the class.

GROUP CONSENSUS FORM

1. Group members

   A.   D.
   B.   E.
   C.   F.

2. Using the lists of 20 items you have made, fill in the following:

   List 10 items listed on differences between you and your parents that all members of the group included on their lists.

   1.   6.
   2.   7.
   3.   8.
   4.   9.
   5.   10.

3. Working as a group, reduce the list to the 5 items you would be least able to do without:

   1.   4.

> 2.   5.
> 3.
>
> 4. From your combined lists, choose 5 items that are not essential but because of your "lifestyle" you would have difficulty doing without:
>
> 1.   4.
> 2.   5.
> 3.
>
> 5. List 3 items that provide you with entertainment or enjoyment:
>
> 1.   3.
> 2.
>
> 6. If you had lived 200 years ago, what would the counterpart to these items have been:
>
> 1.   3.
> 2.

B. General Objective: To develop skills necessary to <u>process</u> information

SPECIFIC OBJECTIVE: Identify the role of political and social events through cause and effect relationships.

1. <u>Cause and Effect Cycle</u>

when: one class period

what: diagrams (next page)

how: (1) Introduce the vicious cycle concept to students.

(2) Reproduce the vicious cycle diagram #1 on the blackboard or overhead. Discuss the diagram.

(3) Have the students hypothesize as to how low crop prices and unemployment may be connected in a vicious cycle (see diagram #2).

(4) Ask the students to make their own diagram of a vicious cycle and share it with the class.

(5) In a follow-up discussion, deal with the idea that many times teenagers (and others) say, "No matter what I do, I'm always wrong." Using a vicious cycle diagram, explore this idea. This could be done in small or large groups.

Diagram #1

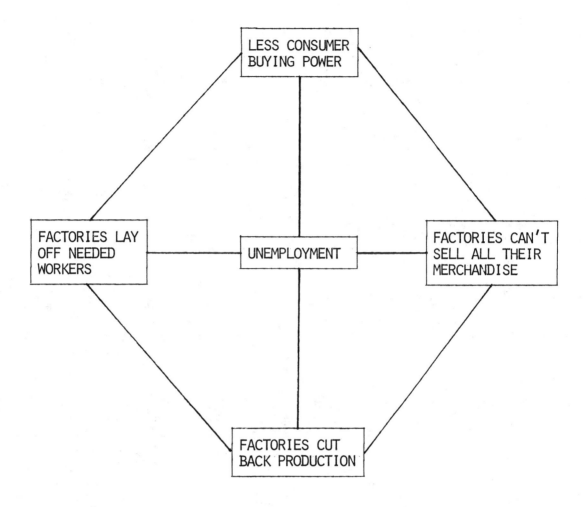

Diagram #2

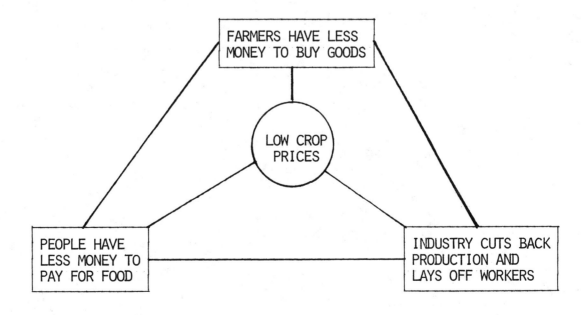

2. <u>Cause and Effect Vocabulary</u>

when: three class periods

what: lists of causes and events

how: Below is a list of terms used to clarify or classify the possible causes that precipitated some event or occasion and the resulting effect.

<u>"Last straw" (decisive) cause</u> (cause nearest to resulting effect)
This is the cause that usually immediately precedes the resulting event.
There may have been several causes building up to this final decisive
one. Causes in this category might be a bombing or assassination that
precipitated a war or a court decision that produced an immediate effect.

<u>First (resulting) effect</u>
This effect is the first result of a single or series of causes. It is
the first noticeable, but possibly not the most important, effect.

<u>Long term or preceding causes</u>
These causes are the ones that lead up to the last straw or deciding
cause. They may occur over a period of some time and sometimes come in
a series. They help to understand the resulting effects.

<u>Following effects</u>
These are effects that may take some time to appear. In other words,
these are effects that do not immediately appear as the result of some
cause. An example of this might be a drug taken in pregnancy that pro-
duces some medical problem when the child becomes an adult, or the dump-
ing of toxic wastes that years later make the land uninhabitable.

<u>Most significant causes and effects</u>
These are the causes and effects that authorities or those studying the
issue deem the most important--the most significant causes producing the
most significant effects.

<u>Less significant causes and effects</u>
These are causes and effects that are believed to be less important or
secondary in nature.

For the following list of events, give examples of causes and
effects that fit the classifications described above. Or
have class develop lists of events that are particularly
relevant to them.

Constitution
Declaration of Independence
Industrialization
Watergate
Supreme Court decisions
Contemporary issue

3.   <u>Gathering School Data: Identifying Cause and Effect</u>

when: one week

what: interview form to gather data on school environment

how: (1) Have students interview the school system finance officer
OR cafeteria manager on operational costs (food, supplies,
etc); principal on cost of vandalism; head of maintenance
on cost of daily upkeep.

SAMPLE INTERVIEW FORM

Name of person interviewed: _____
Position: _____
Area of investigation: _____

Costs - 10 years ago
 	
     Present
 	
     10 years from now

Cause of change: _____ _____ _____
Effect of change: _____ _____
Recommendation of interviewee: _____ _____

(2) Have students present the information in some visual form
such as graphs, etc. for display to rest of class.

(3) Hold class discussion based on information gathered.

NOTE: Costs are related to cause and effect over the years. What
would have to happen to reduce costs, i.e., cafeteria, maintenance, etc.? How does inflation affect the students, both
directly and indirectly?

4.   Analysis of Cause and Effect

when: two class periods

what: political and social generalizations

how: (1) Provide students with well-known political or social
          generalizations or have the students themselves identify
          several generalizations:

       Examples: Absolute power corrupts absolutely.
                   Conflict usually results in society when one group
                      controls another.
       Student
       Example: Athletes in this school get preferential treatment
                      from the administration.

       (2) Have students analyze the generalizations in terms of the
          cause and effect relationships.

       (3) Students should be able to draw on their knowledge of the
          political system to produce examples that support the
          generalization, and then explore the causes and effects
          of the examples.

SPECIFIC OBJECTIVE: Learn to categorize and analyze as a part of processing
                     information.

5.   Government in Your Pocket

when: one class period

what: form (pass copy to each student or place on board, overhead,
       etc.)

how: (1) The activity calls for processing by categorizing items.
          Have students search pockets or purses for items that
          have some connection to the government or laws, i.e.,
          movie ticket stub, sales slip with tax, driver's license,
          social security card.

       (2) Make three columns on the board: local, state, national.
          Or students may do this individually. Can students place
          the name of their items and what connection they have
          with government under the appropriate columns?

       (3) Class discussion: What does the categorizing suggest
          about government regulation?

          (a) Is there regulation at each level?

          (b) How regulated do you feel?

          (c) What would students speculate about the future? Will
              there likely be more regulation or less?

LOCAL	STATE	NATIONAL
local tax	driver's license	money (coins, paper)
bike permit	fishing license	
school I.D. card	sales tax	Social Security card and number

6. <u>Political Cartooning Is the Message!</u>

when: continuous

what: categorizing political cartoons, a form of processing in-
        formation

how: (1) Over a period of time have students clip political car-
            toons and bring them to class. These may be loosely
            divided and categorized: ones of foreign policy to-
            gether, those on economy together, on the President,
            etc. If wall space is available, or on collages, post-
            ers, etc., it is a good idea to display them all.
            Teacher may want to add to the collection.
        (2) Hold a class discussion on each group. Aside from their
            humorous aspect, do the categories have a common message?
            Is the message biased? Is political cartooning an
            effective means by which to suggest social, political,
            and economic problems?

From the <u>Journal and Courier</u>, Lafayette, IN, Sun., 10/30/83.

"OUT OF THE MOTHBALLS"

SPECIFIC OBJECTIVE: Learn how to process persuasive arguments.

7.   Misleading for the Purpose of Persuasion

when: two class periods

what: list of what constitutes a possible misleading argument

how: (1) Tape a class discussion or a TV panel show on a subject
          that will arouse controversy and argument.

       (2) Discuss list of misleading argument terms.

       (3) Replay tape and have class listen for misleading arguments.

Alternative: Give list to groups and have them write an example for
each term, or have them watch a TV panel show where controversy and
argument are likely to be part of the program. As they listen to
the program they can note the examples of misleading arguments they
hear.

       (4) Some questions to ask in class discussion:

           (a) What techniques seem to be most popular? (convergent
               question)

           (b) Suppose you were President of the U.S. and wish to
               persuade others to your point of view, which of the
               misleading arguments might you use on the general
               public? (divergent question)

           (c) Which form of misleading argument is to you most
               compelling? (evaluative question)

MISLEADING ARGUMENT TERMS:

   1. Stereotyping
   2. Generalization from single example
   3. Universal man--everyone wants the same thing
   4. Appeals to authority
   5. Means/End--action good because outcome good
   6. Either/Or--limited choices to two or few when there are many
   7. Complex question--questionable facts in question
   8. Tautology--proving a statement by repeating it in other words
   9. Ethnocentrism--using own culture to judge others
  10. Accepting fact--everyone says so
  11. Single cause--using one cause when there are many
  12. Imperfect Historical Analogy--use past on dissimilar events
  13. Fictional Statement or Question--If this had or had not hap-
       pened, then this would or would not have happened.
  14. Irrelevant proof--evidence has nothing to do with topic
  15. Attack on the Man--personal
  16. Appeal to the Past--tradition
  17. After This, So--because of this B happened after A or A was
       the cause

SPECIFIC OBJECTIVE: Learn how to process biased information.

8. Is the Media Biased? Knowing How to Protect Yourself

    when: two or three class periods

    what: newspapers, news magazines

    how: Presidents in the United States since L. B. Johnson have all
           bitterly claimed they are being misrepresented by the press,
           meaning that the press is biased and therefore unfair.

           (1) Have students search news sources for articles they think
               might be biased (teacher may want to limit this search to
               several specific controversial topics). The articles
               may be on the national, state, or local level. Some good
               places to look are Letters to the Editor, editorials, the
               placement of stories (on front page or on last page), etc.

           (2) Hold a class discussion on what constitutes bias in news
               reports. Students should use their articles as examples
               during class discussion. Some points to look for:

                   modifiers or words with negative meaning:
                       Communist treachery
                       Imperialist Americans
                       Viet Nam Freedom Fighters
                   length of article
                   placement of article in paper or magazine
                   Does news story of specific paper show same bias as
                       editorial in same paper on same topic?
                   Check the cartoons and pictures--Do they add to a
                       biased point of view?

           (3) Summarize discussion by compiling a short list of basic
               things that might indicate bias that students should be
               aware of when reading news articles or watching TV news,
               particularly on controversial topics.

9. Recognizing Bias in Media

    when: two class periods

    what: newspapers or taped news broadcasts

    how: (1) Have students pick out an article or broadcast and list
               all the words that are judgmental in their description.
               Have the students substitute negative words for positive
               and positive for negative to understand how they change
               the article or broadcast.

           (2) Have students compose short paragraphs about an event or
               person using first positive words and then negative
               words.

Example:

> The Soviet leader today in another tirade suggested the aggressive intent of the Soviet Union when he spoke of limited nuclear war. Though his hardline speech was not carried in the Soviet newspapers, the Soviet propaganda newscasts from Moscow emphasized the peace loving tone of the speech. The rubber stamp Soviet legislature greeted his speech with their usual enthusiasm.

Another Example:

> The Soviet and Eastern European women athletes who will be at the Olympics can be characterized as suspiciously broad-shouldered, fuzzy-lipped challengers, typical of the communist bloc sports machine which shoots its athletes with muscle building steroids.

NOTE: Teachers who would coordinate American or English Literature and American Government or Civics will find these two following activities particularly appropriate.

---

10. Political Fables

when: one class period

what: example of political fables

how: Along with the activity on categorizing political cartoons is the reading and writing of political fables. This particular activity would be appropriate for honors and gifted and talented programs with emphasis on analysis and synthesis. Many 19th Century American authors chose to use the fable as one way of expressing political satire. For example, one typical fable was:

> Seated at the gate of heaven, St. Peter observed the approach of a new Soul. The new Soul, having presented himself, was told by St. Peter that he was scheduled for the other place. "Don't be apologetic," said the new Soul, "I merely came here to ask if my old friend _____ was here?" "Not yet," replied St. Peter, "He hasn't died yet." "Well," said the new Soul, "of course he hasn't died. I just thought _____ was here visiting God."

(1) Encourage students to fill in the blank with whatever name would be appropriate: obviously American presidents, congressmen, senators, mayors, or any political personality one might wish to satirize.

(2) Encourage students to write their own fables. Excellent examples of fables were written by America's popular authors, i.e., Mark Twain, Washington Irving, Bret Harte. Why would authors use political fables? Why not just directly attack the person named as in the examples above, by accusing that person of having the pretensions of a "god."

(3) Have students exchange their fables, instructing them to identify and critically evaluate the satirical message.

11. Political Definitions

when: one class period

what: list of definitions

how: It is common practice for texts and teachers to offer authoritative definitions of various parts of the political process. However, many of America's most distinguished authors have also defined parts of the political process in ways which reveal their own biases. An activity to accompany the more traditional definitions is one in which the teacher selects political or literary figures and from those persons' writings identifies definitions that reflect their bias. For example: a Midwesterner, Ambrose Bierce, 1842-1914, author of short stories and a newspaper editor, offers these definitions from his book, The Devil's Dictionary:

Patriotism, n. Combustible rubbish ready to the torch of any one ambitious to illuminate his name.
Politics, n. A strife of interests masquerading as a contest of principles. The conduct of public affairs for private advantage.
Radicalism, n. The conservatism of tomorrow injected into the affairs of today.
Corporation, n. An ingenious device for obtaining individual profit without individual responsibility.

(1) Ask the students to compare these definitions with more conventional ones found in American government texts.
(2) Is Bierce being cynical? Is there a spirit of truth in his definition?
(3) Encourage students to identify their own definitions as part of the critical analysis they apply to the definitions above.
(4) Having read Washington, Jefferson, Jackson, Lincoln, and others such as James Fenimore Cooper, Nathaniel Hawthorne, Henry James, Dorothy Parker, and James Thurber, both in American literature courses as well as in an American government or civics course, students should choose one author and infer from the author's writings a definition of democracy, freedom, patriotism, etc.
(5) Does a general consensus on the definition of freedom, patriotism, democracy, etc. emerge from American

literature? If there seems to be no consensus, then what does that suggest? Should students look forward in the future to a consensus? Should there be consensus?

12. Identifying Differences Between Primary and Secondary Sources

when: one class period

what: list of primary and secondary sources

how: (1) Discuss with the class the terms primary source and secondary source. Primary sources take many forms but they all have one thing in common: they are "firsthand." That means they may be tangible artifacts unearthed at an archaeological dig, taped speeches or speeches printed verbatim in the newspaper, etc. Secondary sources are "secondhand." This means, usually, that someone has examined a primary source and now is reporting on it, but the primary source has been filtered through this person. In other words, this person is interpreting the primary source for you, and you cannot be sure that person has interpreted the source correctly. Of course, we cannot all look at all events firsthand, so we must often rely on secondary sources. That is why more than one secondary source is important for an accurate interpretation.

(2) The following is a list of both primary and secondary sources. Give each student a copy of the list and have them mark P before those they believe are primary sources and mark S before those they believe are secondary. Better yet, have students bring in a list of their own. Make up one central list or have them exchange lists and mark the right answers--the point is to practice identifying.

Sources

P 1. President's televised State of the Union address to Congress.

S 2. Newscaster's televised report on Presidential news conference.

P 3. Congressional record.

S 4. Newspaper account of state legislative session.

P 5. Governor's address to graduating class.

P 6. The Watergate audiotapes recorded in President Nixon's office.

S 7. Book by J. P. Snow on Kennedy family.

S 8. President of Egypt reports on his private conversation with the press.

S 9. Servant in White House reports on conversation he overheard in the Oval Office.

P 10. Servant in White House for past 30 years talks about the problems of serving the First Family.

SPECIFIC OBJECTIVE: Identify techniques to evaluate students' processing
skills

13.   Student and Teacher Evaluation Checklist

when: used at different times

what: project checklist: research paper, creation of a display

how: In evaluating students, it is often helpful to have information on how the students feel about their performance and
participation. The student should complete the checklist
questions alone and then sit down in conference with the
teacher. After analyzing the checklist, what steps could be
taken that would improve student performance in the future?

Checklist

	yes	neutral	no
1. Chosen topic too easy			
2. Chosen topic too difficult.			
3. Was the topic ever boring?			
4. Did you have sufficiant time to spend on topic?			
5. Were research materials for the topic readily available?			
6. Did you find out something that changed your mind about something or someone?			
7. Did you put less effort into your work than you had expected to?			
8. Did you have to spend more time on the topic than you thought was worthwhile?			
9. Did your research uncover any aspect that you would like to explore further but did not have time to because you had to finish the assignment?			
10. Did you have to spend too much time on some one aspect of the assignment and have to skimp on others?			
11. Were you satisfied with your work on the topic?			
12. Did you feel the topic was worth examining?			

Summary: What does this checklist suggest about your performance?

14. Recording Progress Form

    when: every day

    what: form

    how: Have student keep a running "journal" entry on each day's activities concerning a specific topic.

	Specific activity performed	Questions raised	Sources used	Value of activity to your understanding of topic
Date				
Date				
Date				

The journal should be reviewed by both teacher and student to check progress and to make sure student is moving in the desired direction.

15. Group Observation (for teacher)

    when: depends on time available for observation

    what: evaluation chart or checklist (next page)

    how: After observing various groups in action, the teacher might wish to reassign group membership for more effective group work. The teacher may wish to privately counsel students who seem, for whatever reason, to be disruptive in group work.

          In observing a group the teacher should concentrate not on the content being discussed but on how the discussion is taking place. In other words, who talks to whom, who directs the discussion, how are group decisions arrived at, who makes trouble, and who is conciliatory? Group behavior can be divided into three major areas:

          (1) Activity that is directly concerned with the group's assigned task: proposing a line of action or possible procedures, offering information relevant to the problem, helping to define and clarify ideas, proposing solutions or decisions, and examining ideas or decisions for validity.

(2) Activity undertaken by members to keep the group functioning smoothly: mediating differences and disagreements,
easing the sharing of opinions, encouraging others to
share their ideas, accepting criticism and comprising
one's own ideas, and helping to test for possible decisions.

(3) Activity undertaken by members that disrupts group work:
attacking the ideas of individuals or the group as a whole
either overtly or subtly, strongly opposing group's wishes
for personal reasons, attempting to dominate and control
group, seeking attention by refusing to participate but
still remaining with group, and deliberately leading
group astray from its assigned work.

The teacher can develop a chart or checklist along the
following lines to use in group observation.

	Student				
	A	B	C	D	E
WORK RELATED BEHAVIOR:					
proposing procedures					
offering information					
defining ideas					
proposing solutions					
examining decisions					
SUPPORTIVE BEHAVIOR:					
mediating differences					
encouraging participation					
aiding participation					
accepting criticism					
helping achieve solutions					
DISRUPTIVE BEHAVIOR:					
attacking					
opposing					
attempting to control					
refusing to participate					
leading astray					

SPECIFIC OBJECTIVE: Identify and apply the four different levels of
questioning.

16. Learning to Ask Questions in Civics and U.S. Government[6]

when: two class periods

what: materials included

how: Questions are such a vital part of social studies that activities and materials are offered on that skill in this book
in each subject area. The skill of questioning, we have
argued, is not the exclusive domain of the teacher. Students
can learn to ask and answer a full range of questions. Questioning is a skill that can be learned, that can be applied.
Classroom teachers know that good questions from students
stimulate class discussion. What kills discussion and dis-
courages teachers are students who have no questions. Obviously the skill of asking and answering different levels of
questions does not guarantee stimulating useful discussion,
but it is a step in the right direction.

Learning happens when there is give and take between a teacher
and students. Questions are asked and answers are given.
The answers are the same for everyone in the group. Learning
also happens when there is exchange between and among students
dealing with questions that have individual answers and are
not the same for every student. Learning also happens when
students individually process all kinds of questions by themselves. If you agree with the author that questions are an
important part of learning, you should find the following
helpful in teaching your students more about them. "The
basic objective of [questioning] activities is to teach students to recognize the difference between memory/description
type closed questions and speculation/evaluation type open
questions."

Closed Questions:

Closed questions are ones that have specific answers. These ask you
to either remember word for word (Memory) or explain (Description)
something in your own words. The answers to closed questions would
be acceptable for all of us. Here are some CLOSED QUESTIONS about
U.S. government.

Memory	1.	Name the three branches of the federal government?
Description	2.	Explain why the president is head of the armed forces?
Memory	3.	Who was the first President of the United States?
Description	4.	Compare and contrast Teddy Roosevelt with Franklin Delano Roosevelt?

Now write two closed questions of your own about U.S. government,
remembering that:

MEMORY means to identify, define, or answer yes or no.

DESCRIPTION means to compare, contrast, or clarify something.

1. _____

_____

2. _____

_____

Open Questions:

Open questions are ones that have a number of possible answers.
Some of these ask you to imagine (Speculation) how something could
be different. Other open questions ask you to judge (Evaluation)
between things and decide for yourself what is better or worse or
fair or unfair. You have to make up your own mind to answer an open
question. Since everyone has a different mind, they often come up
with several different answers to the same questions. The answers
to open questions, therefore, will not be the same for everyone.
Here are some examples of OPEN QUESTIONS:

Speculation 1. What would happen to the standard of living in the
                 U.S. if the birth rate increased from 2.1 to 3.0?
Evaluation   2. What type of action do you think the government
                 should take to reduce the family size of the poor?
Speculation 3. How might our political system be different if each
                 state elected the same number of Senators and
                 Representatives to Congress?
Evaluation   4. Do you think the seniority system in Congress is
                 beneficial or a deterrent to good government?

Now write two open questions of your own concerning something that
has to do with U.S. government, remembering that:

SPECULATION means to predict, reconstruct, or conclude some-
           thing.

EVALUATION means to judge or choose something.

1. _____

_____

_____

2. _____

_____

_____

17. Mastering the Different Levels of Questions

when: one class period

what: review survey

how: Review students' mastery of identifying the different levels of questions. If students have difficulty identifying the four different levels of questions, review the Chapter on U.S. History for purposes of clarification and practice. Follow-through activities:

(1) Have students find questions in back of each chapter of their social studies text. Have them classify the questions they find into one of the four levels.

(2) On the social studies topics being studied, ask students to write out at least one question at four different levels: Name the three branches of government? Why did the Constitution call for three branches of government? Suppose you were designing the Constitution, what checks and balances might you suggest now? Do you think the checks and balances between the three branches have worked to the benefit of American citizens?

Mastery Test Survey (Matching)

m 1. Name one branch of the federal government?

d 2. Explain checks and balances as applied to the federal government?

s 3. What do you suppose would happen if there were no checks and balances?

e 4. What is your opinion of the checks and balances theory of government?

s 5. What would happen if the federal government were to become a parliament rather than the three branches?

s 6. Suppose you were President of the U.S., what might you think of the separation of powers?

m 7. What is the name of the capitol city of the U.S.?

e 8. What do you think about the power of the Supreme Court?

m = memory question

d = descriptive/convergent question

s = speculation/divergent question

e = evaluation question

18. <u>Answering Open Questions</u>

when: two class periods

what: materials included

how: We need to know how to answer questions. Closed questions
       are easy to answer because once we have located the answer
       the job is finished. Open questions are more difficult to
       answer because they call for one to create or interpret or
       imagine an answer from one's own point of view. To answer an
       open question properly, four steps need to be taken:

       CLARIFY THE QUESTION: tell what the question means to you.

       PROPOSE SOLUTIONS: list several possible answers.

       EXAMINE CONSEQUENCES: explain each possibility.

       MAKE PERSONAL CHOICE AND JUSTIFY IT: choose the one you
           like best and defend it.

<u>CLARIFY THE QUESTION</u>

       Suppose you were asked,

           "What is the best way to succeed in school?"

       Is that question asking you how to make good grades, or how
       to win friends, or how to be elected President of the class?
       You see, there are a lot of meanings we could each give this
       question and <u>that</u> would determine the kind of answer we would
       write.

       This is the important part--that you and the person reading
       your answer both are aware of your interpretation of the
       question.

       You might begin, therefore, by stating the question as follows:

           "To succeed in school means a student must make good
           grades. To make good grades you need to . . . Being
           successful in school means being popular . . ."

       Here are a couple of other open questions for you to practice
       clarifying. Write a sentence after each to briefly state
       what you think the question is asking.

       1. Imagine that you were teaching this class. What would
           you do differently?

           _____

           _____

2. Are you in favor of capital punishment?

_____

_____

PROPOSE SOLUTIONS

The second thing you must do when answering an open question is to propose solutions. Even though you don't necessarily agree, you should examine various possible answers to show that you have fully considered the question.

For instance, if you were answering the question,

"How can you make good grades in school?"

you might suggest the following possibilities:

1. Study hard.
2. Be friendly towards your teachers.
3. Cheat.

All three could be answers, but each would have different consequences.

See how many possible solutions you can propose for this question:

"What would you do if you saw another student steal a teacher's grade book?"

1)

2)

3)

4)

EXAMINE CONSEQUENCES

You can propose all kinds of solutions, but if some make no sense you really haven't accomplished much. Therefore, it is important to show that you have thought about the consequences of each possible answer.

In the example, "How can you make good grades in school?", we suggested three possible ways. Now let's consider the consequences or results of each.

"First, if we study hard we will have less time to mess around or to watch TV. There would be a lot of satisfaction from knowing that every grade has been earned.

Second, to try and bribe the teacher might help, but other kids might find out, and there is no guarantee that the teacher will trade good grades for money. Finally, to cheat might work on occasion, but besides being wrong, it would be hard to do for a long period of time without getting caught!"

MAKE PERSONAL CHOICE AND JUSTIFY IT

Now you are ready for the last step which is to choose the one solution that makes the most sense and to justify it. For instance, you might say:

"I recommend hard study because, even though it isn't fun, it will help me learn more, and that is the real reason I go to school. Good grades will often come as a result of hard study."

Read the following answer to an open question and follow the directions below it. Question:

"Would we be better off without television?

Answer:

"I think this question is asking whether or not Americans would be happier without any television. One possibility is that we wouldn't be happier because we couldn't watch football games, or cartoon programs. We wouldn't know as much because we learn a lot watching TV. On the other hand, we would be happier because Dads would spend less time watching TV and more time playing with their kids. I think we would be worse off without TV because TV lets us see things that interest us."

(a) Underline the three possible answers offered.

(b) Underline twice the consequences of each possible answer.

(c) Circle the sentence that clarifies the question.

(d) What reason is given for the personal choice selected by the writer?

_____

_____

(e) Does the personal choice fit the interpretation of the question?

(f) On a scale of 1 (poor) to 5 (excellent), how would you rate this answer?

1   2   3   4   5

C. General Objective: To develop the skills to examine <u>values</u> and beliefs

   SPECIFIC OBJECTIVE: Learn to value oneself as a source of data and as the identifier of personal social problems.

1. <u>Do We Practice What We Preach? or We Say It, But Do We Believe It?</u>

   when: two class periods

   what: no materials necessary

   how: (1) Write on the board some statement that most Americans accept or support, such as:

   Innocent until proven guilty.

   Separation of church and state.

   Equal opportunity for all.

   All men are created equal.

   (2) Hold class discussion encouraging class to suggest Court decisions, laws, etc. that both go against the statement or support it. Is the statement only given lip service or is it really practiced in America today?

   Questions to discuss:

   (a) Do you think there are such things as American values? (evaluation question)

   (b) Are the value statements above exclusively American? (convergent questions)

   (c) If you had the power, would you require every person in the world to hold American values? (divergent question)

   (d) Are the value statements above in your opinion actually practiced in the United States? (evaluation question)

2. <u>Who Owns the Problem? Who Made the Rules? II</u>[7]

   when: one class period

   what: chart to gather data

   how: Have students list laws, regulations, controls that affect how we live in one column or the other on the chart. They should be prepared to defend their choice of column. Can the class reach a consensus on any necessary or unnecessary rules?

```
┌─────────────────────────────────────────────────────────┐
│                          RULES                          │
│                                                         │
│        NECESSARY                      UNNECESSARY        │
│                                                         │
│     _____              _____      │
│                                                         │
│     _____              _____      │
│                                                         │
│     _____              _____      │
│                                                         │
│     _____              _____      │
│                                                         │
│     _____              _____      │
│                                                         │
└─────────────────────────────────────────────────────────┘
```

NOTE: This activity is important, though in passing it may seem simple and unimportant. This activity is one in a series that calls for the student to be the source of data. The content and the data come from the class, and this is the starting point for a reflective inquiry study. The students own the problem and are one of the sources of data.

SPECIFIC OBJECTIVE: Examine American values in government and evaluate ways government affects life.

3. What Value Student Government?

   when: three class periods

   what: copy of Student Council Constitution for each student

   how: This activity allows students to examine a decision-making body that may directly affect their lives.

   (1) Have students read the constitution of the student government to understand its organization. What values seem to be implied? Are these values the same as those held by the community?

   (2) How are members elected to the student council? Is it a cross-section of the student population? Are any groups of students not represented?

   (3) What concerns does the student council act on? Do these concerns actually affect students? What issues does the class think the council should be concerned with?

   (4) Attend a student council meeting.

4.   Identifying Values: Local, State, and National

when: two class periods

what: newspapers

how: This activity is based on the idea that a newspaper reflects
the interests of the readers, and that interests reflect
values. To know what type of stories are printed, in part,
helps one to know what the readers and their government value.

(1) Divide the students into three groups. Have group members
bring in all the articles they can find that deal in any
way with government (local, state, national) from the
newspaper of a specified date.
(2) Have groups divide the articles into local, state, or
national news and count the number of articles they have
collected. What kind of news is stressed? What does
this suggest about the newspaper?
(3) Study the local news articles and identify the values
that seem to be reflected, i.e., corruption, honesty,
etc. Do the same for the state news articles and then
the national news articles.
(4) How do the values of the three sets of articles compare?
(5) How do the students feel about the values identified?
Do these values have any influence on them at present?
Will these values affect them in the future?

SPECIFIC OBJECTIVE: Identify one's values as reflected in future choices.

5.   Rank the Value of Innovations

when: two class periods

what: magazines, art supplies

how: (1) Have each student write down any 10 technological or
medical innovations; for example, radio, TV, test-tube
babies, vaccines, etc.
(2) Have student cut out a magazine picture or make a drawing
to illustrate each of the 10 innovations they have named.
(3) List and rank innovations from most useful innovation to
least useful, including a reason beside each innovation.
(4) Discuss choices and rankings. Some questions to ask:

(a) Are there gains and losses when we depend on technology?

(b) Does technology own us or do we own technology?

(5) In preparation for a future activity, have students
identify 10 possible innovations or medical break-
throughs that might be developed in the future.

6.   Funding Future Technology Projects

when: two class periods

what: list of 10 possible future technological or medical innova-
       tions from previous activity, or the list supplied below.
       The student list would be preferable.

how: (1) The needs of today's society are many and varied and all
           seem urgent. There are social problems, medical problems,
           and environmental problems, all needing funds for research
           and development. Hold a brief class discussion on above
           issues.

       (2) Divide class into groups. Each group must act as a
           federal government funding agency. Give each group the
           list of technological and medical innovations. Each of
           the 10 projects proposed was in the President's Budget
           and was to receive $10 million so all projects together
           were to receive a total of $100 million. The Congress
           cut the $100 million to $50 million. You must decide
           from which of the 10 projects the $50 million will be cut.
           List the amount you propose to fund each project; no
           project should receive more than $10 million.

Examples of possible projects:

_____ 1. Cancer research

_____ 2. Project on car safety

_____ 3. Project on weather control

_____ 4. Desalinization of sea water into drinking water

_____ 5. Project for manned space visits to other planets

_____ 6. Project to develop solar power

_____ 7. Project on weapons in space

_____ 8. Develop bank to store human organs for transplant

_____ 9. Project to discover inexpensive substitute for gasoline

_____ 10. Project to find safe way to dispose of nuclear waste

$50 million

       (3) By consensus the group must decide the funds distribution.

       (4) Hold class discussion and compare groups' decisions. The
           following questions might be appropriate:
           (a) To what category of projects, people or things, did
               you fund the most money?
           (b) Does your funding tell you anything about what you
               value, and about what the class values?

D. General Objective: To apply knowledge through active <u>participation</u>

SPECIFIC OBJECTIVE: Identify the role of political systems through
participation.

1. <u>How Does a Bill Really Become a Law?</u>

when: one week

what: stages through which a bill must pass from the time it is
proposed until it becomes a law (lobby, quorum, veto, fili-
buster, pork-barrel, logrolling, committee system, and
judicial review should all be included)

how: Mock Congress

Why: Why role-play how a bill becomes law?
Reason: No bill ever became law as described in a text. The
process of law-making is dynamic. To identify that
dynamic process is one reason for using the simulation "Mock Congress."

(1) Class is divided into groups representing the three
branches of government, plus students representing lobby
groups.

(2) Teacher prepares a series of bills to be introduced. The
teacher can use real bills that failed to become laws and
some that made it, or the teacher can make up bills. The
bills should be controversial to show how bills can be
mired down in committee or affected by lobby groups. The
purpose is to show that bills do not all follow the cut
and dried process outlined in textbooks.

(3) Pass out the bills to the groups to be processed into
laws, with groups trying to pass them, groups trying to
change the bills or add to or subtract from them, and
groups trying to stop the bills altogether.

2. <u>Studying the School as a System</u>

when: two class periods

what: copy of the school or school corporation budget

how: (1) Divide the class into groups. Have each group examine
the budget and decide what changes they would make if
they could, and how the changes would affect the rest of
the budget.

(2) Groups can share their decisions with the class for group
discussion.

Why: The budget reflects the school priorities as well as the state requirements. The school is an important "system" which each of the students in the class has experienced and has probably made judgments about. Just how would students change the system if they could? What priorities would they identify and support financially if they had to make choices? Most any system is there to identify, evaluate, and set priorities. Given the community's values and culture, what should be the input of students into the educational system?

3. Participating in the Political Process

when: one week

what: identifying the political process

how: (1) Divide the class into groups. Give or have each group identify a project that is regulated in some way or in which specific steps must be followed. For example:

What steps would an interested group of parents have to take to get traffic lights installed at a dangerous intersection?

What procedures need to be taken to change zoning regulations so a gas station or small store could build in a residential neighborhood, or to keep these businesses from building in an area?

What are the procedures for changing school policy? How would a group of interested citizens approach the school board with their request for reform?

(2) Have groups research their projects stating steps, procedures, and possible solutions or consequences. Students may want to contact government officials or school officials who might be involved with such problems.

(3) Class discussion might be over these questions:
   (a) Are there procedures for filing a request? (cognitive-memory question)

   (b) Do the procedures vary between decision-making bodies, i.e., state legislature, city council, school board? (convergent question)

   (c) What would happen if you and your friends actually tried to bring about change? (divergent question)

   (d) Would you actually participate if your interests were involved? (evaluation question)

4. Creating a Class Human Rights Proposal

when: one week

what: no materials necessary

how: The purpose of this activity will be to present a human rights proposal and have it adopted by a "mock political convention" of class members.

(1) The class should be divided into groups that will each develop and offer its own human rights proposal. A spokesman from each group will present that group's proposal to the class "convention" (posters, visuals, etc. should be encouraged).

(2) The class as a "political convention" must vote on the statements and choose the one they want OR take parts of several in order to create an acceptable human rights proposal.

(3) The class may also wish to suggest appropriate places to send the proposal, i.e., student newspaper, student council. See following activity.

5. Human Rights Participation

when: one period

what: Human Rights Proposal statement agreed on in previous activity

how: Students will prepare letters to accompany the proposal and then send them to the following persons or groups:

Examples: Student Council   State government representatives
           School Board   Congressmen
           PTA   newspapers

or to any group or organization that the class may feel appropriate.

SPECIFIC OBJECTIVE: Identify one's own values and learn to participate in a group concerned with values.

6. Identifying Both Social Problems and a Consensus

when: one period

what: list of social or community problems

how: (1) Provide a list of problems to each student. Have the students rank the problems in order of priority, 1 being the problem student feels is most in need of attention, 2 being second, and so on.

(2) Separate the students into task oriented small groups. Each group will try to reach a consensus on ranking the problems. Consensus is very difficult to reach since every member of the group must agree to the order of ranking established by the group. Suggestions for reaching group consensus:

   (a) Don't change your mind just to go along with the other members of your group, but "bend" a little if you can agree a little with the group's opinion.
   (b) Avoid easy solutions such as majority vote, compromising, etc.
   (c) Listen to all opinions and use logic.
   (d) When group reaches consensus, each member should mark the group's ranking on his/her sheet and then record the difference between his/her own ranking and the group's. For example:

Individual Ranking	Social Problem	Group Ranking	Difference
3	alcoholism	5	2
5	unemployment	11	6

(3) Hold class discussion on:

   (a) Reasons for differences between individual and group rankings.
   (b) Similarities and differences between group rankings.
   (c) For person in each group whose personal ranking came closest to group ranking, were there reasons for this?

NOTE: The following activity is a technique for helping students identify problems.

PROBLEM LIST

	Individual Ranking	Social or Community Problem	Group Ranking	Difference
1.		school safety		
2.		highway safety		
3.		pollution		
4.		crime		
5.		unemployment		
6.		inflation		
7.		race relations		
8.		gun control		
9.		women's rights		
10.		alcoholism		
11.		world peace		
12.		cost of medical care		

7. <u>Inquiry Process II</u>[8]

Why this concern about inquiry when our interest is in citizenship?
Authorities say that the one major goal for teaching social
studies is that of developing citizenship. Remember, when
educators are talking about citizenship, they are not talking
about some vague abstraction but about you. Social studies
educators are primarily interested in your effectiveness as
you participate in a democratic society.

It should be clear that an assumption is being made. Educators ask
the question, "Why is it <u>best</u> for a citizen to inquire?" Not
only do teachers assume an answer to this question, but notice
that teachers also make a value judgment that there is a best
citizen. "The best citizens, according to some social studies
educators, should inquire in a democratic society because
they can discover for themselves the most meaningful proper-
ties of their environment." In other words, the best citizen
is the autonomous person who has gained the skill of checking
ideas about the environment--that is, a citizen capable of
making rational independent judgments.

<u>Inquiry as a Process</u>

Some would say that "the truth shall make you 'free.'" Others
believe that it is the process of seeking truth that makes you "free."
The author casts his lot with the latter belief, that is the process
of gaining knowledge (inquiry) that sets one free to be an effective
citizen, an autonomous citizen. Inquiry is a way of processing
information, and is a particular way to approach life. Inquiry is
one process by which rational decisions are made in a free, rational,
democratic society.

<u>What is Inquiry?</u>

Some authorities suggest that one way to avoid bias, stereotypes, and prejudiced thinking is to apply the inquiry process.
Inquiry merely provides a step-by-step process by which thoughts can
be verified. Inquiry implies a particular way of approaching life,
for true inquirers are critical thinkers who test the information
they gain through a proof process. The following six steps are part
of the proof process.

(1) <u>Experience</u> - The process of inquiry starts with an experience.

(2) <u>State of uncertainty and doubt</u> - The heart of inquiry is
not the established, symmetrical "givens" that generate
inquiry, it is that which does not fit--the irregular,
the confusing.

(3) <u>Framing the problem</u> - The sensing of the problem may lead
you to frame that which you do not know, and it is that
frame which becomes the statement of the problem. The
statement of the problem prescribes the boundaries
within which the conflict is seen and the tension created.

(4) <u>Formulating hypotheses</u> - When you frame a hypothesis you are literally "brainstorming the possibilities." The framing of the problem gives you the limits within which you will hypothesize.

(5) <u>Experiencing and evidencing</u> - The title of this stage almost explains itself. At this stage you gather and evaluate sources of evidence.

(6) <u>Generalization</u> - The final step in the inquiry process is generalization. The generalization is a statement about how well the hypothesis has given meaning to understanding the problem.

when: depends on problem studied

what: Inquiry Form; list of issues

how: (1) Student picks issue to investigate.
        (2) Each student uses Inquiry Form in investigation.
        (3) Individualized instruction--teacher gives help when needed as students work on forms.
        (4) Students' conclusions (generalizations) reported to class.

Suggested Issues

(If these issues do not spark interest, turn back to Activity 6, "Identifying Both Social Problems and a Consensus," and use problems list technique.)

world hunger
    birth control around the world
        problems in the "Fourth World" underdeveloped nations
            problems in the "Third World" underdeveloped nations

problems in the "Second World" developed nations
    problems in the "First World" developed nations
        China's role in the world
            Middle East conflict

use of power reserves
    problems of water and water usage
        growing deserts
            wars and the threat of wars

mining of the seas
    fishing rights
        space exploration
            control and use of space

atomic proliferation
    disease control
        pollution control
            United Nations

INQUIRY FORM

1. Experiencing: What experience have you had with the issue you have chosen from the list that has caused you to be interested in or curious about that issue?

    _____

    _____

2. Uncertainty and doubt: The issue can become a personal as well as a social problem if you feel the need to know. Express as best you can the uncertainty you feel about the issue. What confuses you?

    _____

    _____

3. Framing the problem: What do you know about the issue?

    _____

    _____

    What do you think you know about the issue?

    _____

    _____

    What is it you do not know about the issue?

    _____

    _____

4. Formulating hypotheses: The hypothesis is a proposed point of view on the issue. That view needs to be proved or disproved.

    _____

    _____

5. Exploring and evidencing: Gather and evaluate sources of evidence on the issue. Circle and then name the sources you will use in finding information about your hypothesis.

    books   pictures   newspapers   filmstrips   magazines

    interviews   personal observations   other

    _____

    _____

    List specific pieces of information that deal with your hypothesis.

    _____

    _____

6. Generalization: How does your information prove or disprove your hypothesis?

_____

_____

Evaluating the inquiry: What have you learned? Has the inquiry into the issue provided you with an accurate point of view on the issue? Explain:

_____

_____

_____

_____

_____

NOTE: An important point is that the inquiry process starts with a personal concern. This method is not particularly successful if problems or issues are identified for the student. The motivation to complete an inquiry is intrinsic; that is, the process is one way to study and perhaps develop an appropriate response to life's problems. Inquiry offers citizens in a democratic, complex, interdependent society one process by which to rationally think through problems and issues.

SPECIFIC OBJECTIVE: Identify oneself as part of a political social system (community) and how to effect change through social action.

8. Community Study and Social Action

    when: unit study; time on activity will vary

    what: materials as needed

    how:

> Many civics and government teachers favor community studies and some encourage social action. Community studies often take the form of the historical structure and function of the community, whereas some favor the study of community as a social problem requiring social action. This activity reflects both approaches.

The students' local community is by far the most easily accessible and complete resource available for study. By the time students reach high school they usually know much about their community--at least the parts that directly affect their personal needs and interests.

A CONTEXT FOR COMMUNITY STUDY

General Questions in Preparation for Community Study:

1. Identify what a community is. (see Community Study Branching Wheel below)

2. What is the "hallmark" of a community--that is, why is it the way it is?

3. Who lives in the community?

4. Community services: what are they and who provides them?

5. Compare and contrast communities. Are surrounding communities different?

Community Study Branching Wheel

A community study branching wheel is one way to visually express the concept of community. This example is only part of a wheel and how it can be expanded.

Questions to Ask About the History of the Community

1. What remains from the community's historic past (i.e., buildings, foundations, monuments--don't forget the cemeteries)?

2. What have people in the community saved from the past (i.e., books, pottery, buildings, machines, etc.)?

3. What do these remains suggest about the community's past?

4. Does the past in any way influence the present community?

Questions to Ask About the Present Community

1. Identify the geographic location of the community (maps, land-forms, natural resources, size)?

2. Describe life in the community; include where people live, work, go to school, shop, etc.?

3. Describe community's transportation and where people go and what they do for recreation?

4. What ethnic and racial groups are represented?

5. Is the community changing?

6. What problems will need community action?

Questions to Ask About the Future of the Community

1. Speculate on what your community will be like by the turn of the century?

2. Can you identify any changes now which might be significant to the future of the community?

3. Reconstruct the community in terms of the values you believe people will hold in the future?

4. How would the community have to change if you were to remain in the community?

ACTIVITIES WHICH WILL HELP STUDENTS TO ANSWER THE QUESTIONS:
PAST, PRESENT, AND FUTURE

Past

1. To identify similarities and differences between past generations by collecting data from students and parents, ask student to identify:

    "10 items that you know, see, can do or experience, which were unknown, impossible, or unimaginable for your parents (approximately 20 years ago), grandparents (approximately 50 years ago), great-grandparents (approximately 75 years ago) when they were your present age."

2. Identify historical records of community's past. Examples of sources:

photographs
artifacts (furniture, machinery, books, historic collections, badges, money, stamps)
important memorabilia to community (war monuments, historical markers)
newspapers: picture file, obituaries of important historical community figures, advertisements
senior citizens: oral history, personal possessions from past (clothes, books, jewelry, photos, mementos of local fairs)
old established businesses occasionally have historical records of the company's development
civic organizations usually have historians (Rotary, Elks, Kiwanis, Lions, Veterans organizations)

3. Suggested ways of using resources and questions:

(a) Invite senior citizens to describe community during certain periods of the community's growth and development.

(b) Projects: have students create objects that interpret historical significance, i.e., posters, mobiles, collages, dioramas, models. These displays will be particularly useful when comparing and contrasting with other displays on the present and future community.

Present Community Study

One useful way to think about studying the present community is by discussing the questions identified above as "Questions to Ask About the Present Community." Following that discussion, identify with the class different techniques for gathering information. The following are examples:

1. One of the richest sources about the community is a telephone book. Such a book contains regional maps, advertisements, community services, and, of course, names which reflect ethnic groups.

2. The community is a lab of resource people. Among those who should be considered are: long-term residents, librarians, public officials, newspaper editors, farmers, industrial managers, labor leaders, social workers and/or welfare personnel, ministers, and health officials.

3. Local or regional newspapers are an important source. Keep in mind there are many different kinds of special interest newspapers that might be available besides the local newspaper: ethnic papers, agricultural news, business news, papers serving large metropolitan areas, and papers from surrounding communities.

4. One interesting source about the community is its sounds; the sounds of the community may well reveal some important characteristics and help as a source of data. Suggest tape recording as a data source.

5. A photographic pictorial essay of the community is also an interesting way to study the community. The student photographers could be assigned to identify what typifies the community or to photograph special interests or problems. Of course, the important question to ask the photographer is, "Why choose these pictures?"

6. A popular way to study the community is to survey a selected population. The most available group, of course, would be the families of the students. Such surveys would include identifying employment patterns, social service patterns, volunteer patterns, social living patterns.

Present Social Action

Social action implies the identifying of problems or issues and the acting on those by the class. The assumption is that community action problems are relevant to students because they have experienced the problem and have come to identify or "own" the problem. Active involvement in identifying problems, collecting data, and effecting change are important to a decision-making, self-directive, effective citizen in a democracy. For "Identifying Both Social Problems and a Consensus" and "Inquiry Process," see the previous activities.

One of the more difficult parts of social action, having identified a problem and gathered data, is to develop a plan of action, a strategy. The following questions should help the class develop a strategy:

1. Which people or organizations/agencies are connected or involved with the problems or issues the class has identified?

2. How best can these people or organizations/agencies be alerted to the problems identified by the class? In other words, how best do you get your point across, realizing different approaches might be necessary for different organizations/agencies?

3. What alternatives are possible if people or organizations/ agencies do not respond?

4. What restraints might be encountered and what social action strategy would be an appropriate response? For example, how might publicity be used to arouse public awareness about the problems? Organizing a special interest group or petitioning are other strategies. What strategy works in your community?

Future

Having studied the past and the present community and as part of that study having identified problems and issues, students should begin to identify future problems. One useful way to think about studying the future is by discussing the questions identified above as "Questions to Ask About the Future of the Community."

1. If the students in their study of the present community have identified problems and issues as a study in social action, then an appropriate activity is the study of future problems and issues. These future problems could be treated as were the present problems under "Social Action" above.

2. Design the community as it might look by the turn of the century and about the year 2100. This design might include building materials, growth patterns, and speculation on lifestyles, ecology, and quality of life.

3. A popular futures activity is to prepare a time capsule to be opened in 100 years. The preparation of the capsule might include the following considerations:

    (a) What is important to say about the past and present community so that a criteria might be developed by which items may be selected?

    (b) Students should identify items (artifacts) which reflect how they want their community to be remembered or reflect how they think their community will be remembered.

CONCLUSION: A community study and social action activity contains all four objectives: gaining information, processing, and valuing, with emphasis on participating. This study includes observing, recording, and interpreting, as well as identifying community problems and issues. Community study provides a basis for comparative studies with other communities and illustrates such basic concepts as interdependence within communities as well as between peoples on earth in past, present, and future. Such a study acts as a springboard for many other activities that also aim at the social studies goal of educating for effective citizenship.

Notes

1 Barth, J. L. Advanced social studies education (Washington, DC: University Press of America, 1977), p. 23.

2 This activity was originally published in Elementary and junior high/middle school social studies curriculum, activities, and materials (2nd ed.) by J. L. Barth (Washington, DC: University Press of America, 1983), p. 145, and has been revised for publication in this text.

3 Ibid., p. 146.

4 Ibid., p. 145.

5 This technique has been widely used as a technique to examine change. One example of how this technique has been used to gather data is reported in: Barth, J. L. Understanding change through comparison. Southern Social Studies Quarterly, 1981, 7(1), 21-29.

6 This activity was originally developed in 1980 for "Questions Social Studies Students Ask," a Division of Innovative Education ESPA Title IV-C Research Project of the North Montgomery School Corporation, Linden, Indiana. In particular, the author wishes to recognize the contribution of James Spencer and David Horney in the development of this project. This activity has been revised for publication in this book.

7 Barth, Elementary and junior high, p. 189.

8 Ibid., p. 210.

INTEREST FORM

You have just completed the Chapter Civics and U.S. Government. In an effort to have you identify activities and materials that seem most promising to you in this subject area, please fill out the following interest form.

Instructions:

Identify two activities from this chapter. Name the activities and briefly describe why these particular activities are of interest to you.

ACTIVITY 1

ACTIVITY 2

CHAPTER II

GLOBAL/INTERNATIONAL, WORLD HISTORY, AND GEOGRAPHY

ACTIVITIES AND MATERIALS FOR
GLOBAL/INTERNATIONAL, WORLD HISTORY, AND GEOGRAPHY

ACTIVITIES AND MATERIALS (Cont.)

CHAPTER II

GLOBAL/INTERNATIONAL, WORLD HISTORY, AND GEOGRAPHY

Organization of the Chapter

Each chapter represents a particular subject area, in this case global/ international, world history, and geography. Each chapter consists of three parts: the first part is a brief discussion on courses, topics, and national trends in teaching global/international, world history, and geography through- out the United States; the second part is an example of a state subject area program; the third part has activities and materials for the subject area categorized by the four objectives of teaching social studies--gaining knowl- edge, processing, valuing, and participating.

I. Topics Taught and National Trends in Teaching Global/International, World History, and Geography

One of the emphases in social studies over the past twenty years has been on global studies, studies that have to do with the interdependence of all peoples on the earth. Leaders in the social studies movement have emphasized the importance of global futures which means students need to be global minded, that is have a global perspective on the current problems of the world. This increased interest in global perspective is, in part, a consequence of modern technology, and the desire on the part of some nations to reach out and affect the social, political, and economic affairs of other nations. Global studies includes courses which are normally thought of as electives and encompass some of the following: world history, western civilization, world geography, early and modern world civilization, and area studies such as Asia, Africa, and Latin America. These courses are normally offered at the ninth and tenth grade levels, with world history and geography being offered most frequently in tenth grade.

Course, Topics, and Themes Frequently Covered in Global/International, World History, and Geography

Objectives of the World History Course

The teaching of world history, world problems, and global studies includes a varying pattern of objectives. Three of the most common are:

1. provide students with a traditional coverage of western civilization

2. develop the students' world view by devoting from one-half to two-thirds of the course time to western civilization and the remainder of the course to "area study" units dealing with non-western cultures

3. broaden students' understanding of differing cultures by focusing only on area study units--Asia, Africa, Middle East, China, Russia, etc.

The traditional course intends to provide students with an understanding of the development of western civilization and of the origins of democratic institutions with emphasis on expanding the students' world view through the study of modern European nations. Attention is given to the development of political institutions and their place in modern world affairs. Students will identify the growth of the U.S. in the context of western European and world history. The courses that include area studies intend to promote understanding of major non-western cultures and of the developing nations of Asia, Africa, and Latin America, with emphasis on their role in recent and current world affairs.

Objectives of the Geography Course

The course proposes to expand the students' world view by providing information about physical features, climates, resources, and people of the world. Emphasis is on developing the students' understanding of basic geographic concepts and their ability to interpret maps and globes.

Basic Content of the World History Course

Under the traditional coverage of western civilization, usually from six to twelve weeks are devoted to the topics of pre-history and early civilizations, Greek and Roman civilizations, the Middle Ages, and the transition to modern times. The remainder of the school year focuses on the following topics: the development of European nations, the French Revolution and Napoleon, the Industrial Revolution, the growth of nationalism and imperialism in the 19th and early 20th Centuries, World War I, and the inter-war period with emphasis on the cold war and the work of the United Nations. Some courses will have a short unit on the period before 1789 and then devote most of the year to the period beginning with the French Revolution and carrying on to the present day. These courses are sometimes called "Modern History" or "Modern World History."

Courses that combine western civilization and area studies usually contain chronological units dealing with western civilization during the first half or two-thirds of the year, treating very briefly the ancient and medieval periods. The remainder of the year is likely to be devoted to area study units such as "USSR and its Satellites," "The Two Chinas," "Japan," "India," "Southeast Asia," "the Middle East," and "Africa South of the Sahara." Not all of the units listed will be included, but a selection from them is likely.

Courses that focus entirely on area studies usually depend on multidisciplinary area study units emphasizing history with special attention to geography and governmental institutions, during perhaps one-third of the year's work. Area study units cited above, plus a unit on Latin America, are likely to constitute the remainder of the year's work.

Basic Content of the Geography Course

Attention is usually given to maps and map interpretation and world patterns including landforms, oceans, climates, vegetation, population distribution, and resources. Some courses contain units concerning the geographic influences on international trade and world affairs and regional or culture area studies. Some courses also include attention to historical geography.

Trends in Teaching World History

Evidence as to the proportion of schools that cling to the traditional European-centered world history course and the proportion that are including attention to non-western and Latin American cultures is confused. Review of recent curriculum guides suggests, however, that the traditional course remains firmly entrenched. There seems to be a continuing emphasis on the origins of democratic institutions, and on economic and social history. These are not new, of course, but are aspects that seem to receive continued emphasis. It seems safe to conclude that there is movement toward including study of non-western cultures in the tenth grade course and that this movement will continue at an accelerated pace. It should be noted that there has also been some discussion of moving world history to grade eleven or grade twelve, with the argument that this course is appropriate for more mature students. However, this course remains in grade ten in an overwhelming majority of schools; where it is an elective course, students frequently are permitted to take it when they are in the eleventh or twelfth grade, but it is considered a tenth grade offering.

For the past twenty years world historians and geographers mostly at the university level have been unhappy with the organization and presentation of their particular subject areas. The historians and geographers have been most interested in providing materials and encouraging students to think as would an historian or geographer. They are concerned that their historic or geographic discipline be accurately introduced to high school students. Another trend which we noted earlier was the emphasis by social studies educators on global studies. Their point of view is that all social studies, whether it be in elementary or secondary, should emphasize the interdependence of humanity and that this should be noted in each course and that it not be exclusively the property of world history courses. In other words, the social studies educators are interested in emphasizing world-mindedness as part of every social studies course.

Trends in Teaching Geography

The chief trend seems to be a movement away from "traditional" geography toward a "culture area" approach, with a definite multi-disciplinary pattern being applied, i.e., study of the geographic features, history, government, and economic and cultural patterns of the area.

II. Illustrations of State World History and Geography Courses

There is no one prescribed social studies program throughout the United States. However, one state's description of its world history, geography, and area studies programs will illustrate the content which the state expects to be taught. The following course descriptions identify a state's suggested social studies curriculum which includes such content areas as Early World Civilizations, Modern World Civilizations, Western Civilization, World Geography, and area studies such as Latin America, Asia, and Africa.

Early World Civilizations
The focus of Early World will be on the era of ancient history. Content selected should be in sufficient depth to provide a basis for students to compare and analyze ways of life and patterns of culture, emphasizing both the diversity and commonality of Mankind's behavior. Content should include prehistory, the rise of civilization in the Fertile Crescent, Africa, Asia, and the classical world, among other areas of specialization.

Modern World Civilizations
: Students take an in-depth look at the Twentieth Century world. Students will examine different cultures as they exist in the world today and make comparative analyses of the various kinds of governments, economic systems, and social orders. Foreign relations will be examined from the viewpoint of national interests, and the successes or failures of diplomacy should be examined as well.

Western Civilization
: This course includes a study of some of the significant Western and non-Western world cultures, past and present. Content selected should be in sufficient depth to provide a basis for students to compare and analyze ways of life and patterns of culture, emphasizing both the diversity and commonality of Mankind's behavior. Suggested units are: Prehistory, the Middle East, Western Europe, Russia and the Soviet Realm, Asia, Latin America, and Sub-Sahara Africa.

World Geography
: This course is designed to provide opportunity for students to study the interaction of man and his environment, in space and time. The study includes current developments around the world which affect physical and cultural settings. Cultural settings include people, their political structure, way of life, customs, mores, and past events that affect their environment. Emphasis is also on the geographical processes which affect decisions made concerning interrelationships among nations, production and distribution of goods, use and abuse of resources, and political and economic conditions. Urban analysis and population problems might be a very important aspect of this course.

Latin America Area Studies
: This study is designed to give students understanding and appreciation for the Latin American peoples, their cultures, and achievements. Content which emphasizes Twentieth Century developments includes: environmental and cultural factors that have influenced their way of life; social, political, and economic developments and institutions since 1900; and contemporary inter-American relations. Background information should include at least a brief survey of the major Indian civilizations of Latin America, the Spanish colonial system and European institutions developed in the Americas, and the resulting struggle to establish independent governments and the ensuing problems.

Asian Studies
: This course in Asian Studies is designed to give students some insight into the rich cultures of Asia. It offers students an opportunity to study in depth aspects of culture in one or more of the dominant countries such as China, India, or Japan, emphasizing the role of religions and traditions in shaping people's actions, attitudes, and

response to change. Other aspects of their cultures are explored, such as art, literature, and the development of social, economic, and political institutions. This study should also emphasize the importance of understanding the modernization problems of traditional Asian societies as the student views values and cultures which were not born in the western world.

African Studies

This study is designed to give students understanding and appreciation for the African peoples, their cultures and achievements. Content which emphasizes Twentieth Century developments includes: environmental and cultural factors that have influenced their way of life; social, political, and economic developments and institutions since 1900; and contemporary African-World relations. Background information should include at least a brief survey of the major early kingdoms and cities of Africa, the European colonial systems of Africa, and the resulting struggle to establish independent governments and the ensuing problems.[1]

III. Activities and Materials Categorized by Gaining Knowledge, Processing, Valuing, and Participating

A.   General Objective: To gain knowledge about the human condition which includes past, present, and future

SPECIFIC OBJECTIVE: The purpose of the following series of activities is to help students to identify what a concept is, i.e., a mental image of something; a concept embodies facts or attributes that events have in common. Students should conclude by being able to define and to recognize a concept from data.

1.   Developing the Skill to Identify Concepts

when: two class periods

what: sample concept test below

how: This activity is to help students identify and define concepts.

(1) Have students fill out concept test below.

(2) Discuss answers to concept test with the class using their answers to develop a meaning for the term concept. Have students suggest concepts relating to global or world history and list them on the board.

(3) Have students develop concept test similar to the one below using resource materials available in the room. Compile best questions for use at a later date.

CONCEPT TEST

Instructions: Underline the one word that does not fit with the other words. In the space provided write what the remaining three words (items, etc.) have in common, their relationship (concept).

1. a. teacher; b. janitor; c. PTA president; d. principal

   school personnel

2. a. evolution; b. stability; c. growth; d. modification

   change

3. a. food; b. money; c. shelter; d. clothing

   cultural necessities

4. a. czar; b. king; c. president; d. emperor

   political leaders not elected

5. a. telephone; b. C-B; c. sign language; d. TV

   two-way communication

6. a. hotel; b. igloo; c. tent; d. house

   single family dwelling

Fill in three words (names of items, etc.) that fit the concept (relationship).

1. a. _____ ; b. _____ ; c. _____

   life style

2. a. *food* ; b. *shelter* ; c. *socialization*

   culture

3. a. *exchange* ; b. *survival* ; c. *support*

   interdependence

4. a. _____ ; b. _____ ; c. _____

   systems

5. a. *transform* ; b. *grow* ; c. *alter*

   change

6. a. _____ ; b. _____ ; c. _____
   _____ populations

7. a. _____ ; b. _____ ; c. _____
   _____ dignity of man

8. a. _____ ; b. _____ ; c. _____
   _____ habitat

9. a. _____ ; b. _____ ; c. _____
   _____ sovereignty

10. a. *sun* ; b. *oil* ; c. *coal*
   _____ energy

11. a. _____ ; b. _____ ; c. _____
   _____ scarcity/allocation

12. a. _____ ; b. _____ ; c. _____
   _____ institution

13. a. _____ ; b. _____ ; c. _____
   _____ power

14. a. _____ ; b. _____ ; c. _____
   _____ conflict

15. a. _____ ; b. _____ ; c. _____
   _____ communication

SPECIFIC OBJECTIVE: Identify the cultural universals contained in the
concept of culture and how they vary for different cultures and different
times.

2. Concept Circle

    when: one class period

    what: concept circle (following page)

    how: (1) Have class brainstorm possible characteristics that all
               cultures might share to develop a concept of culture.
               List all responses on the board, then see if the list
               can be categorized. Eliminate characteristics that can-
               not be defended with examples.

           (2) Place characteristics of culture inside little circles
               inside the large circle. This concept circle can then
               be used to study other cultures by filling in specific
               data about the selected country in the appropriate
               circle.

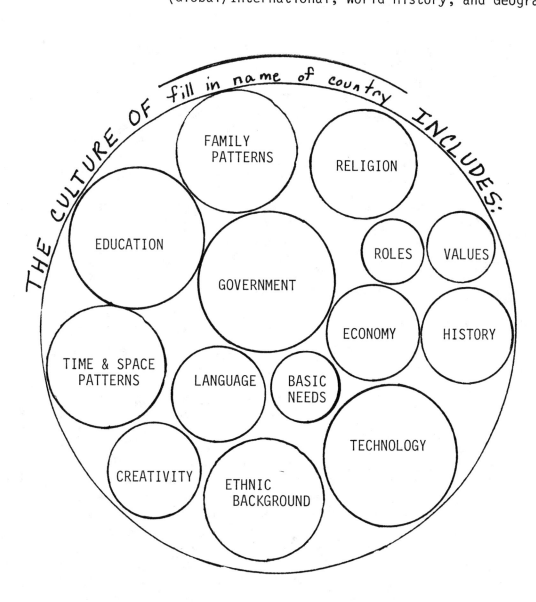

3.   Comparing Cultures

when: two class periods

what: illustrations of cultural exchange

how: (1) Have students look for illustrations of cultural exchange
            (movies, music, etc.) or bring in clippings about cul-
            tural exchanges, sport and music events for example.
        (2) Have students speculate on the influence of the cultural
            exchange they have identified. Examples of cultural
            exchange:
              Books or magazines from foreign countries
              Foreign movies
              TV or radio shows imported from abroad
              Art exhibits from foreign countries touring U.S.
              Trade goods or technology imported for an international
                fair or exhibition
              Clothing imported
              Touring groups (dance, drama, music)
              Sports events featuring foreign teams or individuals

(3) If there is an exchange student or someone the teacher of one of the students knows who is from a foreign culture, invite them to talk to the class. What were the person's expectations and ideas of the U.S. before arriving and where did these ideas come from? How accurate were the person's expectations? What impressions do the students have about that person's country and how accurate are these impressions according to that person?

(4) Students might like to investigate a number of cultural exchange programs to identify what agencies sponsor them, what the qualifications or requirements are, and what the programs hope to accomplish.

4.   <u>Concept Wheel II</u>[2]

when: one class period

what: wheel diagram

how: The following is another method to help students understand concepts.

Place anything you want to understand (event, trend, idea) in the middle of a small circle in the middle of a page. Draw lines spokelike out from the circle at the end of which are written implications, consequences, associations, etc. If you wish, you can then run out consequences of the consequences and so forth. This gives another orientation to the understanding you generate from the original idea in the middle of the circle. For example:

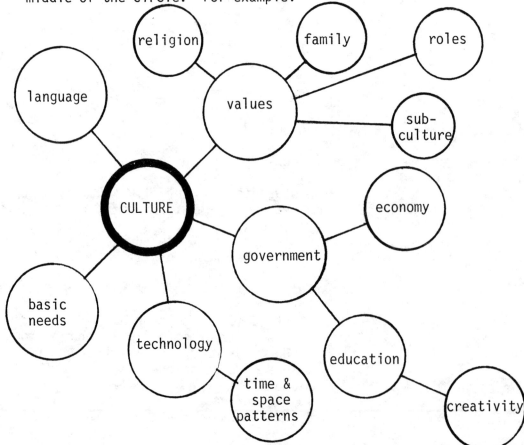

SPECIFIC OBJECTIVE: Investigate basic beliefs of various religions/moral philosophies and their impact on cultures; generalize about the common characteristics of these religions and their functions.

5.   World History Through the Study of World Religion

when: three class periods

what: list of world religions

how: (1) Divide the class into groups.
(2) Assign a religion to each group and have them research
the symbols or the way in which the specific religion
decorates its place of worship.
(3) Have groups prepare a display of what they have discovered,
using illustrations of things they have made.
(4) Hold class discussion on the meaning of the various
symbols and decorations. Do all religions have some
symbols in common?

Major World Religious Groups

Christians	Confucianists
Roman Catholic	Buddhists
Eastern Orthodox	Shintoists
Protestant	Taoists
Moslems	Jews
Hindus	

6.   Identifying and Comparing World Religions

when: five class periods

what: sample chart below

how: (1) Hold a class discussion on what students would need to
know about religions or philosophies (moral) in order to
compare them. Write suggestions on the board. Using
the suggestions, prepare an outline or set of questions
the students can follow (see below).
(2) Divide the class into groups. Have each group select a
religion or philosophy to research using the outline or
questions as a guide.
(3) Compare the findings of the various groups by discussing
the similarities and differences between the religions
or philosophies.

_____
name of religion or philosophy

1.   Is it monotheistic (one god)?
2.   Is there a written text?
3.   How does it explain creation and man's purpose on earth?
4.   Does it project a future beyond death?
5.   Does it have an organized assembly or structure (hierarchy)?
6.   etc.

Follow-up Activity: See activity "Identifying a Personal
   Philosophy or Religion" under Objective C. Develop the
   skill to examine values and beliefs in this chapter.

7.   Wanted for Interviewing: Dead or Alive

when: two class periods

what: interview form (below)

how: Have students each select one famous, distinguished, renowned,
        or notorious person from ancient, medieval, or modern times
        whom they would like to interview. Did this person have a
        particular religious or moral philosophy that led them to
        act in a way that has made them famous? Students can use the
        interview form either while they are researching their
        choices or as a class assignment when their research is
        finished.

INTERVIEW FORM

_____
        name of person being interviewed

dates: _____ _____   occupation: _____
        born   died

1.   Why should I know you? What are you famous for?

     _____

     _____

     _____

2.   What should I learn from your experience?

     _____

     _____

     _____

3.   Suppose you could live in another time, what would that time
     be, and how would you have changed history?

     _____

     _____

     _____

4.   Did you contribute to the progress of mankind? What was your
     philosophy?

     _____

SPECIFIC OBJECTIVE: Define nationalism and other "isms"; describe and
evaluate the influence of these isms on how one would view the world

8.   Knowing Your "isms"

when: three class periods

what: list of terms: Nationalism   Imperialism
                        Sectionalism   Colonialism
                        Internationalism/Globalism   Jingoism
                        Ethnocentrism   Protectionism

how: (1) Have students research definitions for these terms.
        (2) Have students make displays, i.e., collage, poster, etc.,
            on one of these terms.
        (3) Discuss the terms as they apply to countries or cultures
            previously studied.
        (4) Discuss the role and activities of the United Nations in
            relation to these terms.
        (5) Give students a list of the "isms" above. Ask them to
            identify those isms which might represent a cause and
            effect relationship. For example:

nationalism/ethnocentrism/jingoism/imperialism/protectionism/nationalism

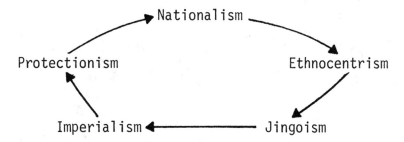

        (6) Using the "isms" from the list of terms above, identify
            which ism fits the following statements:

            1. We are all traveling together on the   _____
               spaceship earth
            2. America, love it or leave it   _____
            3. Differences are only skin deep   _____
            4. Strict immigration laws   _____
            5. We must all learn to become brothers   _____
            6. All men are created equal   _____
            7. Buy American   _____
            8. There is no second best in the arms race   _____
            9. We will save our little brown brothers   _____
           10. I'd rather be dead than red   _____

        See the following activity, "National Concept Wheel," as an
        example of how one could diagram (represent) the relation-
        ships that could flow from a concept such as nationalism.

9. <u>National Concept Wheel</u>[3]

    when: one class period

    what: concept wheel (see below)

    how: (1) Hold a class discussion on nationalism, helping the class
                identify what fits with the concept of nationalism.
          (2) Develop a concept wheel with nationalism as the center.
          (3) When completed, have students apply the wheel to the
                United States and two other countries from different
                parts of the world. Does the concept wheel need to be
                changed or altered to fit the three different countries?

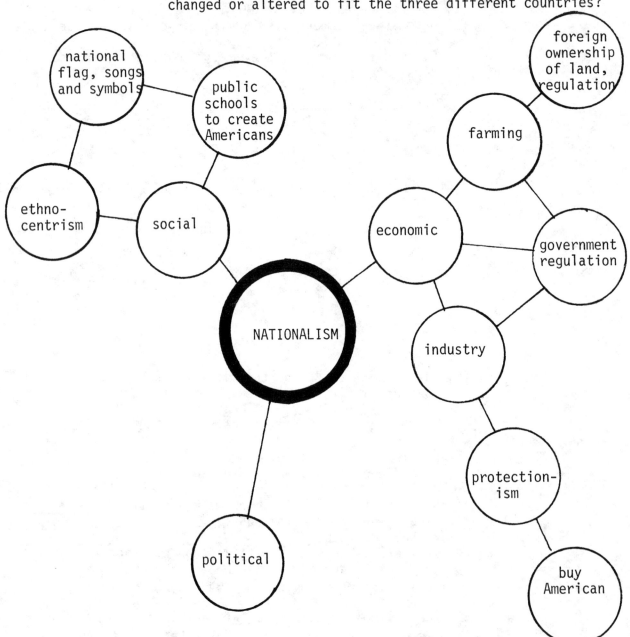

10. <u>National Anthems and Nationalism</u>

when: one class period

what: recordings of national anthems from four or five countries
        with a translation of their lyrics, i.e., France, Great
        Britain, Russia, Canada, United States, Germany, Australia
        (see lyrics below)

how: (1) Distribute copies of the lyrics and have class listen to
            the records.
        (2) Identify how the music and lyrics affect listener and
            whether they instill feelings of nationalism.
        (3) Which of the anthems do the students find most inspiring?
            Rank the anthems according to a criteria developed from
            the "identified effect" above. Could the class write
            lyrics for a national anthem? Are there certain words
            and thoughts that are common to all anthems? Do lyrics
            suggest a national message? Can the class clearly
            identify that message?

SAMPLE LYRICS

FRANCE   La Marseillaise

Ye sons of France, awake to glory
Hark, Hark, what myriads bid you rise:
Your children, wives and grand-sires hoary,
See their tears and hear their cries,
See their tears--and hear their cries!
Shall hateful tyrants mischief breeding
With hireling hosts, a ruffian band
Affright and desolate the land,
While peace and liberty lie bleeding?
To arms, to arms, ye brave!
Th' avenging sword unsheathe!
March on! March on!
All hearts resolved on victory or death.

GREAT BRITAIN   God Save The Queen

God save our gracious Queen,
Long live our noble Queen,
God save the Queen;
Send her victorious, Happy and glorious,
Long to reign over us:
God save the Queen.

RUSSIA

Unbreakable Union of free-born Republics,
Great Russia has welded forever to stand;
Created in struggle by will of the peoples,
United and mighty, our Soviet Land!

Sing to our Motherland, glory undying,
Bulwark of peoples in brotherhood strong!
Flag of the Soviets, peoples' flag flying,
Lead us from victory to victory on!
Lead us from victory to victory on!

CANADA   O Canada

O Canada! Our home and native land!
True patriot love in all the sons command.
With glowing hearts we see thee rise,
The True North strong and free;
And stand on guard, O Canada,
We stand on guard for thee.
O Canada! Glorious and free!
We stand on guard, We stand on guard for thee,
O Canada! We stand on guard for thee.

GERMANY (West)

Unity and right and freedom
for the German fatherland;
let us all pursue this purpose
brotherly, with heart and hands.
Unity and right and freedom
are the pawns of happiness.
Flourish in this blessing's glory
flourish, German fatherland.

11. Promoting the Nationalistic Feeling

when: two class periods

what: texts of speeches by political leaders

how: (1) As a class have students identify a number of political
           leaders (not necessarily contemporary or current leaders)

       (2) Have students study texts of speeches of several of these
           leaders to determine how they created unity and stirred
           feelings of nationalism in their listeners. How did their
           actions promote nationalism?

Following are some quotes from well-known political leaders.
These may be analyzed in class discussion and used as a
starting point for students' individual research on political
leaders.

The only thing we have to fear is fear itself.

                              Franklin D. Roosevelt
                              First Inaugural Address
                              March 4, 1933

Victory at all costs, victory in spite of all terror,
victory however long and hard the road may be; for
without victory there is no survival.

I have nothing to offer but blood, toil, tears and sweat.

> Winston Churchill
> First Statement as Prime Minister
> House of Commons
> May 13, 1940

Never in the field of human conflict was so much owed by
so many to so few.

> Winston Churchill
> Tribute to Royal Air Force
> House of Commons
> August 20, 1940

MANKIND HAS GROWN STRONG IN ETERNAL STRUGGLES AND IT WILL
ONLY PERISH THROUGH ETERNAL PEACE.

GERMANY WILL EITHER BE A WORLD POWER OR NOT AT ALL.

> ADOLF HITLER
> MEIN KAMPF, 1933

The New Frontier of which I speak is not a set of promises--
it is a set of challenges. It sums up not what I intend to
offer the American people, but what I intend to ask of them.

> John Kennedy
> Speech Accepting Democratic
>   Nomination
> July 15, 1960

And so my fellow Americans, ask not what your country can
do for you; ask what you can do for your country.

> John Kennedy
> Inaugural Speech
> January 20, 1961

Discipline is the soul of an army. It makes small numbers
formidable, procures success to the weak, and esteem to all.

> George Washington
> Letter of Instruction to the
>   Captains of the Virginia
>   Regiments
> July 29, 1759

To be prepared for war is one of the most effectual means of
preserving peace.

> George Washington
> First Annual Address to Congress
> January 8, 1790

SPECIFIC OBJECTIVE: Identify the geography of a country through the study of a single resource or cultural factor.

12. The Study of Nations Through Exchange Rates and the Value of Money

when: one class period

what: catalog of foreign imports, illustrations of imported goods as found in newspapers and magazines or catalogs from specialty stores such as Pier I or Italian Imports, list of current money exchange rates from the bank (some newspapers carry the rates)

how: (1) Price the items in the illustrations in terms of their own currency.
(2) Assign students or groups of students to certain countries and have them "buy and sell" using the exchange rates to change the currency when goods "move" from one country to another. (Local banks will either have this information or can get it for you. Remember that exchange rates can and do change daily.)
(3) Next, have the currency rates fluctuate severely. What happens, then, if prices are not adjusted? Some items may be too expensive and thus unattractive to the buyer.
(4) Ask the class: If the American dollar is "strong" overseas, who would be happy in the U.S.? Who would be happy in Europe and Asia? If you were to visit France this summer, which would you want, a strong dollar or a weak dollar? If your family builds cars, what strength of dollar would they want overseas?

13. The Study of Nations Through Comparison of a Single Resource

when: three class periods

what: chart below

how: Select a single natural resource such as coal, water, iron, or oil. Compare that resource between selected nations using the chart below. (Use a new chart for each resource studied.)

OIL	COUNTRIES				
	U.S.	LIBYA	NIGERIA	MEXICO	ETC.
How much is available?					
Quality?					
Export?					
How important is it to that nation?					
(Categories selected by students)					

14. <u>Learning About the World Through "Adopting an Animal"</u>

    when: three class periods

    what: no materials necessary

    how: (1) Divide the class into groups and give each group a conti-
             nent or section of a continent to research in the area
             of animal life, i.e., What animals are native to the
             region? Is the animal useful or harmful? Is any animal
             an endangered species and why? Economic value of animals?
             Domestic and wild?
        (2) Compare group findings. Is there much overlapping?
        (3) Invite a representative from the zoo to come and speak to
             the class: Where does the zoo get animals from? What
             special problems do they have with care and feeding?

        <u>Alternative</u>: Have each student "adopt" an animal (select a
        specific animal preferably not native to the U.S.) and re-
        search that adopted animal.

        These two activities promote the study of geography through
        the students' research on climate, location, etc.

15. <u>The Study of Nations Through Comparison of Transportation Systems</u>

    when: three class periods

    what: maps and chart below

    how: Select countries with different types of land forms and
        varied geographic features (see chart). Have students re-
        search those countries' internal transportation system for
        shipping goods by rail, road, air, water, etc. After the
        students have identified the problems in transportation faced
        by the selected countries and the solutions arrived at, have
        them fill in the chart.

Countries	Problems				Solutions		
	mountains	desert	rivers	unique problem	tunnel	bridge	unique solution
ALGERIA							
PAKISTAN							
JAPAN							

16. <u>What if the Nation's Geography Was Different?</u>

when: two class periods

what: sample chart below

how: The objective of this activity is to select a single manufactured or processed product and note how that product affected the history of the country.

   (1) Have students identify in what countries steel production (for example) is a <u>vital</u> industry. (May want to limit this to one continent such as Europe.)
   (2) On a map determine the steel production centers and their relationship to the areas where the natural resources of coal and iron are mined. How close are the manufacturing centers that use the steel? Do the Common Market countries cooperate? Do the Eastern European countries cooperate? Which is more heavily industrialized, Eastern or Western Europe? How does this compare with population statistics?

<u>Drawing inferences</u>:
   Geography plays a decisive role in the development of a country. How might the history of the selected countries below have been different if their geographic placement had been different? Suppose the citizens of West Germany were miraculously transferred to Saudi Arabia, how would the climate, natural resources, religion, and attitude of Middle East Arabs affect the lifestyle of the West Germans? On the other hand, speculate on the effect the West German culture might have on the Arabs. Use responses as a source of discussion on the role of geography on a country's development.

	Cold (Alaska)	Desert (Middle Africa)	Rain Forest (Central America)	Isolated Island (New Zealand)	Varied Climate (Middle Europe)
Germany					
Russia					
Burma					
Etc.					

17. Home Sweet Home

    when: one class period

    what: pictures from magazines or other materials of dwellings from different parts of the world

    how: (1) Show the pictures to the class using an opaque projector.

        (2) Class discussion:

            In what country or particular area of the world would each of the dwellings be found?

            What influences what a dwelling looks like, i.e., climate, available materials?

            What can you infer from a person's house/home?

            Are there characteristics that all dwellings have in common?

            What dwelling appeals to the students the most?

SPECIFIC OBJECTIVE: Identify how each individual is linked (related to other parts of the world).

18. Newspaper Ads Provide Information About Local Links to the World[4]

    when: one week or longer

    what: local newspapers

    how: (1) Have students clip newspaper ads for products or services from another country.

        (2) Students should compile these ads into a collage. Ads could be from one day or a week or longer. The students could compile individual collages over a long period of time, or each student could bring an ad on one day and make a class collage. Over a longer period of time, you could make a very large class collage. As the collages are put together, either individually or as the class, the teacher might have students indicate on a map the places of the world that are represented.

        (3) Display the completed collage(s) and have students discuss ways their locale is linked to the world. Possible discussion questions:
           (a) In what categories can we place these links to the world?
           (b) Why do we have these links to the world?
           (c) Which are the most important to you? To your parents? To businesses? Farmers? Workers? Professional people?
           (d) Which links affect the most people? How are they affected? Is it a positive or a negative effect? Explain your answer.

19. Around the World With a Daily Newspaper

when: two class periods

what: Each student (or group of two or three, if class works well that way) should have one copy of a daily newspaper. Since it is usually not practical to have Sunday editions in the classroom, the larger weekday issues are recommended.

how: (1) Have each student (or group) clip all articles that deal with something related to a foreign country and affect him or her personally. See what kind of articles they pick out based on this bare-bones instruction. (If they cannot find anything that they believe affects them personally, then they really need this unit!) If they get bogged down, a few questions like this will get them started again:
  • Is anyone from here going to (or has anyone come from) another country?
  • Do you see anything about foreign products which you might use?
  • What country mentioned in the paper is farthest away from here? (OR: farthest in terms of how people live?) Can you think of anything at all that you know about that country? Can that possibly have anything to do with our country?
  • Can you find anything in the grocery ads (OR automobile ads OR want ads, etc.) that relates to a foreign country?

(2) As articles are located, they can be mounted around a large world map on the bulletin board, with string linking the article with the country involved. Have each student pick one article and tell why he is interested in it and how it affects our lives. Limit the talks to two minutes. More than one student may choose the same article, if the reasons are different.

As the study progresses, a collage of articles can be added to the map or to a globe which can hang as a mobile, thus reminding students of the wealth of information about the world available each day in the newspaper. It will continually excite and stimulate research on the part of the students.

Alternative

(1) Have the students keep a daily log of their local newspapers for a period of a week or longer. Maps should be posted as compiled.

(2) At the end of this period, the class should be ready for this type of analysis:
  (a) Rank the parts of the world according to the amount of coverage each had in your local paper at this

time. Regional divisions such as these could be used: West Europe, East Europe, Asia, sub-Sahara Africa, South America, Central America, Canada, Middle East . . .

(b) What part(s) of the world seem to be having the most consequences for your future? Note the "circled" event(s) on each map.

(c) Take your pile of articles which reported events you felt were most likely to have vital consequences for you in the future. Categorize these articles into the types of events they represent (human rights, distribution of natural resources, energy, etc.). What kinds of global problems do you see that you are most concerned about? What have other classmates chosen? Prepare an argument for your choice and debate with someone who has made another type of choice.

(d) Do you feel your local newspaper has provided you with adequate coverage of this vital global problem? What else do you think you should know about it? Make a list of the possible sources in your community for receiving this kind of information (possible individuals, as well as organizations, communication media, etc.).

(3) If your community has both weekly and daily newspapers, follow the above procedure in analyzing both. Compare the findings.

(4) Do you feel your local newspapers are providing you with adequate global coverage? What suggestions would you like to make to the publishers?

Perhaps members of the class would like to become contributors to the newspaper to better inform the local community about their global community. Such a contribution might take the form of an information column which, in each issue, presents an overview of a different country or city abroad, with special emphasis on events that are likely to affect local residents, however indirectly. Or, students may wish to "profile" organizations, industries, and individuals whom the class has discovered to be especially active globally.

20. What You Eat is What You Are: National Recipes

when: two class periods

what: recipes or cookbooks from various countries collected by the teacher or supplied by students--recipes from Italy, Germany, Spain, Nigeria, Japan, Mexico, etc.

how: (1) Have students examine recipes to see what they reveal about the cultures from which they come, i.e., what foods are probably plentiful or widely grown? Does the method

of preparation reveal anything about the culture? For
example, what do these ingredients suggest about the
nations from which they come? Do students know of any
foods eaten in foreign countries that seem strange or
unusual to us? For example, Bird's Nest Soup (Chinese):

Ingredients for the "Unofficial" Royal
Recipe of Thailand for Bird's Nest Soup

6 whole nests or 1¼ oz. "dragon's teeth"
   (dragon's teeth are broken bits of
      nests that are cheaper than whole
      nests)
8 cups chicken broth
2 cups of chicken
1 cup of ham
½ cup of pork
3/4 cup bean sprouts
8 quail eggs
2 egg whites (chicken)
1 cup chopped watercress leaves
coarse crystal sea salt

(2) If students are interested, have individuals or groups
volunteer to prepare several of the recipes and bring
them to class. Why not ask the home economics teachers?

Alternative

Have students search supermarkets, import food stores, and
specialty stores (Vietnamese, Korean, Greek, Asian) for foreign foods. Students can copy ingredients from the packages
or cans. What do the ingredients say about the culture where
they are produced?

21. Ethnic Restaurants in Your Town or City[6]

when: two class periods

what: yellow pages of the telephone book

how: (1) Have the students work in small groups (two to four) with
someone bringing a phone book for each group.

(2) Have the students quickly skim the restaurant section for
clues about ways restaurants are linked to the world.
Have them list the clues on scratch paper and discuss
these clues with the group or the class. Some clues might
be cities (such as you would infer from the Acapulco Inn),
countries (such as Doro's Excellent Italian Cuisine), or
other geographical locations (such as the Mediterranean
House). An inference might be based on the food adver-
tized, as in "gyros" (from Greece).

(3) Based on the clues discussed, have the groups work with the phone book to list at least 10 places in the world with which your community is linked via its restaurants. Have the groups report their findings to the class. The teacher might want to record the countries listed on the board or mark them on a map.

(4) Then, ask students to survey the yellow pages of the telephone book and identify sections other than the restaurant section that have evidence of global ties. List the clues that they used to identify other sections.

(5) After completing the activity, the following are possible discussion questions:
   (a) To what parts of the world do restaurants in our community tend to be linked, based on the evidence in the phone book?
   (b) Identify two or three reasons why these ethnic restaurants may be located in your community.
   (c) How much are these ethnic restaurants or foods a part of your life?
   (d) Describe at least five other procedures you might use to gather further evidence of world links in your community by making some firsthand field observations in your community. (In a very small community, the teacher might also have students use a phone book from a city nearby and make comparisons.)

Alternative

Repeat this exercise with other sections of the telephone yellow pages. Look under headings such as: automobiles, cameras, churches, television sets, travel agencies, sports equipment, manufacturing firms, civic and professional organizations.

22. Tracing a Family Tree[7]

when: one week

what: any family tree chart will do, see example following

how: Have students construct a family tree tracing their family's history as far back as possible. They will present these family trees to the class. Students might also compare family histories. (Since certain students might be sensitive about this, it would be best if they volunteer this information.) Students should be encouraged to discuss specific family customs and to compare these with the customs of other students' families. Students might be asked to speculate on:
   How living in the United States has affected the customs of their family.
   How their cultural/ethnic heritage has affected their family life.
   Why specific family customs developed.

How their ethnic group has influenced life in their community.
The impact of members of their family on the community.

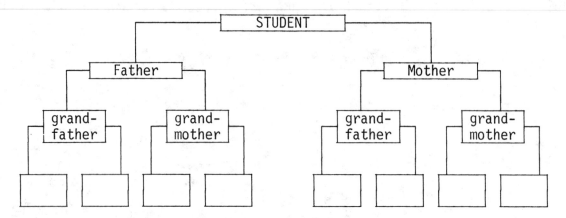

The following is a lesson that can be developed to supplement student efforts in the above activity.

Ethnic Smorgasbord

On a particular day, have students bring in a food or artifact representative of their ethnic background. They should describe each "ethnic dish" or artifact. You may want students to speculate on the origin of particular recipes or artifacts. To conclude the activity, have students discuss the similarities and differences between the various foods and artifacts.

23. Our Ethnic Ties--Then and Now[8]

when: one week

what: Information on their state or community is available from the tourist office of the state department of commerce or local chamber of commerce. Information on historical sites is available in travel guides, such as those published by oil companies and available in libraries. You might also check to see if there is an international center in the state capital.

how: (1) Have students collect data on festivals in the state that celebrate ethnic origins of citizens both now and in the past.

(2) Have students also collect data on cities in the state that have historical reminders of the ethnic background of citizens.

(3) After students have collected their information (to save time you might want to write to these places for them), the following are possible ways to use their data.
(a) Make bulletin board displays on the "parts of the world" that can be visited in their own state without

leaving the state.
(b) Report or demonstrate to the class crafts, customs, or styles of architecture from other parts of the world that can be found in cities in their state. (Consider guest speakers, if they are available.)
(c) As a class project, prepare a travel guide on how to "see the world" without leaving your state. This could be as simple or complicated as the class time and interest allows. If it is possible, have the class visit one of the places in their travel guides.
(d) Make a large map and indicate with appropriate pictures where the national or ethnic festivals are located in your state. Students in small groups (two or three) could be responsible for one picture.

(4) Any of these activities could be followed with some of the following questions for class discussion.
(a) Based on our information, from what parts of the world have people come to our state?
(b) People from what countries tended to settle in which parts of our state?
(c) What visible influences have these people had on the areas they settled?
(d) What reasons can you give for why they chose these places? (Jobs, resembled their homeland, others were already here, climate, etc.)
(e) Name some famous people from the groups we have identified that settled in our state. Indicate the contributions made by these people.

24. Proverbs II[9]

when: two class periods

what: proverbs and sayings (following), chart

how: Almost every culture has "sayings" that express beliefs or customs of that culture. Often sayings are similar from one culture to another.

(1) Have students examine the following sayings.

(2) Have students match up as many sayings as they can in chart form.

(3) Are there foreign sayings that have no equivalent in another language?

(4) The point of the lesson is that complex ideas in most societies are "summarized" into proverbs. Are those summaries universal? If so, what could one infer about human experience?

For example:

AFRICAN	EUROPEAN	UNITED STATES
By the time the fool has learned the game the players have dispersed. (Ashanti)	When the horse has been stolen, the fool shuts the stable. (French)	It's useless to lock the barn door after the horse is gone.
Death does not sound a trumpet. (Congo)	Death does not blow a trumpet. (Danish)	Death comes in on silent wings.
Rain does not fall on one roof alone. (Cameroon)	When it rains, it rains on all alike. (British)	
No matter how long the night, the day is sure to come. (Congo)		It's always darkest before the dawn.
	Money talks. (French)	
	Still waters run deep. (German)	
	Ebb and flood waits for no man. (German)	
		It's who you know not what you know.

The following are other proverb sayings. Can students match any of the following with sayings that are familiar to them?

A learned man has always riches in himself. (Latin)

Like father, like son. (Latin)

The pot does not call the kettle black. (British)

Knowledge is always better than riches. (Ashanti)

When you follow the path of your father, you learn to walk like him.
     (Ashanti)

One camel does not make fun of the other camel's hump. (Guinea)

One falsehood spoils a thousand truths. (Ashanti)

It is the calm and silent water that drowns a man. (Ashanti)

Wood already touched by fire is not hard to set alight. (Ashanti)

If you are in hiding, don't light a fire. (Ashanti)

The ruin of a nation begins in the homes of its people. (Ashanti)

If the palm of the hand itches, it signifies the coming of great luck.
     (Basutoland)

She is like a road--pretty but crooked. (Cameroon)

You do not teach the paths of the forest to an old gorilla. (Congo)

Two birds disputed about a kernel, when a third swooped down and carried
it off. (Congo)

A close friend can become a close enemy. (Ethiopia)

One who recovers from a sickness forgets about God. (Ethiopia)

Unless you call out, who will open the door? (Ethiopia)

When spider webs unite, they can tie up a lion. (Ethiopia)

You cannot build a house from last year's summer. (Ethiopia)

A blade won't cut another blade; a cheat won't cheat another cheat.
     (Ethiopia)

Where there is no shame, there is no honor. (Ethiopia)

If there is no elephant in the jungle, the buffalo would be a great
animal. (Ghana)

Knowledge is like a garden: if it is not cultivated, it cannot be har-
vested. (Guinea)

After a foolish deed comes remorse. (Kenya)

He who is unable to dance says that the yard is stony. (Kenya)

There is no medicine to cure hatred. (Ashanti)

B.   General Objective: To develop skills necessary to <u>process</u> information

SPECIFIC OBJECTIVE: Learn to locate, select, and evaluate from sources such as charts, maps, globes, outlines, and illustrations for the purpose of processing information.

1.   Clarifying and Organizing Cultural Inferences

when: three class periods

what: description of country following

how: (1) Have students read description of country. From this available information, student should infer as much about the people and culture as they can (i.e., family structure, work, education, technology, etc.). Support the inferences with facts from the description of the country. The following chart may help to clarify and organize the inferences and evidence.

	Cultural Inference	Evidence
family structure		
work		
education		
technology		
etc.		

(2) Having filled out the chart and noted the inferences, then identify a country that closely fits the description below and test out the students' inferences.

Country Description

Geography

It is a hot country with a growing season limited by the rainfall. For the most part the land is low and flat, although there is a plateau area where the weather is cooler and more pleasant. The country is surrounded on three sides by countries of like geography; the fourth side is bounded by the sea.

The seashore for the most part is marshy; farther inland is rain forest. As one moves inland the land changes slowly to savanna and finally to desert. Rainfall is heavy in the rain forest. In the savanna, however, the rain only falls from April to October.

The country is as large as Texas, Oklahoma, and Arkansas combined, but the population is four times the number of people that live in those states, and the population continues to grow.

Oil is the most abundant natural resource. There is some industry. Groundnuts is the largest cash crop. There is some cotton grown. Tropical fruits are abundant in some locations but are difficult to ship because of their perishibility.

Effects of Geography

Housing: cement and bricks are the most common building materials. In the villages houses are made of mud with thatched roofs.
Clothing: for the most part light weight cotton. Sandals are the usual footwear.

Many people live in the cities working in some kind of industry. People in villages farm and raise some livestock.

When oil is selling well, technology is imported at a great rate, along with many consumer goods. Food must also be imported to feed the growing population.

Goals

Raise the standard of living for all citizens.
Control population and increase food production.
Politically educate citizens to develop a more sophisticated democratic process.

2. Identifying, Classifying, and Inferring from Maps, Charts, and Graphs

when: three class periods

what: resource material in the form of maps, charts, etc. on an area such as Africa or South America (a continent)

how: (1) Have students use the materials to describe the area:

climate
economic situation
etc., depending on information available

(2) Have students speculate on the future growth, perhaps comparing two regions.

Encourage compare and contrast, a convergent thinking exercise, but also encourage analysis and synthesis, a divergent higher form of thinking which calls for identifying, interpreting, classifying, and inferring. Inferring is encouraged by asking students to speculate on future growth.

3.   Maps and How They Work

   when: two class periods

   what: classroom maps

   how: (1) Hold a class discussion on the important elements that
              make up a map:
                 Title of Map - what type of map is it and what is its
                          purpose
                 Scale - the ratio of the differences between places on
                         the map and the same places on the area being
                         mapped
                 Orientation - longitude and latitude, north and south,
                         etc.
                 Legend or Key - description and examples of map symbols
                 Date - expresses the time to which the map applies

              Examine and display different types of maps.

         (2) To apply this information, have the students produce maps
             of some small area, i.e., wing of the school, location of
             tables and chairs in the library, room at home, pets in
             the neighborhood, trees in a designated park area.

         (3) Have students display maps by grouping them into cate-
             gories according to the content of the map, i.e., school,
             community, home.

4.   Maps and Geography

   when: two or three class periods

   what: four maps of the same region showing the following geographic
           information:
              map 1 - topographical map with location of unnamed rivers,
                      mountains, etc. Also should have climate, rain-
                      fall information, etc.
              map 2 - map with location of natural resources
              map 3 - outline map
              map 4 - map showing location of cities and major indus-
                      tries--farming to manufacturing

   how: (1) Give first three maps to students. Place students indi-
              vidually or in small groups.

         (2) Using the information from maps 1 and 2, have students
             decide where major cities might be located and why, and
             what industries might have developed and where. Their
             decisions should be marked on map 3.

         (3) When the students have filled in their outline map 3,
             have them compare it with map 4. Were the students
             accurate? What might account for the difference?

(4) The following questions would be appropriate for class discussion:
   (a) Do you recognize the region?
   (b) Why do you think cities and industries are placed where they are?
   (c) Where would be the best location of cities, parks, city center, suburbs, etc.?
   (d) Do you think that the geography of a region in contemporary times affects the placement and growth of communities?

5.   It's a Small World, After All II[10]

when: two class periods

what: maps and folders from travel agencies; plane, bus, train schedules

how: (1) Discuss with students the idea of the world seeming smaller because of modern travel--mostly by plane. Plane routes are planned to take the shortest distance between two cities. Have students view globe from the North Pole. See why planes may use the polar route. For example, planes from Los Angeles fly over the Pole to reach England and northern Europe.

In past years students have studied how long it took pilgrims to reach America, or how Fortyniners moving west to California had to leave early enough in the spring to get over the Rocky Mountains before the snows of late autumn trapped them. The time of year and weather are no longer the major concern of a traveler. Quite often we no longer measure how far one place is from another in miles, we measure it in time (Grandma lives two hours away).

(2) Have students measure some distances by time. For example, one can travel, on the average:

                4 miles in an hour walking
               50 miles in an hour by car
               25 miles in an hour by ship
              500 miles in an hour by plane

A number of maps give not only the number of miles between cities but the length of time it takes to drive that distance. Plane, bus, and train schedules all give departure and arrival times enabling one to determine the time spent traveling.

How long would it take to get from (for example) Lafayette, Indiana to Chicago, Illinois, which is about 125 miles, by:

        foot _____

        car _____

bus _____

train _____

plane _____

   (3) Obtain travel folders from a travel agency, including
     cruise folders. Have students pick an overseas trip they
     would like to take. Students must figure the distance
     from one stop to the next in both miles and time (by
     whatever means they would be traveling).

6. Geography of Developed and Undeveloped Areas

  when: one class period

  what: aerial photos of one developed area, possibly known to stu-
     dents, and of one undeveloped area

     (One popular and available source of aerial photographs is
     National Geographic. For example, see "Satellites that
     Save Us," September 1983, 164(3), p. 281.)

  how: (1) Show the photo of the developed area first, and discuss
     with class why homes, schools, businesses, etc. are
     located where they are. That is, what effect has
     geography had on the photographed area?

     (2) Show undeveloped land photograph. Where would the class
     place homes, schools, industries, waste disposal, etc.
     and why? Summarize the activity by identifying those
     geographic factors which seem to affect the location of
     developed areas, i.e.,

       Transportation
       Work force
       Resources (power, materials, etc.)
       Etc.

     (3) Which of the factors are most important and which are
     least important? Rank the factors according to an in-
     ferred hypothesis (good guess). Check the validity of
     the ranking with the community's own commercial leaders.

SPECIFIC OBJECTIVE: Analyze the development, expansion, and/or decline of
 selected cultures in terms of their patterns of development using such factors as geographic features, population growth, density, and resources in
 processing the information.

  7. Save the Children and Encourage the Growth of the Desert

    when: three class periods

    what: no materials necessary

how: Developing nations have many needs: education, improved
       health, agricultural development, industry, etc. Have stu-
       dents research a developing country, focusing on its problems
       and what that country will have to do to solve those problems.

       It is important to examine not only the needs but also the
       consequences of proposed solutions. Many well-meaning pro-
       jects which introduced medical/health and agricultural tech-
       niques have been a mixed blessing. The following is an
       example of a mixed blessing:

           Many developing nations have encouraged the growth
           of technology as one answer to their pressing prob-
           lems. In a number of Third World nations, some
           less than twenty years ago, life expectancy was 36
           years for females and 37 years for males. Middle
           age for many Africans and Asians was 20 years of
           age, and old age was past 30.

   (1) Suppose you lived in a village on the edge of the Sahara.
       Your village population was directly related to the
       climate and vegetation. Suppose further that medicine
       was introduced and also supplementary foods. As a conse-
       quence, a third more children lived past their first year
       of life and half of the older males and females lived on
       past their normal life expectancy. The village no longer
       was directly related to the environment. There is in the
       village a need for more food, more firewood, more chickens,
       goats, and cows. What effect do you believe the increased
       gathering of firewood and the increased grazing of chickens,
       goats, and cows would have on the Sahara environment?
       What would you infer the effect of the increased population
       to be on the Sahara Desert? Is it at all possible to
       believe that the intervention of technology has helped to
       expand the desert?

   (2) Can the class identify other possible "mixed blessings"?
       Just to stimulate thinking, what would the effect be on
       the desert culture above if a tractor and plow were given
       to the village? Other mixed blessings: electrical power,
       clean water, a hard surface road.

8. Population Growth Near the Sahara Desert

   when: one class period

   what: cause and effect model (following)

   how: The use of a cause and effect model can enhance the students'
          understanding of global interdependence. Many factors can
          be included in creating such a model. Also, a series of
          models can be developed and tied together showing overlapping
          interdependence.

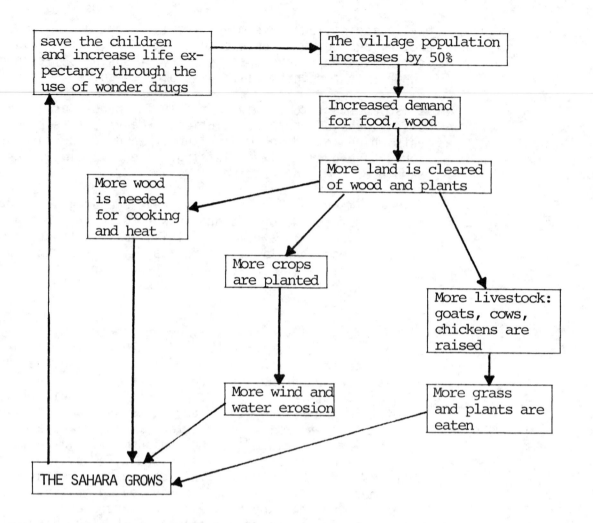

9.   Exploring An Underdeveloped Nation

when: one class period

what: materials as needed

how: Divide the class into groups. Each group must plan a trip
        from a major port of entry to a distant city in one of the
        countries or regions which is to be studied, Egypt would be
        an example, keeping a detailed log (record) of the trip in-
        cluding land forms, weather, climate, vegetation, animal life,
        etc. For example: Cairo to Alexandria
                            Cairo to Port Said
                            Cairo to Aswan
                            Port Said to Alexandria

Example of report: Cairo to Aswan

Sept. 13:   Arrived at Cairo Airport on outskirts of city. Weather
            hot, but low humidity. Very dusty. Must bargain with
            taxi drivers for fare into city or find one who will use
            his taxi meter. City crowded. Car horns blow incessantly.
            Water unsafe for drinking.

Sept. 14:   Make arrangements for train trip to Aswan. Try to make
            some local purchases before leaving. Arabic is official
            language; some English is spoken.   (cont.)

Sept. 15:   Leave on train for Aswan. Travel along edge of Nile or close to it a good part of the time. All land that can be irrigated in any way possible from the Nile is farmed. Animals seen are water buffalo, horses, mules, goats. Moving right along the edge of the Sahara Desert--still hot and dry but cooling off toward evening.

etc.

SPECIFIC OBJECTIVE: Identify and categorize cultures by time, place, and cultural characteristics.

10.   <u>Identifying and Categorizing Cultures by Time and Place</u>

when: one class period

what: pictures of people from different eras and cultures, include some group shots; sample chart below

how: Number the pictures. Use an opaque projector to enlarge the picture so everyone can see it at the same time.

(1) Have students examine the pictures. Can they identify the time and place of the picture by the way in which the people are dressed and the composition of the picture? Can the students identify the dominant person in a group picture? What makes that one person more significant or outstanding than another? Have students fill in the chart as they view the pictures.

(2) How accurate were the students? What clues did the students look for and how did they arrive at their choices of time and place?

(3) Is there any one picture that represents a time or a place in which the students wish they might have lived?

PICTURES	TIME	PLACE	DOMINANT PERSON IF GROUP PICTURE
1			
2			
3			
4			
5			
6			
7			
8			

11. Common Cultural Categories

when: ongoing activity

what: sample chart below, either page size for each student to fill
in or one or more large poster size

how: (1) Through class discussion have students suggest categories
that all cultures share or have in common, such as language, shelter, etc. After the categories have been
established, make them into a chart.

(2) Apply the chart to cultures previously studied or to cultures in the process of being studied.

COMMON CULTURE CHART

Instructions: In each of the boxes under the name of the country
place a picture, small collage, or list that fits the specific
cultural category.

Common Cultural Categories	COUNTRIES				
	Nigeria	Japan	France	Mexico	etc.
1. Language	English and 200 other local lang.		French: list of dia- lects		
2. Shelter					
3. Food	rice yams chicken				
4. Government	Demo- cratic Repub- lic				
5. Religion	Christ. and Moslem				
6. Etc. Education Transportation Medicine					

SPECIFIC OBJECTIVE: Identify and categorize people, places, and things.

12. <u>Foreign Fast Food Menu</u>

   when: one class period

   what: restaurant menus, preferably ones that list foreign dishes

   how: (1) Have students examine menus and list foods that mention a
              foreign culture. (For example, the most common is French
              fries.) Also see ads in newspapers for gourmet cuisine.

          (2) Have students categorize the foreign dishes by country.

          (3) Have students speculate on how the food got its name and
              if it actually originated in that particular country.

          (4) What foods do the students eat at home that come from
              another culture?

          (5) What foods are associated with a particular country?
              (Polish sausage, Italian spaghetti)

          (6) How many fast food restaurants serve only ethnic or
              foreign dishes? (Mexican, Greek, English Fish and Chips,
              Chinese, etc.)

13. <u>Guess Again!</u>

   when: one class period

   what: no materials necessary

   how: Play "20 Questions" using famous people in history. This
          activity, of course, necessitates enough prior study of the
          person so that the student can answer Yes or No to the class
          questions.

          One student starts the game by being "it." That student has
          someone from history (not U.S. history) in mind and other
          students are allowed to ask Yes/No type questions until they
          guess the identity of the person from history. Usually a
          limit of questions (20) is set. Whoever guesses the correct
          name can be the next "it."

          Illustrations of questions that identify and categorize
          people:

             Gender question: Are you a male (female)?

             Time in History question: Did you live before the 1900s?

             Location: Did you live in Europe?

             Occupation: Did you work for the government?

SPECIFIC OBJECTIVE: Analyze cause and effect relationships through the
process of modeling.

14. <u>Identifying Patterns of Revolution Using a Relevance Tree Model</u>

when: three class periods

what: identifying the patterns of revolution using relevance tree

how: (1) Divide the class into groups. Give each group a revolution, i.e., American, French, Russian, etc.
(2) Have groups identify the steps or stages in their revolu-
tions, starting with the cause.
(3) Compare groups' findings and identify a general pattern
or criteria, if they emerge, that will fit most revolu-
tions. Simply, can the class identify those parts of
an event which seem to be essential to the making of a
revolution?
(4) Have the class apply the general pattern to a current
"revolution" possibly in Central or South America, the
Middle East, Asia, or, of course, Africa (actually, if
you think about it, almost anywhere). Does the pattern
fit? According to the pattern, what does the class predict will happen next?

<u>The Relevance Tree Model</u>: This is one form of diagramming relation-
ships between events much like a concept wheel. The "tree" shows
the probable cause and effect relationships but adds a dimension beyond the concept wheel. A relevance tree model identifies both the
problem, issue, or topic and answer, response, or goal. The problem
and answer are placed opposite each other with suggested action
branched between. Suggested actions (cause and effect) are plotted
or branched to demonstrate how alternative answers could lead from
the problem to the goal or answer. This model is particularly appropriate for divergent level thought where emphasis is on inferred
relationships.

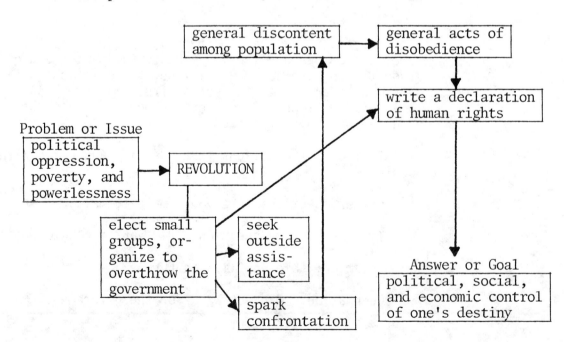

SPECIFIC OBJECTIVE: Develop the ability to communicate effectively in written papers including the processing of ideas and the preparation of papers.

15. Effective Reading, Effective Thinking

when: when needed

what: Effective Reading Through Processing Information Form

how: One of the vital skills necessary for good citizenship is processing information. In the chapter on U.S. Government and Civics, inquiry was identified as one way to process information. Also, activities on identifying bias and propaganda were suggested. The skill to process information is learned. It must be practiced. The following simplified form is one additional technique for teaching students to process the content they are reading.

EFFECTIVE READING THROUGH
PROCESSING INFORMATION FORM

Procedure: Use this processing form when reading the assignment.

I.   Briefly state the question, problem, theme, issue, or point of view.

_____

_____

_____

II. Place the question, problem, theme, issue, or point of view into an If/Then statement with the intent of identifying the effect, outcome, or result.

_____

_____

III. Offer at least two objective facts to support your identified effect, outcome, or result.

1. _____

_____

2. _____

_____

IV. Offer at least two objective facts that tend to rebut, deny, reject, or disprove your identified effect, outcome, result.

1. _____

2. _____

16. Papers Evaluation[11]

> when: one class period or at end of writing assignment
>
> what: evaluation form
>
> how: This form may be used as an exercise in evaluating an essay selected by teacher or student may use it to self-evaluate his/her own paper and then check evaluation with teacher.

Papers Evaluation

_____   _____
        student's name   title of paper

Content:	excellent	good	suggestions for improvement
1. Sources: number selected and quality			
2. Thoroughness of investigation			
3. Exactness of data			
4. Subject covered to extent required			
Style:			
5. Form: table of contents footnotes bibliography titles and subtitles			
6. Spelling and punctuation			
7. Student's expression of content			
8. Proofread			

SPECIFIC OBJECTIVE: Develop the ability to communicate effectively in groups: analyze group roles, assume roles which help maintain the group and which help accomplish the task.

17. Oral Report Checklist and Teacher Evaluation[12]

      when: time length of report determined by teacher

      what: oral report checklist

      how: (1) Students must choose topic related to what class is studying.

            (2) Students must outline report and get teacher's approval of outline. Students should check out anything they do not understand at this time with teacher.

            (3) Students must use more than one source to obtain information from more than one point of view.

            (4) Teacher should give copy of oral report form to students so they can use it as a guide. Teacher will use form to evaluate student while he/she is giving report and then will give checklist to student after report.

Oral Report Checklist			
student's name	well done	satisfactory	needs attention
1. Approved outline			
2. Write subject on board			
3. Face class, speak slowly			
4. Identify sources			
5. State time and place of subject			
6. Relate subject to what class is studying			
7. Give report from notes (no reading)			
8. Write difficult names on board or on overhead			
9. Summarize			
10. Be ready for class questions			
11. Comments:			

18. Oral Report Evaluation Form for Students[13]

   when: at time of oral reports

   what: oral report form for students

   how: Students are encouraged to evaluate performance of other
         students presenting oral reports. The following form will
         allow students to evaluate an oral report and add comments.
         Have students fill out form either during or after report.

Oral Report Evaluation Form for Students

student giving report

evaluator	very weak	fair	good	very good	superior
1. Introduction was interesting					
2. Student related topic to what we are studying in class.					
3. Student was able to make report interesting with personal opinions yet stuck basically to facts.					
4. Student summarized briefly.					
Comments:					

C. General Objective: To develop the skills to examine values and beliefs

  SPECIFIC OBJECTIVE: Identify and rank values and evaluate the effect on
                      one's own life.

   1. Identifying and Analyzing Your Values

      when: one class period

      what: Personal Preference Form - One of the first steps in identi-
             fying oneself as a citizen, not only of the country but of
             the world, is to sort out how one might feel about (that is,
             value) events. This is one of those activities where the
             student is the source of data.

      how: (1) Have student complete the Personal Preference Form

PERSONAL PREFERENCE

I. Preference Ranking: Rank the statements below from 1 to 10, 1 being the statement you feel is most important to you to 10 which you feel is least important. Rank each group of 10 statements separately.

II. Strength of choice: After each of the statements below, circle how you feel about that statement as follows: A = strongly like, B = like, C = neutral, D = dislike, E = strongly dislike.

Rank	Statement	Strongly Like	Like	Neutral	Dislike	Strongly Dislike
SOCIAL/PERSONAL						
____ 1.	a good job	A	B	C	D	E
____ 2.	own many things, i.e., car, house, boat	A	B	C	D	E
____ 3.	be in good health	A	B	C	D	E
____ 4.	a lot of leisure time	A	B	C	D	E
____ 5.	a healthy environment	A	B	C	D	E
____ 6.	to be rich	A	B	C	D	E
____ 7.	hold an important position in the community	A	B	C	D	E
____ 8.	successful children	A	B	C	D	E
____ 9.	be recognized as an important person with high status	A	B	C	D	E
____ 10.	have a loving family	A	B	C	D	E
NATIONAL						
____ 1.	free education according to the person's need	A	B	C	D	E
____ 2.	protect the environment	A	B	C	D	E
____ 3.	free public transportation system	A	B	C	D	E
____ 4.	space programs	A	B	C	D	E
____ 5.	jobs for all	A	B	C	D	E
____ 6.	the best military defense system	A	B	C	D	E
____ 7.	social justice for all	A	B	C	D	E
____ 8.	raise the poverty level so that all citizens are above subsistence	A	B	C	D	E
____ 9.	free medical care	A	B	C	D	E
____ 10.	crime prevention and cure	A	B	C	D	E

		Strongly Like	Like	Neutral	Dislike	Strongly Dislike
INTERNATIONAL						
____ 1.	raise subsistence standards throughout the world	A	B	C	D	E
____ 2.	increase cooperation on global and space problems	A	B	C	D	E
____ 3.	ban the use of war in space	A	B	C	D	E
____ 4.	provide source of electrical power to those who do not have it	A	B	C	D	E
____ 5.	distribute world's natural resources so all may share	A	B	C	D	E
____ 6.	improve the world's ecology	A	B	C	D	E
____ 7.	ban the use of war as way to settle disputes	A	B	C	D	E
____ 8.	increase the military growth and authority of the United Nations	A	B	C	D	E
____ 9.	provide education to all people in the world	A	B	C	D	E
____ 10.	medical care for all who need it	A	B	C	D	E

(2) Have a small group of students tally the results in preparation for class discussion.

(3) Possible questions for class discussion:
 (a) Which of the statements were most important to you personally, to the class as a whole at each level: social/personal, national and international? What was least important?
 (b) What relationship do you see between your personal choices and your choices for the nation and the world?
 (c) Should national or international concerns be of most importance to our government? How concerned should the U.S. be about developing countries?

2. Identifying a Personal Philosophy or Religion

 when: one class period

 what: compiled findings of groups from Activity A-6, "Identifying and Comparing World Religions," in this chapter

 how: Have students identify items from the findings of the groups who researched the religions or philosophies in the activity mentioned above which the students would like to combine to form a personal religion or philosophy--individual activity.

3.   An Inquiry Introduction to Global Futures[14]

when: two class periods

what: Global Future Prediction form; Consensus Global Futures form

This activity is one of those where students' values and preferences supply the data. This particular approach is important when initiating an inquiry lesson for the inquiry arises out of the values expressed by the students as they categorize and rank the importance of their ideas.

how: (1) Have the students individually fill out the entire Global Futures Prediction form.

GLOBAL FUTURES PREDICTIONS

Instructions: Please complete the following statements.

By the year 2000 the world will be concerned with:

    1.
    2.
    3.
    4.
    5.

By the year 2000 my nation will be concerned with:

    1.
    2.
    3.
    4.
    5.

By the year 2000 my community will be concerned with:

    1.
    2.
    3.
    4.
    5.

By the year 2000 my neighborhood will be concerned with:

    1.
    2.
    3.
    4.
    5.

By the year 2000 my family and I will be concerned with:

    1.
    2.
    3.
    4.
    5.

(2) Divide the class into small groups. Give each group a prediction section from the entire Global Futures Prediction form and have them complete the first two sections of the Consensus Global Futures form.

CONSENSUS GLOBAL FUTURES

Instructions

Each group member should individually rank in importance the five predictions from the selected section above. Then as a group a consensus must be reached in ranking the predictions. Finally, a class consensus must be reached in ranking the predictions in order of importance.

I. Rank order at least 5 predictions that <u>you</u> identify:

1. (most important)

2.

3.

4.

5. (least important)

II. Rank order at least 5 predictions that your <u>group</u> identifies:

1. (most important)

2.

3.

4.

5. (least important)

III. Rank order at least 5 predictions that the <u>class</u> identifies:

1. (most important)

2.

3.

4.

5. (least important)

---

(3) Through class discussion reach a consensus on global futures predictions.

SPECIFIC OBJECTIVE: Identify cultural values and infer how they would
                      fluctuate in various times and places.

4.   Time Machine II[15]

    when: one class period

    what: chart

    how: Imagine that the following people have been carried through
space and, in some cases, time. John Kennedy finds himself
taking the place of William McKinley during the Spanish-
American War in 1898. Ghandi is to replace Lenin during the
Russian Revolution in 1917. Socrates replaces Abraham Lincoln
during the Civil War in 1860. Hitler finds himself in the
place of George Washington at the time of the American Revolution in 1776, and Joan of Arc takes the place of Martin
Luther King, Jr. at the time of the Bus Boycott in Montgomery,
Alabama in 1965. The list, of course, is endless. What
would be the reaction of the above people? What problems
would they face if they tried to use the practices they normally used? Use the following chart.

★ ★

What are the consequences of these people applying their values and methods
to the times to which they are transported?

Name	Values & Methods	Location to Which Transported and Person Replaced	Time to Which Transported	Consequences
Kennedy		McKinley Spanish-American War	1898	
Ghandi		Lenin Russian Rev.	1917	
Socrates		A. Lincoln Civil War	1860	
Hitler		Washington Amer. Rev.	1776	
Joan of Arc		M. L. King Bus Boycott Montgomery, Alabama	1965	
?				

★ ★

SPECIFIC OBJECTIVE: Identify how one values one's links with the world.

5.   You and the World: What Links Are Important to You?[16]

when: two class periods

what: strength of feeling form

how: (1) Ask students to list at least 10 (more if they can) ways
           their own lives are linked to the world. Then ask them
           to indicate how important these things are to them per-
           sonally. Arrange the items in the following categories:
           very important, no strong feeling either way, not very
           important (see form below). Then have the students write
           a short paragraph on how their links to the world affect
           their lives.

10 LINKS TO THE WORLD			
10 WAYS MY LIFE IS LINKED TO THE WORLD	VERY IMPORTANT	NO STRONG FEELING (NEUTRAL)	NOT VERY IMPORTANT
1.			
2.			
3.			
4.			
5.			
6.			
7.			
8.			
9.			
10.			

Possible Variation: Try to have students list 10 ways their
lives are linked to the world and indicate importance before
they have done any activities. Save the list; have them make
a second list after you have completed the activities. Return
the first list and have them compare the two lists and discuss
in their paragraphs what they have learned about how important
the world is to their lives.

(2) Have students ask a parent or adult to list 10 ways their
    lives are linked to the world and indicate how important
    they are. Have the students compare their list to the

adult list. Are the links similar or different? Do the adults value the same things as they do? How might they explain this?

Speculate how the links they listed affect the lives of people in other countries; or how these links affect their community. Do any of the links listed provide opportunities to influence some worldwide activity? How?

Examples--hosting a foreign student; contributing to disaster relief; presenting an argument for a particular policy; joining a coffee boycott; planning a trip abroad; purchasing a foreign-made product.

6. Map and Word Association

when: one class period

what: map of the world and word list
This activity was originally developed by the Center for War and Peace Studies in the early 1970s. The activity depends upon students associating a specific word, i.e., enemy, with certain regions of the globe. In particular it is a good technique for pre- and post-testing of attitudes, and offers an opportunity to quickly survey the students' knowledge about the world. Finally, the teacher might ask, "How might you fill out the word association list if you were a (Russian, Chinese, Iranian) citizen?" or "How might you fill this out as an American in the 21st Century?" Depending on how the activity is used, it could be gaining knowledge if used as pre- or post-test, valuing if preference patterns are examined, and processing if students are asked to categorize.

how: (1) First outline a map of the world in simple form (on board or transparency) labeling each region of the world with a letter of the alphabet. For example, North America might be labeled A, Central America B, South America C . . . Russia H . . . China K, etc.

(2) Provide the students with a word list and have them associate the word with the region of the world that best fits their interpretation of the word. For example, when you think of the word freedom, what region of the world comes to mind? When you think of the words hunger, racism, unfriendly, what regions of the world come to mind? The following is an example of the words that have been used. Teachers might wish to construct lists which would be most appropriate for their students.

COMMENTARY: This is characteristic of those activities in which the students provide the data. As a summary activity, have a small group collate the class's responses to determine whom the class feels is free, the enemy, friendly, etc. The students' responses may be a good starting point for discussion about global relationships, world history, or area studies.

Word List

1. ___Freedom	13. ___Pollution	25. ___Lack of freedom
2. ___Enemy	14. ___Racism	26. ___Highly skilled labor
3. ___Missiles	15. ___War	27. ___Universal education
4. ___Exotic	16. ___Change	28. ___Traffic congestion
5. ___Stable	17. ___Terrorism	29. ___High crime rate
6. ___Friendly	18. ___Revolution	30. ___Slavery
7. ___Hunger	19. ___Developed	31. ___Patriotic
8. ___Poverty	20. ___Weak	32. ___Environmental crisis
9. ___Dictatorship	21. ___Unfriendly	33. ___Population explosion
10. ___Religious people	22. ___Mineral wealth	34. ___Technically advanced
11. ___Women's lib	23. ___Industrialized	35. ___Healthy people
12. ___Generation gap	24. ___Underdeveloped	36. ___Beautiful people

D. General Objective: To apply knowledge through active <u>participation</u>

SPECIFIC OBJECTIVE: Identify standards of living, evaluate the effect of those standards on people, and participate by applying those standards to one's own life.

1. Eating by Third World Standards

    when: one week

    what: calorie chart (diet books and some cookbooks usually carry these charts), caloric intake chart below

    how: (1) Discuss with the class how food production and widespread Hunger and starvation are desperate problems in some countries. What is the difference between hunger and starvation?

          (2) Have each student select a country from the chart below. Using a calorie chart, students must prepare menus for several days. The calories must not exceed those listed for the selected country. Have students compare this to what the average U.S. caloric intake is.

Daily Caloric Intake as Compared to U.S. (3300 calories)	
Upper Volta	1710 calories daily
Algeria	1730 calories daily
Haiti	1730 calories daily
Indonesia	1790 calories daily
Somalia	1830 calories daily

MENUS:	country		U.S.	3300
	calories			calories
	FOOD	CALORIES	FOOD	CALORIES
Day 1				
Day 2				
Day 3				

(3) Speculate on what life must be like where the population is always hungry and malnourished. Questions to ask:
Do calories really matter?
Is there a direct relationship between number of calories and creativity, ambition, production, and health?
Some say that one-half the world's people are either hungry or malnourished. Is this a problem?
Is there hunger in the United States? If so, how would you explain that?
Is there a different definition of hunger in the U.S. than in Haiti?

Example for using charts: Students selecting Upper Volta would choose foods for one day not exceeding 1710 calories (daily intake for Upper Volta). Then they would plan the foods available for the U.S. daily intake (3330 calories) and compare the two countries.

	Upper Volta		U.S.	
breakfast	1 cup cooked cereal	270	2 scrambled eggs	250
	2 yams (sweet pot.)	280	2 pieces buttered toast	350
			1 cup milk	170
			1 cup orange juice	133
		550		903
lunch	1 cup rice	140	1 hamburger & fixings	400
	1 cup stew	250	French fries	200
			Milkshake	450
		390		1050
dinner	2 cups rice	280	2 pieces fried chicken	650
	1 slice chicken	100	potatoes w/sour cream	200
	2 cups milk	340	½ cup cooked peas	100
			2 cups milk	340
			small dish ice cream	100
		720		1390
	TOTAL	1660	TOTAL	3240

Alternatives

(1) Ask students to go one week or less not eating one meal
a day (reduce calorie intake). Some students may go
without breakfast or lunch regularly, but that does not
count. They must miss a meal that they would normally
consume.

(2) After a week of reduced calories, discuss with the class
their feelings during the week and their reactions to the
lack of food. Did they tire easily or become angry about
little annoyances more quickly? What would life be like
if they always had to eat that way?

2. Living on Third World Standards

when: one class period

what: no materials necessary

how: (1) Propose to the class that they individually are going to
live for a year on a hypothetical Third World nation's
per capita income of $350. The $350 must pay for every-
thing that they must use to sustain themselves: food,
clothing, power, transportation, entertainment, etc.

(2) Have each student prepare a list of those items which
they now use or are used in their behalf such as heat,
light, water, etc. that they could no longer use on a
$350 budget. For example, if they own a car, they could
not use it because of the cost of insurance and maintenance. If they take hot showers, they could not afford
both the heat and the water. Forget snacks, and most
items which require power.

(3) Within time available, collate students' lists of items
they would have to give up, then ask some of the following questions:

(a) Does it make a difference whether you can take a
shower or bath?

(b) Would you act differently if you knew you could not
afford medical care and medicines?

(c) How might you think about the developed world if you,
in fact, had to give back all the items you listed?

(d) Now that the students are living on $350 a year, they
have come close to joining the majority of the people
throughout the world. What would they suggest as
ways to improve their standard of living? What might
prevent their suggestions being realized?

SPECIFIC OBJECTIVE: Participate in surveying the community to identify the interdependent links between cultures.

3.   Links Between One Community and the World: The Meaning of Interdependence[17]

   when: depends on the depth and number of surveys conducted by students

   what: sample survey form

   how: This activity requires the students to look closely at their own community and the degree to which people and goods from other areas of the world are a part of that community.   The activity can vary from a simple approach, such as the counting of foreign-made cars in the school parking lot and the number of foreign food restaurants listed in the yellow pages, or it can be extended to an in-depth study of the community.   An in-depth study would involve the class going into the community over an extended period of time to study such factors as: monetary value of foreign trade; number of foreign-born in the community; number of foreign visitors yearly; number of applications for passports; bank loans to foreign sources; monetary value of church donations to foreign areas; location of ethnic neighborhoods.   Several classes, as well as people outside of the school, might be involved in such an undertaking.

   You may want to begin this activity with a survey of your school.   Then, after initially involving the students in their own "world," proceed to a wider study of the community. The depth in which you survey is dependent upon the time you allot to the study, the needs of your students, and the availability of source material.

   (1) Conduct a survey of any or all of the following facets of global interdependence in the school (see sample survey form on next page):
      (a) Number and home country of foreign exchange students attending school.
      (b) Number and makes of foreign-made cars in the school parking lot.
      (c) Country of manufacture of equipment used in school:
         audiovisual equipment   industrial arts equipment
         sports equipment   home economics equipment
         science equipment   secretarial equipment
      (d) Conduct a survey of the number of people in school who have traveled abroad.   List some of the reasons for their travel and the areas of the world visited.
      (e) Construct a survey to discover the extent to which foreign-made items are in the homes of students.

SURVEY FORM										
	Countries Represented									
ITEMS SURVEYED	Japan	Taiwan	Phillipines	China	Germany	France	Great Britain	Italy	etc.	Location
foreign-made cars	16				7	1		3		school parking lot

(2) Analyze the data received from the surveys by having student groups organize the data into tables, graphs, and charts. Analyze the data through class discussions in the following terms:
   (a) How much interrelationship exists between the United States, other countries, and the students?
   (b) Who is involved in bringing about these exchanges of people and goods?
   (c) How dependent are the school and its students on foreign-made equipment?
   (d) How do such exchanges affect the lives of those involved?

(3) Have students develop a map to show the transnational interactions that affect their school. Use outline maps of the world, having the students draw lines from the country of origin of a piece of equipment to the port of entry into the United States to the school. The students should hypothesize about the meaning and effect of this interdependence in terms of jobs created, money flow, use of natural resources, benefits received by all involved, and any other concepts that would aid your class.

(4) Have the students then write an individual definition of "interdependence."

(5) Divide the class into groups of five to eight students. Each group is to discuss their definitions and then come up with a group definition for "interdependence."

(6) Have the class as a whole discuss each group's definition and then write an acceptable class definition for "interdependence." Remember that a clear definition should contain terms, the meanings of which are also clear to the class. To define an unclear term using other vague concepts does not represent progress.

4. <u>Collecting Information About International Links of Local Civic and Service Organizations</u>[18]

when: one week

what: Lists of local, civic, and service organizations and their presidents. These should be available from the local Chamber of Commerce. The questionnaire is included. (You may want to revise it to suit your needs.)

how: (1) Have students individually or in pairs contact the various organizations and arrange to meet with a representative to complete the questionnaire. Make sure students give an explanation of the objectives of the questionnaire, and the kind of information desired. This could be done on the phone or by mail, though personal contact would be preferable for more complete information and a larger percentage of responses.

(2) The information from the completed questionnaires should be tallied and placed in charts or tables that can be used by the class. On a world map, indicate national headquarters with one color; use another color to indicate countries visited or countries that have sent visitors or countries where organizations have projects.

After compiling the data, the following discussion questions could be used:
(a) To what areas of the world are local civic and service organizations linked?
(b) In what kinds of world projects or programs are local civic and service organizations involved?
(c) What reasons do these organizations have for being involved with the world?
(d) How great an impact do these organizations have on the world? Other countries? Your state and community?

QUESTIONNAIRE

This questionnaire is part of a social studies activity to determine how civic and service organizations in __(community)__ are linked to the world. The class will compile the results to show ways organizations are linked to the world and countries with which they are involved. You are welcome to see our compiled data. Thank you for helping us find out how organizations in our community are linked to the world. If you have any questions, please call me at _____ or come to the school.

Thank you,

_____
(Teacher)

Name of Organization _____

Is your membership international?   ○ Yes   ○ No

Do you have an international headquarters?   ○ Yes   ○ No

If so, where is it located? _____

In what country did your organization originate? _____

In what kinds of international projects does your organization participate? Please list and give a short explanation.

_____

_____

_____

Have any of your members in the last year visited members in another country?   ○ Yes   ○ No

If so, what country? _____

If any of your members have traveled outside our country and would be willing to talk to our class about their experiences, would you please indicate their name, the country they visited, and how they could be contacted.

5. **Why are Organizations Involved in International Interactions?**[19]

when: two periods

what: institution cards (at least one per student); reason cards (at least two per student)

how: (1) Have students work individually or in small groups of two or three. Students should draw one institution card and two reason cards. They are to select one reason and use it to give an explanation of why their institution is involved in international activity. Students must identify specific examples of ways their institution could be involved internationally.

(2) Have students report on their institutions and the reason for that institution's international involvement either orally or by role playing.

Alternative

Have students present a short role play giving the class the institution they represent and see if the class can identify their reasons for becoming involved in international activity.

Use 3 x 5 cards cut in half or quarters (or any other handy materials) and print one institution on each card. Make enough so each student can make one blind draw. Print one reason for international activity on separate cards, making enough so each student can make two blind draws.

Institution Card Subjects | Reasons for International Activity Cards

Church
Business
Service Organization
Military
Schools
Government

Disseminate Knowledge
Family Ties
Cultural and Ethnic Ties
Acquire Status
Personal Friendship
Save Souls
Help Others
Curiosity
Mankind Identity (interest in other people as human beings)
Make Money
Control Finances and Resources
Acquire Material Needs
Acquire Knowledge

Notes

[1] Barth, J. L. _Advanced social studies education_ (Washington, DC: University Press of America, 1977), pp. 3-28.

[2] This activity was originally published in _Elementary and junior high/middle school social studies curriculum, activities, and materials_ (2nd ed.) by J. L. Barth (Washington, DC: University Press of America, 1983), p. 230. It has been revised for publication in this text.

[3] Ibid.

[4] This activity appears in _Indiana in the world_ (Indiana Department of Public Instruction, 1978), p. 10, and has been modified for publication in this text.

[5] Ibid., p. 6.

[6] Ibid., p. 14.

[7] Ibid., p. 10.

[8] Ibid., p. 13.

[9] Barth, _Elementary and junior high_, p. 234. This activity has been modified for publication in this text.

[10] Ibid., p. 225.

[11] Ibid., p. 240.

[12] Ibid., p. 239.

[13] Ibid., p. 240.

[14] This activity originally appeared in an occasional paper of the Center for War/Peace Studies, 1973, and has been adapted for publication in this text.

[15] Barth, _Elementary and junior high_, p. 245. This activity has been modified for publication in this text.

[16] _Indiana in the world_, p. 6. This activity has been modified for publication in this text.

[17] Ibid., p. 5.

[18] Ibid., p. 40.

[19] Ibid., p. 36.

INTEREST FORM

You have just completed the Chapter Global/International, World History, and Geography. In an effort to have you identify activities and materials that seem most promising to you in this subject area, please fill out the following interest form.

Instructions:

> Identify two activities from this chapter. Name the activities and briefly describe why these particular activities are of interest to you.

ACTIVITY 1

ACTIVITY 2

NOTES

CHAPTER III

U.S. HISTORY

ACTIVITIES AND MATERIALS FOR
U.S. HISTORY

CHAPTER III
U.S. HISTORY

Organization of the Chapter

Each chapter represents a particular subject area, in this case U.S. history. Each chapter consists of three parts: the first part is a brief discussion on courses, topics, and national trends in teaching U.S. history throughout the United States; the second part is an example of a state U.S. history program; the third part has activities and materials categorized by the four objectives of teaching social studies--gaining knowledge, processing, valuing, and participating.

I. Topics Taught and National Trends in Teaching U.S. History

Eleventh grade social studies, much like the fifth and eighth grades, as distinct from other grade levels is "reserved" for U.S. history. This did not happen by chance; it was planned as part of a fifth grade, eighth grade, and senior high U.S. history cycle by the 1943 Committee on American History in the Schools and Colleges commonly known as the Wesley Committee. Knowing about the Wesley Committee is necessary to understanding the K-12 social studies curriculum because school systems by and large have followed the recommendations of the Committee. The Committee not only established the three cycles but also recommended appropriate historical periods and topics to be taught in each cycle. The fifth grade was to emphasize discovery, colonization, colonial period, becoming a nation, and the movement west, with in-depth study up to the 1850s followed by a rapid survey to the present. The intention was that history and geography were to be integrated into telling the story of the development of the North American continent in the 17th, 18th, and early part of the 19th Centuries, with special emphasis on the United States and often

Canada.

Eighth grade U.S. history, according to the Wesley Committee, was to be concerned essentially with the 19th Century with special emphasis upon the Constitution, development of the nation, sectionalism, slavery, Civil War, industrialization, immigration, and America's emergence as a world power. This was to be followed by a rapid survey of contemporary U.S. history. The third and final cycle, senior high U.S. history, offered usually in eleventh grade, was to emphasize the 20th Century, stressing the World Wars, economic problems, and social movements, with at least one-third of the time devoted to today's contemporary problems. The general recommendation was that (a) all three cycles (grades five, eight, eleven) should offer rapid surveys and (b) would emphasize a particular historical period. The intention of the recommendation was to discourage teachers from attempting to cover (in depth) all of American history in each cycle. Teachers who have attempted the in-depth approach from discovery to the present in one year found that the school year runs out somewhere around the Depression and the Second World War. If one assumes that the study of history was intended to help students identify appropriate lessons from the past to help understand contemporary events, then U.S. history was not achieving the desired goal, because instruction rarely reached contemporary times. The course, in practice, remains a survey from discovery to modern times with little or no class time devoted to contemporary problems or to the application of historical understanding to real social problems. Hence the student question: "Why do [students] have to take history? What is it for?"

Course, Topics, and Themes Frequently Covered in U.S. History

Objectives of the Course

The course intends to expand the students' knowledge of their nation's history and traditions with the objective of strengthening their appreciation of the American heritage. Emphasis is on (a) developing students' understanding of the historical backgrounds of political, economic, and social institutions and problems of the nation today, and (b) helping students identify the increasing role of the U.S. in world affairs in recent decades and become informed about major problems in American foreign relations.

Basic Content of the Course

The course is usually presented as a chronological survey of United States history, with brief attention to the colonial period, an extended treatment of the Constitution, and about one-half to two-thirds of the year's work devoted to the period since 1876. The following list of units, with time allotments, is not untypical:

      A New Country in a New World - 3 weeks
      Formation of the Federal Union - 4 weeks
      Launching a New Government - 3 weeks
      Nationalism vs. Sectionalism - 4 weeks
      Division and Reunion - 4 weeks
      Emergence of Modern America - 6 weeks
      The United States Becomes a World Power - 2 weeks
      Prosperity and Depression - 4 weeks
      American Foreign Policy, 1921-1980s - 3 weeks

Less frequent topical units are also used in the course. The following are illustrations of units recommended by some state guides:

      Territorial Expansion
      Relations with Other Countries
      Growth of America as an Industrial Power
      Role of Labor
      Growth of Political Parties
      America's Cultural and Social Growth

Trends in Teaching U.S. History

In a few states and school systems, the eleventh grade course treats U.S. history to about 1900, and a second year of American history in grade twelve is devoted to "contemporary" U.S. history. The twelfth grade course may, in these schools, include some units similar to those found in Senior Problems, Problems of Democracy, and U.S. Government courses.

The effort to differentiate senior high school U.S. history from the junior high/middle school course usually seems to take the form of major emphasis on: the Constitution and political systems, the recent period (since 1900); economic developments, including big business and big labor; and U.S. foreign relations, with attention to the U.N. and NATO. Recent surveys of teaching practice in U.S. history show an increasing emphasis on foreign affairs. The following units are typical:

United Nations	Cold Wars, Hot Wars
U.S. and Contemporary World Affairs	World Peace and Understanding
Current American Foreign Policy	International Trade and Aid

The U.S. history course as taught in the three cycles will continue to be considered a capstone course; capstone in the sense that the course is a summarizing of social studies from preceding grades. For example, fifth grade is the capstone for grades one through four summarizing self, family, school, neighborhood, community, region, and state. Eighth grade American history is the capstone for sixth and seventh grades, providing a content to which all world and global studies are related. Eleventh grade U.S. history will act as a capstone for ninth and tenth grade electives and provide a foundation for Problems of Democracy and U.S. Government courses in twelfth grade.

Social studies teachers will probably continue to ignore efforts of the curriculum planners and recommendations of the Wesley Committee to limit senior high U.S. history to a brief survey followed by an in-depth study of the 20th Century with emphasis on application to contemporary social problems. In-depth ground covering of "all significant" events from discovery to the present will continue to prevail even though that organization receives considerable criticism from both teachers and students.

As the comments on grades five, eight, and eleven indicate, many school systems are seeking a clearer differentiation of U.S. history content to be presented in three cycles. Some curriculum developers have discussed a 2-2-2 sequence in grades seven through twelve: grades seven and eight devoted to "American studies"--U.S. and state history, geography, civics, economic life; grades nine and ten devoted to a "world view"--either through world geography in grade nine and world history in grade ten, or a two-year sequence of area study units; and grades eleven and twelve devoted to the United States in a world setting--U.S. history, government, problems, economic system, and world affairs or "world problems."

II. Illustration of a State U.S. History Course

There is no one prescribed social studies program throughout the United States. However, one state's description of its U.S. history program will illustrate the content which the state expects to be taught. This illustration identifies a state's suggested social studies curriculum for U.S. history.

> This course should serve as a capstone course building upon those basic concepts developed in the general overview of American history offered in the eighth grade. It should deal primarily with twentieth century American history. The approach should allow a great deal of flexibility in developing certain themes from America's past as they relate to life in America today. Whenever appropriate, students should be encouraged to develop skills of inquiry by using expository accounts, documentary and primary sources, etc. Interpretations of problems, issues, and events should, wherever relevant, emphasize the diversity, cultural pluralism, and multicultural approach to American society past and present.[1]

As a special note, the reader should be aware that many of the topics and activities that would normally be found in this chapter have already been covered by activities in other chapters in this book and in the companion book, Elementary and Junior High/Middle School Social Studies Curriculum, Activities, and Materials. In particular in this book, Chapters I and II have extensive activities on nationalism, Constitution and political systems, separation of powers, U.S. as a world power, international organizations and foreign policy, and community study and social action. For an extensive number of activities on discovery, colonization, becoming a nation, and global studies see Chapter Fifth Grade and Chapter Eighth Grade in the abovementioned book. The activities identified in this chapter follow the recommendations of the Wesley Committee by emphasizing an application of history to 20th Century social problems. The emphasis for senior high school U.S. history is on processing and valuing, skills which will be necessary for twelfth grade American government, senior problems, or social science courses.

III. Activities and Materials Categorized by Gaining Knowledge, Processing, Valuing, and Participating

A. General Objective: To gain knowledge about the human condition which includes past, present, and future

SPECIFIC OBJECTIVE: Learn to identify, explain, and predict events based on differing theories of history with emphasis on acquiring a critical view of the application of history.

1. Historical Points of View

    when: three class periods

    what: theories of history below

    how: (1) Divide the class into groups and give each group a different theory of historical development from the list below.
    (2) Give all the groups the same historical event such as the Civil War, the Great Depression, etc. The group must view the event from the point of view of the particular theory which it has been assigned (who, what, where, when, why, and how).
    (3) Have each group report on its theory to the class. What theory does the class think best fits this particular event? Do the students think that different theories would be better for different events?

Popular Theories of History

History texts are often written with a particular theory of history in mind. The following are examples:

1. CLASS STRUGGLE is the main reason for historical development and economics is that which fuels the struggle.

2. SOCIAL MASSES are the prime instigators of historical development.

3. SIGNIFICANT INDIVIDUALS have directed the course of historical development. It is the significant people who make and shape the world.

4. CONSPIRACIES of small groups of people have influenced the course of historical development.

5. CYCLES of history repeating themselves down through time.

6. MAN IS EVIL is the belief that history is a demonstration of man becoming more evil throughout his development and this evil will lead to complete destruction of the human race.

7. PROGRESS is the belief that history is a demonstration of man progressing toward ever greater development. Man is perfecting himself toward an ultimate good.

8. NO MEANING means history does not illustrate either good or bad. Not knowing the meaning of creation and development, there is no way to know the meaning of events; they just happen.

Some questions to think over:

Which one of the eight theories above is most useful to your thinking about the history of the United States? Which is the least useful?

Why do you suppose that many historians adopt a particular theory of history?

Can you think of a theory of history that is not included in the eight above?

2. Historians Draw Inferences

when: one class period

what: collected artifacts (from one culture or comparative cultures) Artifacts can be such simple things as a coat hanger, rubber band, paper clip, clothes pins, to such things as a tool, machine, etc. from another culture.

how: (1) Divide the class into groups and give each group one or more artifacts. If possible, use artifacts from different cultures: one culture uses plastic, the other uses natural wood materials. Are the objects permanent or disposable, used up or preserved and passed on?
      (2) Have students role play they are from another planet or a lost culture on this planet. They should suggest hypotheses about their artifacts. The following questions should be considered:
          What is it?

How was it produced?
Who used it?
How did they use it?

(3) After the groups have presented their "findings" to the class, raise the following questions:
  (a) Do historians think a special way--a way that is different from ordinary people? (convergent question)
  (b) Suppose you were a historian, what questions would you ask about an artifact? (divergent question)
  (c) Would it be useful to think like a historian when reading historical material? (evaluative question)

3.   What Do You Know For Sure?

when: one class period

what: This activity is one in a series that encourages students to think divergently. One technique that encourages divergent thinking is to ask students to consider a set of historical events which could challenge their preconceived notions. Processing information means, literally, "What do you know for sure?" This activity should encourage students to "check out" their own knowledge.

All of the acts listed below were performed by a specific society as acts against the freedom of religion. These acts were:

- a series of laws which encouraged the confession of one's own sins and the reporting of sins in an open meeting (which is an important step in the process we now call brainwashing)

- the hanging of a number of Christians who expressed their beliefs forcefully

- outlawed Christmas as a religious holiday

- tortured a number of men and women on the basis of hysterical confessions of adolescent informants

A. Soviet Russia
B. Fascist Spain
C. France under the Louis
D. New England Puritans
E. Mainland China
F. Spain during the In-quisition
G. Germany under Hitler

how: (1) Have students identify one of the societies listed that most likely practiced all of the acts above. Have them briefly explain their choice.
(2) Have students identify the society they believe would be least likely to practice all the acts above and explain their choice.
(3) Quickly tally results on board. The correct answer is New England Puritans. Are the students surprised by the correct answer? Why? Do they have a different image of what Puritans did?

4. Collecting History

   when: one class period

   what: any "collections" that students, parents, or friends would be willing to bring to school to display to the students

   how: Collecting seems to be almost a natural instinct for people the world over. Some of the most common collections are of books, records, stamps, postcards, Christmas cards, and antiques. Often we read in the paper about extensive and expensive collections such as works of art, antique automobiles, coins, etc. Almost any collection that has objects extending over a long period of time offers a lesson in history.

      (1) Have students examine the collection (if possible) or at least observe a display of the collection.

      (2) What do the objects in the collection tell us about the time in history when they were produced, the materials available to make the object, etc.

         Stamps are a good example because even current ones commemorate past events and people. Questions can be asked about why that particular person or event should be remembered. What were the reasons (causes) for the event or what were the conditions in the country at the time that produced the individual commemorated on the stamp?

      (3) One of the characteristics of the gifted is their "passion" for collecting objects--model boats, beer cans, keys, bottles, bottle caps, pets, pictures, etc. which are in many cases historical collections. A historical collection is a rich source to tap. Granted, interest in the objects collected may offer a very narrow perspective for the collector, but the objects provide an opportunity to develop the sense of place and time in history. The collector in a sense is a historian with a visual demonstration of objects that are from a particular time and place and represent a particular unique design.

5. Interpreting History Through Sayings and Slogans

   when: two class periods

   what: list of sayings

   how: Every so often throughout history phrases originate that are repeated, become known, and often turn into sayings that are still used in present times. Most of the time these phrases are repeated without a thought as to where they came from. Some sayings are so well known that they can be parodied because people will be aware of the original saying and what it has come to mean. But all sayings, whatever their current meaning, originated at a certain time and place in history and have a certain meaning. In other words, these phrases were said for a specific reason, and in may cases represent the time in which they were said or written.

Below is a list of sayings, the date, and author. Mix up the sayings and give a list omitting date and author to each student. Can they put the sayings in chronological order and speculate on what was going on in the country at the time that would prompt the feeling that produced the phrase?

Alternative Activity

Just give the list of sayings, dates, and authors to students. Have them speculate on the meaning and on why that saying may have been particularly appropriate at the time it was written.

"Nothing is certain but death and taxes."

> 1789 - Benjamin Franklin

"Go west, young man."

> 1851 - John Babsome Lane Soule
> popularized by Horace Greeley

"Tippecanoe and Tyler too!"

> 1840 - Political campaign slogan
> for Wm. Henry Harrison-John Tyler

"The mass of men lead lives of quiet desperation."

> 1854 - Henry David Thoreau

"War is hell."

> 1863 - General William T. Sherman

"The only good Indian is a dead Indian."

> 1869 - General Philip Sheridan

"The public be damned."

> 1882 - William H. Vanderbilt

"Laugh and the world laughs with you; weep and you weep alone."

> 1883 - Ella Wheeler Wilcox

"I'm from Missouri, you've got to show me."

> 1899 - Willard Duncan Vandiver

SPECIFIC OBJECTIVE: Identify the geography of the U.S. stressing westward
expansion, nation building, and sectionalism.

6.   Acquiring and Sectioning America II[2]

when: one week

what: large outline map of U.S. (This can be done by throwing a
transparency outline map onto a large sheet of paper and
having students trace the outline and cut it out.) The map
should have the outline of the following:

(a) U.S. of 1783   (d) Oregon Territory in 1846
(b) Louisiana Purchase of 1803 (e) Mexican Cession in 1848
(c) Texas Annexation in 1845   (f) Gadsden Purchase in 1853

how: (1) Divide the class into six groups and give each group a
section of the map.
(2) Each group will research its section to discover the circumstances surrounding the purchase or acquisition of
the section and the effect of the purchase on the rest
of the country.
(3) The students should examine the states within their
region, i.e., the circumstances surrounding being granted
statehood and any unusual history that might be connected
with the states. Outline the states and mark the
capitals and give date of when each became a state.
(4) Starting with the U.S. of 1783, have the groups report
on their findings in the order of the purchase or
acquisition, putting the map together as they go.

7.   Sectionalism

when: two class periods

what: newspapers, magazines, TV news

how: (1) Divide the continental U.S. into the following sections:
Northeast, Southeast, Middle West, Northwest, and South-
west.

(2) Divide the class into five groups and give each of the
groups one of the sections. Students should list the
states in their section and then gather past and present
population figures for those states.

(3) Have groups report briefly on their findings.

(4) Hold a class discussion:

(a) How has the population shifted in the past 40 years?

(b) What has been the cause of population shift?

(c) What do students predict will be the future population
migration trends?

(5) Have students bring in examples from newspapers, magazines, or TV of population shifts or industry shutdown
or relocation and how these affect population.

8.   Manifest Destiny[3]

when: two class periods

what: map and list of acquisitions

how: Definitions: manifest - clearly apparent, reveal
                    destiny - pre-ordained, inevitable course of
                              events

All TV weather broadcasters use outline maps of the U.S. We
all take that outline for granted when, in fact, the outline
was developed following a series of acquisitions throughout
the 200 year history of our country. Were all these acquisitions cases of manifest destiny?

(1) Have students answer the following questions:

   (a) What are two reasons Americans wanted to expand?

   (b) What in your opinion caused the U.S. to stop at the
       borders as they are today?

   (c) What do you think the chances are of changing our
       borders again?

   (d) Where might we add or lose territory?

(2) Have the students write a one-page essay on the following
    question:

           "Do you believe anything in history was pre-
           ordained?"

    (See activity 1, "Historic Points of View," for suggested
    theories of history that might stimulate some thought on
    beliefs about "destiny.")

NOTE: The essay should apply the four recommended steps for

       answering open questions. (See activity "Answering

       Open Questions" in Chapter I and the activity "Review

       on Answering Open Questions" in this chapter.)

9.   Examining the Frontier[4]

   when: one class period

   what: quotation and background statement

   how: (1) Divide students into groups. Have them read the quotation
            and statement below and then answer the following ques-
            tions.

         Quotation from a Nameless Frontiersman of 1850

   ". . . I spent three years in the land of the mountain men. Sometimes we had plenty of food. In the summer we ate buffalo until our
   stomachs nearly burst. But sometimes we starved. When things got
   really black, we would boil a batch of large black crickets. When
   they stopped kicking, we ate them. I saw one old mountain man boil
   his moccasins. When they got soft, he closed his eyes and chewed
   away. But in many ways those were good years. I learned a lot. I
   became a new person--more rugged and independent. I learned how to
   take care of myself. I became more clever than the Indians who
   followed my trail. I learned how to get by without comforts. I
   became more practical. But, most of all, I learned to judge people
   for themselves . . ."

   In 1893, Frederick Jackson Turner, a history professor from the University of Wisconsin, gave a speech to the American Historical
   Society in which he announced that the census of 1890 demonstrated
   that the frontier was no longer a part of America. For the past 86
   years historians have been looking back on those frontier days as
   being particularly significant in the development of the U.S.

   Why study the frontier? Why not just let it die as it did in 1890?
   Why dig it up again? Well, a part of the answer is that behind the
   myth and the legends of the West there may be a clue to understanding
   Americans today.

         (2) Group discussion questions:
            (a) What was the frontier?
            (b) What special qualities do people need to survive on a
                frontier?
            (c) Which of those characteristics are most prevalent in
                America today? Which are most noticeably missing?
            (d) Space, the sea, medicine, and nuclear energy are all
                called the new frontiers. Why is this so? Can the
                students name any other new frontiers?
            (e) Are there always new frontiers--is the notion of
                frontier a state of mind, a place, a thing?
            (f) Is there a relationship between frontier and manifest
                destiny? Are they both states of mind, one support-
                ing the other? See activity 8, "Manifest Destiny."

         (3) Have groups share results of their discussions if time
            permits.

10. <u>Women's Work Is Never Done!</u>[5]

   when: one class period

   what: matching exercise below

   how: (1) Have students complete matching exercise.

MATCHING: Column A contains descriptions of pioneers of the American West. Column B contains the names of pioneers. Place the correct letter next to the description.

COLUMN A

___1. Guide for Lewis and Clark, 1800-1806

___2. Missionary to Oregon, 1836

___3. Idaho miner, sheepherder, horse tamer, sharpshooter, and cattle rancher, 1870s

___4. Wyoming justice of the peace, 1860s

___5. Western outlaw whose 20-year career was ended with shot in back in 1889

Answers: 1 - d; 2 - i; 3 - g; 4 - c; 5 - a

COLUMN B

a. Belle Starr
b. Buffalo Bill
c. Esther Morris
d. Sacajawea
e. Bat Masterson
f. Jesse James
g. Josephine Monoghan
h. Sitting Bull
i. Narcissa Whitman
j. Wyatt Eart

(2) In addition to the few women whose names stand out in the settling of the American West there were the thousands of nameless, but equally important, women whose lives read like the following diary excerpt from Washington state in the 1830s:

". . . rose about five. Had early breakfast. Got my housework done about nine. Baked six loaves of bread. Made a kettle of mush and have now a suet pudding and beef boiling. My girl (American Indian) has ironed and I have set my house in order. May the merciful Lord be with me through the unexpected scene. Nine o'clock was delivered of another son . . ."

Hold a discussion on the following:

In view of the obviously vital role women played in the settling of the west, how do you explain the fact that men get most of the space in history books?

Consider these possibilities as you discuss:

___ Only men did important things.

___ Women mostly preferred to work in the home and that is not very important historically.

___ Women were not permitted by law and by custom to take an active part in the public life of the West.

___ Men, by and large, have written the history books.

___ Other reasons? _____

SPECIFIC OBJECTIVE: Identify and critically evaluate how labels influence or define a point of view.

11. Word Association with Key Names and Labels

when: one class period

what: list of collective nouns for specific groups of animals below

how: (1) Everyone is familiar with the following terms for groups of animals:

herd of cattle	pack of dogs
gaggle of geese	pride of lions

BUT have you heard of:

1. a parliament of owls	6. a murder of crows
2. a knot of toads	7. a sloth of bears
3. a drift of hogs	8. a paddling of ducks
4. a peep of chickens	9. a muster of peacocks
5. a rafter of turkeys	10. an exaltation of larks

All of the above are legitimate collective nouns for the animals mentioned. Could one also "think up" collective nouns for historical events?

(2) If we apply these descriptive and colorful words to animals, can we also apply such words to people and events? For example: What could we call the group of "Indians" who dumped tea in Bostom Harbor at the Boston Tea Party? Of course, the first word that comes to mind is TRIBE of Indians.

(3) Below is a list of synonyms for the word "group." Looking back in American history, what groups of people or events would these words best fit? (There are no right answers—individual choice.)

clutch	some possible key word groups:
assembly	war hawks
company	Minutemen
association	troops at Valley Forge
clique	gold seekers in '49
set	frontier settlers
collection	plantation owners
cluster	peace doves
congregation	
bunch	
parcel	For example:
lot	a collection of minutemen
troop	a clutch of gold seekers
arrangement	a troop of "War Hawks"
flight	a flight of "Peace Doves"

Students may wish to make up new words or give an old word new meaning to fit a group or event. The point of the activity is to single out key words and to encourage the use of the word using the students' own choice of noun.

(4) Have students share their favorites with the class.

12. <u>Your Title Is Your Point of View II</u>[6]

    when: one or two class periods

    what: list of titles for Civil War:

                The War for States' Rights
                War Between the States
                The Great Rebellion
                American Civil War
                The Yankee Invasion
                The Lost Cause
                Mr. Lincoln's War
                The Brothers' War
                The Second American Revolution
                The War for Southern Independence

    how: Give list to students. Have students identify several reasons why each of these titles applied to the Civil War. Which of the titles would the northern states have been more likely to use? Which of the titles would fit the southern point of view? Rank order the 10 titles above according to class choice. Does that rank order suggest a bias for a particular view of the Civil War? Can the students identify what that bias might be? Would that ranking be the same in Ohio and Texas? If not, why not?

SPECIFIC OBJECTIVE: Use knowledge to speculate and categorize information of the historic treatment of selected minorities with emphasis upon a critical evaluation of the application of civil rights.

13. <u>To Be a Slave II</u>[7]

    when: two class periods

    what: resource materials on slavery and chart following

    how: (1) Provide source materials for students to read about slavery and the conditions of slavery and the reaction of slaves to those conditions. Teacher may wish to distribute a chart to students to help them focus their thinking while they are doing their reading.

           (2) Have students fill out chart listing slaves' reactions to slavery, reasons behind actions, and results or consequences of those actions.

           (3) At the bottom of the chart have students rank their own choice of reaction.

	FIRST CHOICE OF SLAVES	SECOND CHOICE OF SLAVES	THIRD CHOICE OF SLAVES
Reaction of slaves to condition of slavery	(example) Acceptance		
Reasons why slaves took the above action	well treated by owner; afraid of being caught escaping		
Resulting consequences	remain well treated; remain with family		
Student ranking of personal choice			

Instructions: Below is a list of possible actions taken by slaves toward their condition of slavery. On the chart above list the actions from most frequently taken to least frequently taken. Then fill in the rest of the chart. On the bottom line rank your own choice of actions.

    acceptance
    revolt
    escape
    passive resistance (hindering work on plantation by
                        doing work slowly)
    active resistance (sabotage; hindering work by doing
                       work badly or being destructive)

(4) Hold class discussion:
    (a) Of the five actions listed, which was the one most
        often followed by most slaves?
    (b) Did the reactions of slaves change noticeably after
        the start of the Civil War?
    (c) Suppose you had been a slave, what action would you
        have chosen?
    (d) What conditions would have prompted your actions?
    (e) Is it ever right to own another person as a slave?
    (f) Do you believe there is slavery anywhere in the world
        today?
    (g) Is slavery an issue today anywhere in the world?
    (h) Do all people have a right not to be a slave? If so,
        when was that right granted and by whom?

14. <u>Defining Key Words</u>

    when: one class period

    what: word list and chart

    how: (1) Have students define briefly each of the words in the word list.

WORD LIST

1. Jim Crow laws _____

2. Reconstruction _____

3. Civil Rights _____

4. Segregation _____

5. Carpetbagger _____

           (2) Have students place words in the sections of the chart where they think the words fit. They must defend (give reasons) for their choice of word placement in the chart.

Advantages for Blacks	Advantages for Whites
1. _____ (word) (reason) _____ 2. _____ _____ 3. _____ _____ 4. _____ _____ 5. _____ _____	1. _____ (word) (reason) _____ 2. _____ _____ 3. _____ _____ 4. _____ _____ 5. _____ _____
Disadvantages for Blacks	Disadvantages for Whites
1. _____ _____ 2. _____ _____ 3. _____ _____ 4. _____ _____ 5. _____ _____	1. _____ _____ 2. _____ _____ 3. _____ _____ 4. _____ _____ 5. _____ _____

<u>Note to Teacher</u>: The words are examples. You may very well wish to suggest other words appropriate to the content being studies. The form above could be modified to fit other word definition series where there is a definite advantage to one group and a definite disadvantage to another group, i.e., employer/ employee (Industrial Revolution), Imperialist/Imperialism, Subjugated/Subjugator, etc.

15. Separate and Unequal by "Jim Crow"[8]

when: two class periods

what: resource materials on "Jim Crow" laws; chart below

Briefly, Jim Crow laws referred to laws that restricted
Blacks such as:
separate waiting rooms at train and bus depots
separate rest rooms
restricted to special Jim Crow sections at back of
  street cars, trains, buses
school segregation
segregated theaters, hotels, restaurants, barber shops,
 etc.
race etiquette: act inferior to Whites
                 doff hat and get off sidewalk for Whites
                 respond to term "boy"
                 be called by your first name only
                   during your entire life
etc.

how: (1) Have students research and identify as many Jim Crow laws
          and restrictions as they can.
      (2) Have students fill in chart below to demonstrate how Jim
          Crow laws would affect one's weekly activities.
      (3) Hold a class discussion. Are these laws and restrictions
          a part of the past or are there "hold-overs" in today's
          society? What are some major events and Court decisions
          that did away with many Jim Crow laws and restrictions?

LIST OF ACTIVITIES FOR ONE WEEK (examples)	JIM CROW LAWS	
	PROHIBITED	RESTRICTED
1. ride bus to school		must sit in back
2. dinner in restaurant	White only rest.	
3. went to movie		sit in section reserved for you
4. got haircut		
5. went to shopping mall		
6. drink from public fountain		
7. went to public library		
8. went to local motel to reserve rooms for visiting relatives		

16. Civil Rights Time Line II[9]

  when: four class periods

  what: resource materials on laws pertaining to treatment of Blacks
         (slave codes, voting laws, Supreme Court Decisions, etc.)

  how: (1) Have students, individually or in groups, research the
             laws and Supreme Court decisions. What was the date the
             law was passed or the Court decision handed down? What
             were the immediate causes for the passage of the laws and
             what were the short and long term effects of the law or
             decisions?

         (2) Have students place laws and decisions in chronological
             order and create a time line with an illustration or
             short description of each law in its place on the time
             line.

         (3) Hold class discussion on the direction of the laws and
             Court decisions.
               What factors have brought about significant changes and
                 reversals in laws and Court decisions?
               What relation do these laws have to other minorities
                 such as Mexican-Americans, women, old people?
               What direction will laws and Court decisions take in
                 the future and why?

         (4) Where does Civil Rights start, with contemporary rights
             movements or in early history of the century? In other
             words, the time line on Civil Rights could start in
             colonial times, modern times, or contemporary times.
             Where the time line begins, in part, is determined by the
             scope of the topic under study.

17. Genocide as a Fact of Modern Life[10]

  when: three or four class periods

  what: The term "genocide" comes from two words, the first of which,
         gen, is a Greek term meaning "somthing that is born or pro-
         duced," hence a people. The second term, cide, is a common
         suffix meaning destruction or killing (as in homocide, sui-
         cide, patricide). The term "genocide" had the meaning of a
         deliberate attempt to destroy an entire group of persons; it
         appears to have come into use after World War II to describe
         the destruction of the entire European Jewish community among
         other religious and ethnic groups.

         In recent years, the tendency has been to extend the term to
         mean not just the physical destruction of a people, but also
         moral, cultural, or psychological destruction. According to
         this conception, a majority may wipe out a minority in the
         sense of not letting them speak their own language, enjoy
         their own theater, train their own religious leadership, etc.
         This is not the sudden, sharp murder of thousands but it does
         eventually lead to the death of a culture.

how: Class discussion questions:

(1) Can you produce evidence of genocide directed in this country against a particular group of persons? Be specific and provide evidence.

(2) In the mid-1920s the Supreme Court declared (later reversing itself) that it was constitutionally proper to prohibit the use of the German language in certain schools in which most of the children and teachers were German. What is your response to this Court ruling? Why was it originally made?

(3) A teaching practice that has become common, "bilingual education," has been criticized because it is thought not to teach the student to speak English. Bilingual education begins with the students' native language and, in theory, gradually teaches them to speak English. However, it clearly does make use of the students' first language. What is your reaction to this practice?

In the past, Black leaders have accused Whites of genocide, that is, the deliberate destruction of Black culture. Can you analyze this accusation, breaking it into a number of sub-questions:

(1) Is there in reality a "Black" culture?

(2) If so, can one describe it?

(3) Do Whites deliberately attempt to destroy it? If so, how?

(4) Can one argue that Whites have borrowed elements from the Black culture? If so, what elements? How?

(5) Can one point to the destruction of whole groups of Blacks by Whites? If so, where and when?

(6) Can one point to something less than violent murder and destruction by Whites of Blacks? That is, can one identify slow destruction rather than what we have called "rapid genocide"? If so, where and when?

18. Let's Clip Their Wings[11]

when: two or three class periods

what: Brief review and reminder to class that America is a nation of laws--laws to protect the rights of citizens and laws to limit the power of authority, those elected or appointed to rule.

how: (1) Have the class choose a minority, i.e., Mexicans, Jews, Blacks, women, age groups such as over 65, teenagers, and children under five, a distinguishable minority that during the course of this activity will lose their rights. For example, elementary "kids" should not have the same rights as high school students. Old folks should not have the same driving privileges as younger, more alert people. Surely fools, idiots, imbeciles, simpletons should not share equal rights with those who are normal responsible citizens. There must be many citizens who because of their strange ideas ought not to have their rights protected.

(2) Divide the class into groups and have them consider what rights could be removed from the identified minority, what stands in the way of removing these rights, and what means can be used to "get around" the barriers to re-moving the rights: for example, muzzling the press by prior review of copy; a look at the treatment of religious and ethnic minorities in Germany before and during World War II; review the "Jim Crow" laws as noted earlier in this chapter--these should give the class ideas.

(3) After the groups have made their reports to the class, the following questions will stimulate class discussion:

(a) Would it be possible--in a democracy with the Bill of Rights--for a given group of citizens to be stripped of their rights?

(b) If, in fact, a given minority were stripped of its rights, would the society then be a democracy?

(c) Does the presence of a written law, such as the Con-stitution, actually prevent a group from being stripped of rights?

(d) Many dictatorships around the world have an elaborate written bill of rights which grants freedom and liberty to all their citizens. If this is true, how can we account for the fact that most countries are dictatorships?

(e) Can one point to groups of individuals who were--with or without "due process of law"--stripped of their rights? (For example: deportation of "Reds" during the Palmer Raids of 1919.)

(f) Can one argue that some of the wilder fringe groups during the 1960s and 1970s (i.e., Yippies, followers of Mao, Che Guevara, etc.) whose phones were tapped and whose mail was systematically intercepted by the FBI and the CIA were deprived of their rights? Would such groups fit under the generalization that most accept: in a democracy, a minority may not have its rights summarily stripped away?

SPECIFIC OBJECTIVE: Identify and critically evaluate past and present attitudes, opportunities, and restrictions on immigration.

19. Immigration

when: one class period

what: Immigration: A Right or a Privilege form

how: This is as much a valuing activity as it is one for gaining knowledge, because it asks the students to identify their strength of feeling. This is one of those activities where the teacher intends to gather data from students as an introduction to the activities on immigration.

(1) Have students fill out following form.

Immigration: A Right or a Privilege Form

INSTRUCTIONS: Read the statement. Decide how you feel about the statement and place the number of the statement on the strength of feeling scale at the point that best expresses your feeling.

1. If you want to become an American, you should adopt the American culture.

2. Being a hyphenated American (Polish-American, Black-American, Irish-American, Japanese-American, Mexican-American, Native-American) is being a good American because it reminds us of our family heritage.

3. "Give me your tired, your poor, your huddled masses yearning to breathe free . . ." should no longer guide Americans' thought on immigration.

4. America is a pluralistic society, but, if you want to be a real American, there are certain basic ideas you must accept.

5. Opportunity for success will be lost for many Americans if the country continues to be open to all foreigners who feel oppressed in their own country.

6. A mixture of different races, religions, and customs adds strength to the American society.

Strength of feeling scale:

strongly agree	agree	neutral	disagree	strongly disagree

---

(2) It is well known that immigration groups once settled and established tend to wish immigration restricted to a qualified few. Do students follow that wish or do they idealistically propose to open the door to all who would enter?

(3) Determine where class as a whole falls on the scale. Are there inconsistent beliefs marked on the strength of feeling scale?

As a final note: When studying unit on immigration, refer back to students' attitudes. This scale could be used as a post-evaluation.

20. When Immigration Became a Privilege II[12]

when: two class periods

what: readings on immigration laws

how: (1) Have students study immigration laws, keeping a record of the date the law was passed and briefly what the law contained.

(2) Hold a class discussion. Make a chronological list on the board of the law and the date it was passed. The students can supply this information from their notes. For example:

Chinese workers, insane, diseased criminals, paupers prohibited	1882
Japanese workers prohibited	1907
literacy test required	1917
application of quota system based on national origin	1921
quota revised to 2% of number of people from that nation living in U.S. in 1890 (meaning mostly northern Europeans); Canadians and Latin Americans excluded from quota regulation	1924
Displaced Persons Act	1948
quota established for Chinese and Japanese	1952
Refugee Relief Act	1953
Limit of 20,000 from any one country, total limit of 170,000. Immediate family members not part of limit. Preference given to relatives and skilled laborers.	1967
limited Mexico to 20,000 a year	1976
world-wide limit of 290,000 with preference to family members, those with needed skills, and refugees	1978

QUESTION: Suppose the immigration law of 1978 was in effect when your family some generations ago was trying to enter the United States? Would your family have been allowed to stay and become citizens? Explain your answer.

(3) Hold class discussion on the laws.
What were the reasons for the laws?
Were the laws justifiable at the time they were passed? If not, have they been corrected in more recent times?
Are current regulations adequate and fair?
Can students predict events or circumstances that might make new regulations necessary?
By some counts there are 7 to 10 million illegal aliens in the United States, most of whom are not identified and will not be returning to their native lands. Should the continuing flow of illegal aliens be counted as part of the total number admitted by 1978 law?

21. Identifying Immigration Guidelines

    when: two or three class periods

    what: resource materials on immigration laws

    how: (1) Divide class into groups.

           (2) The groups must play the role of the Immigration Review Board and establish the conditions and requirements for persons wishing to immigrate to the U.S.

               Students should understand that they are setting up GUIDELINES, conditions under which people may immigrate to the U.S.

               Factors students might consider:

nationality	health, mental and physical
race	religion
age	criminal record
relatives in U.S.	wealth
leaving native land	employment skills
because of flood,	
famine, persecution, etc.	

           (3) Groups should report their conditions and requirements to the class.

           (4) Hold class discussion on similarities and differences between group reports and the significance of those similarities and differences.

           (5) By combining group lists and through class discussion, prepare a master guideline for immigration.

           (6) Have students research actual immigration laws and regulations. (See activity "Who Is Acceptable, You Decide II" in this chapter.)

           (7) Hold class discussion on a comparison of the class guidelines and the actual laws and regulations. Do they differ markedly? If they do differ, how do they differ? What reasons for this difference can the students identify?

22. Change Your Country, Change Your Name[13]

    when: one class period

    what: list of names

    how: (1) Changing one's name is a common practice in the U.S. partly because the immigration authorities thought foreign names should be Anglicized. People change their names to make them easier to pronounce, such as movie stars, or to Americanize the name for social as well as political and business reasons. For example, would you be less likely to vote for Spiro Theodore Anagnostopoulos and more likely to vote for him if his name was Spiro Agnew (Vice President 1969-1973)? The students themselves often use a nickname or a shortened form of their name, or just their initials. Have a quick show of hands in the class of those who do not normally use their full name.

(2) The following is a list of names and what they have been changed to. Mix the new names up and give the list to the students. Can they match the new name to the original?

Original Name	New Name
1. Nathan Birnbaum	George Burns (actor/comedian)
2. Lucille Le Sueur	Joan Crawford (actress)
3. Issur Danielovitch Demsky	Kirk Douglas (actor)
4. Walter Matuschanskavaskyj	Walter Matthau (actor)
5. Rodolpho d'Antonguolla	Rudolph Valentino (actor)
6. Cornelius McGillicuddy	Connie Mack (baseball player)
7. Goldie Mabovitch	Golda Meir (teacher/Prime Minister of Israel)
8. Joe Yule, Jr.	Mickey Rooney (actor)
9. Israel Baline	Irving Berlin (composer)
10. Krikor Ohanian	Mike Conners (actor)
11. Suzanne Mahoney	Susanne Somers (actress)
12. Leonard Rosenberg	Tony Randall (actor)
13. Spiro Theodore Anagnostopoulos	Spiro Agnew (politician)

(3) Hold class discussion. Run through the list with the students to speculate on why the individual changes his/her name and what country their family might have emigrated from. Do students see any trends in name changing; will it be more or less confined to movie stars? Are immigarnts from certain countries more apt to change their names than others? How much does the type of name you have affect the opportunities offered you?

(4) Do the students know of name changes from their own experience with family, relatives, or friends? Be sure students suggest why the name was changed.

23. Immigration: When and Why?

when: class periods as needed

what: research materials; list of famous Americans

how: (1) If possible, invite several immigrants to discuss with
the class:

Why they immigrated and when?

What their job was before they came to the U.S.?

What is their job here in the U.S.?

What do they like most about the U.S.? Like least?

What do they miss most from their native land?

(2) Below is a list of famous foreign-born Americans. Have
students match each person with the country from which
they emigrated by putting the letter representing the
country (in the right column) in the space provided before each person's name in the left column.

___ 1. Andrew Carnegie (millionaire/industry)   a. Germany

___ 2. Knute Rockne (football)   b. Great Britain

___ 3. Albert Einstein (science)   c. Scotland

___ 4. Wernher Von Braun (science)   d. Norway

___ 5. Alexander Graham Bell (science)

___ 6. Henry Kissinger (teacher/government official)

___ 7. Tom Payne (revolutionary)

(answers: 1 - c, 2 - d, 3 - a, 4 - a, 5 - c, 6 - a, 7 - b)

(3) Have students identify each person's age and the date at
the time they immigrated to the U.S. What were the
probable circumstances that caused the individual to come
to the U.S.? For example, would a Tom Payne be permitted
to immigrate to the United States today? What about
Andrew Carnegie, would he have been acceptable by today's
immigration standards?

24. Who Do You Choose?[14]

when: one class period

what: description of four prospective immigrants

how: (1) Give students the description of the four prospective immigrants. Only two of the four may be granted visas and each student must make a decision on which two of the four to choose and give reasons for the choice.

NGO DIEM THIEU

42-year-old male from Danang Province, Vietnam. Worked for the American military as a filing clerk. Speaks some English. Widower with five children. Roman Catholic.

PEDRO CABRILLO DESANTIAGO

18-year-old male from Juarez, Mexico. Speaks no English and has only an elementary school background. Has worked as a farm laborer for nine years. Single. Roman Catholic.

KEMU LESUTO

35-year-old male from Nairobi, Kenya. Educated at the Universite Nationale. Speaks fluent French, English, and Swahili. Holds a medical degree in obstetrics. Married with two children. Moslem.

ANNA GABRIELLA

25-year-old female from Sweden. Speaks fluent English and French. Experienced as a professional singer. Divorced with one child. No religious affiliation.

My choices would be:

_____
(name of immigrant)

_____
(reasons for choice)

_____

_____

_____
(name of immigrant)

_____
(reasons for choice)

_____

_____

(2) Determine (by a show of hands vote) which of the two prospective immigrants would be granted visas by the majority of class members.

SPECIFIC OBJECTIVE: Identify from contemporary events social-personal issues and problems which arise from cultural conflicts.

25.   <u>Questionnaire on Family Mobility</u>

     when: two class periods

     what: questionnaire below modified by teacher

     how: (1) Discuss mobility of American family life and how the mobility has increased throughout the history of the United States.

               (2) Have students fill out questionnaire and use it for class discussion particularly to search out comparisons and trends.

               (3) National trends on family mobility suggest that families are not "staying put" but are, in fact, moving around the country, if not around the world. Approximately seven moves are average for most families. Would that number of moves have the potential to change the country? Can students think of ways that the country might change, i.e., which states will lose representation in Congress because of lost population; what states will lose industries; where are the future good (high paying) jobs?

MOBILITY

1. Where were you born?
2. Where did you live before you moved to your present address?
3. How many places have you lived?
4. Where do your grandparents live?
5. How long have they lived in that location?
6. Where did your grandparents live previously?
7. Where did your great-grandparents live?
8. How many generations of your family have lived in the U.S.?
9. How many times have your parents moved?
10. How many times have your grandparents moved?

26.   <u>Who Is Acceptable, You Decide II</u>[15]

     when: two class periods

     what: description of prospective immigrants prepared by teacher (see sample below); quotas and criteria government uses for admitting immigrants or guidelines prepared by students (see activity "Identifying Immigration Guidelines")

     how: (1) Divide class into groups. Supply each group with the sample description of prospective immigrants.

(2) The groups, using actual government criteria or the class guidelines (prepared for another activity) must reach a consensus on which people on the list may enter the U.S. Ten of the fifteen on the list may be allowed to enter and stay.

(3) Have groups list their choices on the board. The comparison of choices may produce heated debate and force groups to justify their choices. Did emotions play any part in reaching choices?

(4) Were there hidden criteria which we call bias? Were there biases in favor of people from particular countries? Do the 10 persons chosen represent the small group's values? Do the 10 arrived at through class consensus represent the values of the community served by the school?

DESCRIPTIONS OF PROSPECTIVE IMMIGRANTS

(10 may enter and stay)

1. Twenty-one-year-old male Russian Jew who wants to be a Rabbi and claims religious persecution in his mother country
2. Young university student who has taken part in demonstrations against his government in Poland
3. Sixteen-year-old Muslim female, member of the Palestianian Liberation Organization army, who lost both parents during an Israeli raid on their village in Lebanon
4. Twenty-four-year-old daughter of minor party official who believes she cannot be creative in her homeland
5. Thirty-five-year-old Black African farmer from the Sudan who was driven from farming by the recurring drought in that part of Africa
6. Thirty-nine-year-old Viennese musician who lost his hand
7. Five-year-old Vietnamese boy whose parents were massacred by pirates while the family was trying to escape to Hong Kong
8. Pregnant woman from underdeveloped nation who wants her baby to be born and raised in America
9. Fifty-year-old doctor from Mansoura, Egypt, who wants to make money in the U.S.
10. Thirty-seven-year-old military officer who took part in an attempted overthrow of his country's government in South Africa
11. Wealthy seventy-year-old Indian guru who in his declining years wishes to join his followers in the U.S.
12. Forty-two-year-old medical doctor who speaks no English
13. Twenty-eight-year-old mother of two children from Great Britain whose American husband died before she could claim American citizenship
14. Thirteen-year-old child who lost both parents in a civil war
15. A farmer and three members of his family who have always been poor as have his ancestors, because they worked marginal lands in Central America

27. <u>A Case of Mistaken Identity</u>

    when: a few minutes each day

    what: following statements (clues)

    how: Each day give the students one of the following statements in the order listed (clues). How quickly can the students find out to whom the statements refer?

        (1) A society, proud of its democracy, stripped members of a certain ethnic group of their Constitutional rights within this century.

        (2) This society rounded up members of this distinguishable ethnic group who were professing to be loyal citizens of this society and required them to live in what they called "Relocation Centers" during the years 1942-1945.

        (3) The highest court in the land heard the case and in 1945 decided that it was Constitutional to do what the chief executive officer had already done in 1942--that is, send members of this ethnic group to the "Relocation Centers."

        (4) The Supreme Court decision is usually known as the Korematsu Case after Fred Korematsu. The full title is <u>Korematsu vs. the United States</u>.

        (5) The official reason given for sending all of the members of this ethnic group to the "Relocation Centers" was that they showed great potential for spying against us during World War II. However, the members of the two other ethnic groups with whom we were fighting--Italians and Germans--were not treated in this fashion. They were not rounded up and not stripped of their civil rights and not sent to camps.

28. <u>"Let the Best Man Win"</u>

    when: two class periods

    what: source materials, list of presidents and their political opponents

    how: "What if" situations or events are always interesting to re-search and speculate about. Particularly appropriate for gifted students who seem to respond to speculation/divergent activities.

        (1) Have students select one of the presidents and the political candidate he defeated from the list.

        (2) Working on the assumption that the defeated candidate would have made a better president than the man elected, explain why this would have been so and the results or consequences of this reversal of history.

President	Date	Defeated Candidate
Richard Nixon	1968	Hubert Humphrey
Herbert Hoover	1928	Alfred E. Smith
Calvin Coolidge	1924	John W. Davis
Warren G. Harding	1920	James M. Cox
James A. Garfield	1880	Winfield Hancock
Rutherford B. Hayes	1876	Samuel J. Tilden
Ulysses S. Grant	1868	Horatio Seymour
James Buchanan	1856	John C. Fremont
Franklin Pierce	1852	Winfield Scott
Zachary Taylor	1848	Lewis Cass

SPECIFIC OBJECTIVE: Identify and inquire into the causes and effects of America's involvement and growth as a world power.

29. Going It Alone or Together II[16]

when: two class periods

what: newspapers, magazines

how: (1) Discuss with the class the concepts of "alone" and "together." In everyday life what do people do to stay alone or to keep themselves separate from others? What do people do who want to be with other people and share? What would students do in school to stay alone or to get together with others? List their suggestions on the board. For example:

Separate
  eat alone at lunch
  keep to oneself
  don't participate

Together
  sit with friends
  take part in discussions
  go places together

(2) Broaden the discussion to what nations do to remain isolated or to become involved. Much of the world is interdependent, but some nations also fear the consequences of too much interdependence and try to remain somewhat isolated. How do they try to stay isolated? What do some nations do to interact with others? Again list the students' suggestions on the board. For example:

Separate
  make it difficult to
    enter or leave country
  close country's borders
    (Berlin Wall)
  strict import laws

Together
send military hardware to
  country under attack
join trade organizations,
  make trade agreements
Olympics
world organizations

(3) Have students look in newspapers and magazines for examples of America remaining separate or working together with other countries. Are some countries trying to remain separate from the U.S.? Why? How do the students feel about America's overseas involvement? The U.S. has developed an interdependent relationship with much of the rest of the world--how do you feel about that

dependence? Is interdependence a positive or a negative development? Ought the United States be independent of natural resources from other countries? What would happen in the United States if all trade were stopped?

30. A Foreign Policy Study II[17]

when: five class periods

what: list of U.S. foreign policies

how: (1) Divide students into groups and assign one foreign policy to each group from the list below or allow groups to select one of the policies so long as they each pick a separate policy.

(2) Have each group research its choice to identify the historic causes that brought about the policy and the results (both short and long term effects).

(3) Have each group prepare a visual (map, poster, charts or graphs, collage, time line, etc.) when it presents its findings to the class. At the end of this activity there should be a collection of visuals on each of the policies.

Examples of U.S. Foreign Policies

Manifest Destiny	Monroe Doctrine	World Policeman
Detente	Domino Theory	Isolationism
Shuttle Diplomacy	Good Neighbor Policy	Make world safe
Camp David Accords	Arms Limitations	for democracy
Containment		

(4) Hold class discussion on current U.S. foreign policy. Does U.S. policy differ depending on the country or area? Do we follow the same foreign policy in Central America as we do in the Middle East? What about Asia and Europe? Has the United States treated one group of countries different than others?

(5) Of those policies listed and any others that can be identified--choose the policy you believe has been the most effective, then defend your choice.

31. Review of Eras II[18]

when: two class periods

what: suggested list of eras (next page)

how: (1) Historians, and people in general, label time periods and separate them into neat categories. In consequence, different eras in our nation's history have acquired labels.

(2) Give students list of eras below. They should identify
the dates encompassed by the era label, one fact or event
that seems to support the label, and one fact or event
that seems to prove the label inaccurate.

(3) List on the board eras, dates, supportive facts, and un-
supportive facts as supplied by students from their individual lists. Tally the number that chose the same event
or fact and put the number beside the fact. Does the
class think the era deserves the label? If not, what
would be a better label, i.e., was the era of good feeling in reality the era of the "Bankers' Rip Off"?

ERA LABELS

	Era	Dates	Supporting Fact	Disproving Fact
1.	Progressive Era			
2.	Age of World Power			
3.	Age of Imperialism			
4.	Gay Nineties			
5.	Period of Industrialism			
6.	Age of Manifest Destiny			
7.	Age of Sectionalism			
8.	Era of Good Feeling	1816-20s	eastern states prospered	the frontier had hard times
9.	Federal Period			
10.	Era of Revolution			
11.	Period of Salutory Neglect			
12.	Roaring Twenties	1920-29	substantial urban growth	rural areas economy de-pressed
13.	Atomic Age			
14.	Etc.			

32. American Social Thought: How Has It Changed?

when: three class periods

what: research materials: old newspapers, magazines, and problems chart

how: Students should be made aware of how attitudes and values shift from year to year and generation to generation. (See activity "Measuring Change Through the Generation Gap" in Chapter I.)

(1) Divide class into groups and give each group a topic in which there have been recognizable shifts in attitude or values in the last generation or so, i.e., women's rights, crime and punishment, ecology, etc.

(2) Have groups research how attitudes have changed for their topics and the outlook for the very near future. Observing how the media treated the subjects in old magazines and newspapers makes a good starting point for identifying what values and attitudes were in the past. What circumstances or events may have spurred the changes and shifts identified?

(3) Have groups report on their findings.

To help the process of identifying change in attitudes and values, start the activity by having students fill in as much of the chart as they can. (Students need to know how these different generations thought about the problem.)

Problems	Grandparents' Generation 1920-30	Parents' Generation 1950-60	Your Generation 1980s
Population control	big families	planned parenthood	combine family with career; children optional
Hunger			
Environment			
Unemployment			
Energy			
Crime			
Education	higher ed. a goal, a sign of status	higher ed. important to get a good job	education is important but higher ed. is an option

33. <u>Where We Stand Today</u>

when: one class period

what: George Orwell's predictions from his book <u>1984</u> listed below

how: George Orwell's book <u>1984</u> was published in 1949. He pictured
a future society. Below are some of his predictions. Can
students match the predictions Orwell made with actual
current events or world situations?

PREDICTIONS 1984

1. ORWELL PREDICTED A WORLD OF THREE MAJOR SUPERPOWERS.

2. THE THREE SUPERPOWERS WOULD WAGE CONTINUOUS WAR, NEVER RESORT-
ING TO NUCLEAR WEAPONS. THE AREA OF THE WAR WOULD CHANGE AS
WOULD THE RELATIONSHIPS OF THE THREE POWERS; NO SINGLE SUPER-
POWER WOULD BE STRONG ENOUGH TO CONQUER THE OTHER TWO.

3. THE PEOPLE IN ORWELL'S WORLD ARE CONTROLLED BY TELESCREENS
WHICH CAN MONITOR THEIR BEHAVIOR. REBELLION CAN BE IMMEDIATELY
IDENTIFIED AND SUPPRESSED.

4. HISTORY AND THE LANGUAGE ARE CONTROLLED AND MOLDED TO FIT THE
LATEST PARTY POLICIES.

5. ADHERENCE TO THE PARTY LINE IS MAINTAINED BY THE THOUGHT POLICE
WHO USE PSYCHOLOGY AND TORTURE TO KEEP THE POPULACE IN LINE.

Questions:

(1) Do any historical events since World War II support even
one of the predictions?

(2) Which of the predictions are most likely to happen in the
future?

(3) How would the United States need to change to become
Orwell's predicted future society? Will your grand-
children live in that society?

B.   General Objective: To develop skills necessary to <u>process</u> information

SPECIFIC OBJECTIVE: Identify and apply the four different levels of questioning, having ranked preferences, and practice writing questions.

Asking Questions[19] - Prologue

Questioning, which is a processing skill, belongs to both teacher and
students. Teachers have long known that relevant questions from students
normally reflect a good understanding of the content to be learned. It is not
unusual for up to 80% of the interaction time between teachers and students in
a social studies class to be used for asking questions. Because of the heavy
emphasis on teachers' questioning, most text materials are organized and
written to answer questions.

An analysis of social studies textbooks made some years ago revealed that
approximately 95% of all questions asked in the text were cognitive-memory or
description-convergent. Similar studies have been run on teachers' questions
in the classroom. It is not surprising that 85% of all questions teachers ask
are cognitive-memory or description-convergent. In other words, social studies
teachers have a strong tendency to ask students to recall information either
verbatim (cognitive-memory) or in their own words (description-convergent).
But in either case the result is approximately the same; students believe
that social studies is primarily the recalling or recitation of content. A
pattern of questioning which only requires cognitive-memory or description-
convergent thinking will not ordinarily encourage higher level thinking. But
then, why should it be a problem that students are asked to think at low
levels? It is a problem because the decisions a citizen has to make in a
democratic society call for higher levels of thought.

Traditional Teaching vs. Inquiry Teaching

Some educators believe that students enter formal schooling with a wide
range of different levels of questions, yet by the end of their schooling the

students' range of questions asked in school seems to be significantly narrowed. Learning in school has become a pursuit, something different from the real world of students. The traditional emphasis on schooling as distinct from education has tended to narrow a student's perspective in social studies to a low range of questions so that there are school type questions which center on closed fact and convergent type thinking, i.e., "What are the two reasons for the First World War?" or "Why did the League of Nations fail?" or "What was the N.R.A.?" There is, on the other hand, inquiry type thinking which emphasizes the whole range of four levels of questions from fact ("When did Columbus discover the new world?") to description-convergent ("What are reasons for his wanting to sail toward the west?") to speculation-divergent ("Suppose Columbus had not discovered the new world and it remained undiscovered for another 200 years, what effect would this have had on Europe?") to evaluative ("Do you believe it is good that western man has had the urge to discover?").

Suppose students have the capacity to ask inquiry type questions. Then is it not reasonable to think that teachers should stimulate students to ask inquiry questions because inquiry is based upon the students' perception of their needs and interests in the world? The difference is not over inquiry but over who asks the inquiry questions, the student or the school. The point is that students probably do not ask the same questions as does the school about the content. For example, the school asks, "Who is Christopher Columbus?" The student may ask an evaluative question, "Why do you make a big point about Columbus? Wouldn't the new world have been discovered eventually anyway?" In summary, it would be fair to say that social studies teachers tend to deal with the first question "Who is . . .?" and not the second question that asks "Why do . . .?"

If it is true that both teachers and students "own" the process of questioning, then one activity to start with would be to identify one's preference.

Of course, one can learn the four different levels of questions as a mechanical exercise, but it is quite another to be able to think at the different levels. Often teachers and students have a preference for different levels of questions. Some teachers may never ask anything other than closed questions, whereas some students will answer only questions that call for a memorized response.

1. <u>Ranking Preference for Different Levels of Questions</u>

   when: one class period

   what: Preference Attitude form

   how: (1) Distribute to each student the preference form. It would be useful if the instructor would also mark the preference form. The intent is to gather data both on the teacher's preference and on the students'.

   (2) Once the students have ranked their preferences on the forms, collect the forms and have a small group tally the preferences for class totals and report the tallies to the class.

   (3) Ask questions similar to the following:

   (a) What do the tallies suggest about the class?

   (b) Does the class tolerate the four levels, that is, would the class answer all four levels?

   (c) Should all four levels be used in class?

   (d) Would learning be different if the four levels were used as a regular practice in the schools? If so, how might you as an individual learn differently? How might the school be different/changed?

   Note to teacher: You may wish to finish the prototype questions on the following form with the content being studied. However, the purpose of this activity is to rank the preferred level of question, and inserting content might prejudice the response.

PREFERENCE ATTITUDE

Instructions: The following are some ways people ask about things. We are not concerned right now about how you would finish these questions, but would like to know which kinds of questions you would most like to ask.

There are no right or wrong answers. Your answers should simply tell how you feel about that kind of question. Remember, whatever your answers are, you can be sure that many other people feel the same way.

I. Preference: For each group of questions below, tell which one you would most like to ask by placing a "1" in front of it, a "2" in front of the next, a "3" in front of the next, and a "4" in front of the question you are least interested in.

II. Strength of Choice: After each of the questions below, circle how you feel about that question as follows: A = strongly like, B = like, C = neutral, D = dislike, E = strongly dislike.

use this column only after ranking level of question	Rank		Strongly Like	Like	Neutral	Dislike	Strongly Dislike
(examples)							
E	4	1. How do you feel about . . .	A	B	©C	D	E
M	2	2. When was the first . . .	A	B	C	D	©E
D	1	3. What is your . . .	A	B	©C	D	E
E	3	4. In your opinion . . .	A	©B	C	D	E
		1. Why did the . . .	A	B	C	D	E
		2. In your opinion . . .	A	B	C	D	E
		3. Describe the . . .	A	B	C	D	E
		4. What would happen . . .	A	B	C	D	E
		1. What would you predict . . .	A	B	C	D	E
		2. When did . . .	A	B	C	D	E
		3. Do you believe . . .	A	B	C	D	E
		4. Explain how this . . .	A	B	C	D	E
		1. What do you think about . . .	A	B	C	D	E
		2. What would it be like if . . .	A	B	C	D	E
		3. How are they similar . . .	A	B	C	D	E
		4. Identify the . . .	A	B	C	D	E
		1. Name the . . .	A	B	C	D	E
		2. Compare the . . .	A	B	C	D	E
		3. Suppose the . . .	A	B	C	D	E
		4. Why do you think . . .	A	B	C	D	E

Now that you have ranked preference and strength of choice, use the following guide to mark each of the questions in the four sets either M for memory, D for description/convergent, S for speculation/divergent, or E for evaluation, so that you can know the level of question you have ranked.

Key to type of
  questions   Totals

D 1.

E 2.   Closed   (Memory)   M _____

M 3.   Questions   (Description/

S 4.   Convergent)   D _____

S 1.

M 2.   (Speculation/

E 3.   Open   Divergent)   S _____

D 4.   Questions

E 1.   (Evaluation)   E _____

S 2.

D 3.

M 4.

M 1.

D 2.

S 3.

E 4.

Interpreting Your Response:

    How did you respond? Inspect the preference side (left side) of the form. Remember you ranked your preference with one (1) being the highest and four (4) the lowest. From each group of questions add the preference ranks for each level. For example, suppose you marked the Speculation question second in the first set of questions, third in the second set, first in the third set, and second in the fourth set. The total would be eight (8). The lower the total number, the greater your preference for that type of question. Now look at strength of choice (right side of form), in other words, your attitude toward the different types of questions. Perhaps all you need to do at this time is to look at your positive, neutral, and negative feelings toward certain types of questions.

    2.   <u>Identifying and Writing Four Levels of Questions</u>

            when: one period

            what: Identifying and Writing Four Levels of Questions form

            how: Give each student a copy of the following form. For other sources of practice, see Chapter I, "Mastering the Different Levels of Questions."

IDENTIFYING AND WRITING FOUR LEVELS OF QUESTIONS

CLOSED QUESTIONS

Fact-Memory level questions require the reproduction of factual information after rote memory from an authoritative source. Often this lowest
level of thought question asks for recall of definitions, time, or
place. It is a closed question because there can be only one right answer. For example:

1. Name the current President of the United States?
2. According to the text, what is the definition of the words
   "honest graft"?
3. Is it true that Washington, DC is south of Chicago?
4. Identify on what date and on what city the first atomic bomb
   was exploded?

Key words to ask fact-memory questions:

CLOSED QUESTIONS	FACT-MEMORY	RECALL	IDENTIFY	YES/NO	DEFINE	NAME

Writing exercise: Using the key words, write at least two examples of
fact-memory level questions.

1. _____

   _____

2. _____

   _____

Description/Convergent level questions require the recalling of facts or
ideas and the association or organization of those facts into one's own
words. For example, "Compare World War I with World War II?" The
teacher asking this question is looking for the two wars to be compared
on specific points which are known to both the teacher and student.
This is a closed question because there are right answers but answers
need not be rote memory. For example:

1. Explain the three reasons the United States entered World
   War I?
2. Compare Presidents Harding and F. D. Roosevelt?
3. Why did Japan bomb Pearl Harbor?
4. Describe the wartime relationship between Churchill, Stalin,
   and Roosevelt?

Key words to ask description/convergent questions:

CLOSED QUESTIONS	DESCRIPTION/ CONVERGENT	DESCRIBE	EXPLAIN	COMPARE, CONTRAST	WHY	STATE RELATIONSHIP

Writing exercise: Using the key words, write at least two examples of
    description/convergent questions:

1. _____

_____

2. _____

_____.

OPEN QUESTIONS

<u>Speculation/Divergent</u> level questions require original and creative responses. This level question often confronts one with a problem situation, i.e., "Suppose you were President Wilson, what might you have done to persuade senators to support the League of Nations?" The answer to the question requires a uniquely personal combination of facts and ideas. The answer would be a hypothesis, an educated guess, inferred from the known facts about Wilson's attempt to persuade senators. Though there is no one right answer and it is classified as an open question, the answer is based on well founded, valid, accurate information. For example:

1. How might the League of Nations have acted toward imperialist nations in the 1920s if the United States had been a member?
2. What inference would you make about the role of world organizations in preventing wars given the history of the League of Nations?
3. Predict the future of the United Nations as a "peace keeping" organization?
4. How would you reconstruct the United Nations so that it could settle disputes between the superpowers?
5. What would you hypothesize about the future of the United Nations?

Key words to ask speculation/divergent questions:

| OPEN QUESTIONS | SPECULATION/ DIVERGENT | HOW MIGHT | INFER | PREDICT | HYPOTHESIZE | RECONSTRUCT |

Writing exercise: Using the key words, write at least two examples of
    speculation/divergent level questions:

1. _____

_____

2. _____

_____

◆ Evaluation level questions require answers that call for judgment and choice. Judgment is usually based on some evidence, a personal value, a personal concept of good against which some item is measured, i.e., "How did you like the movie?" The answer to this question requires a personal standard as to what is a good movie. Judging the movie asks one to compare the movie against what one thinks a good movie is. The answer is personal judgment and therefore open--for there is no right or wrong, only one's opinion or choice. For example:

1. What do you think about the "arms race"?
2. In your opinion should there be an "arms race"?
3. Do you believe there should be an "arms race"?
4. Justify your beliefs about the "arms race"?
5. Defend your opinion on the "arms race"?

Key words to ask evaluation level questions:

OPEN QUESTIONS   EVALUATION   OPINION   DEFEND   JUDGE   JUSTIFY

Written exercise: Using the key words, write at least two examples of evaluation level questions:

1. _____

   _____

2. _____

   _____

3.   Post-Evaluation on Identifying Levels of Questions

   when: one class period

   what: evaluation form

   how: Distribute post-evaluation form to students and have them complete both the identification and explanation.

   Key: Level   Reasons for choice
   1.   M   calls for yes/no response
   2.   S   calls for inference or speculation on what might happen
   3.   E   calls for opinion, judgment
   4.   S   calls for hypothesis based on inferred, known facts about the Depression
   5.   E   calls for personal concept of good against which Roosevelt can be compared
   6.   M   calls for one right answer
   7.   D   calls for closed answer put in one's own words over known facts
   8.   D   calls for closed answer over known facts
   9.   E   calls for personal judgment based on concept of a good society
   10   M   calls for one right memorized date

POST-EVALUATION ON IDENTIFYING LEVELS OF QUESTIONS

Instructions: Mark the question M (memory), D (description/con-
vergent), S (speculation/divergent), or E (evaluation). Give reason for choice of level.

1. ___ Did the Great Depression occur only in the United States?

_____
(reasons for choice)

2. ___ What do you suppose would have happened if the Depression
had continued after World War II?

_____

3. ___ Defend your opinion of the New Deal?

_____

4. ___ What changes do you predict would have occurred in the
capitalist economic system if there had been no World
War II?

_____

5. ___ Do you believe F. D. Roosevelt was a good President?

_____

6. ___ Name one of Roosevelt's Brain Trust?

_____

7. ___ Describe the N.R.A.?

_____

8. ___ Compare the Republican and Democratic party platforms in
1932?

_____

9. ___ What do you think of economic reforms such as Social
Security?

_____

10. ___ On what date did World War II start for the United States?

_____

4. <u>Review on Answering Open Questions</u>[20]

   when: one class period

   what: list of historic firsts below

   how: (1) Distribute copies of "Historic Firsts of the 1960s" to
          the students and have them answer questions at the bottom
          of the page.

HISTORIC FIRSTS OF THE 1960s

   First landing on the moon: 1969
   First human heart transplant: 1967
   First working model of a laser beam: 1960
   First nuclear showdown between U.S. & USSR: 1962
   First Roman Catholic President elected: 1960
   First birth control pill approved: 1960
   First nationwide federal aid to public schools: 1965
   First Negro appointed to Supreme Court: 1967
   First supersonic transport: 1968
   First experimental "cracking" of genetic code in DNA model: 1961
   First military draft lottery: 1969

   Questions:

   a. *Circle the one of the above "firsts" that you think had the
        biggest impact on life in America.*

   b. *Give four (4) reasons or <u>pieces</u> <u>of</u> <u>evidence</u> to support your
        choice.*

       (2) When students have finished the above assignment, give
          them the following question and have them answer that
          question in a written essay. That essay should use the
          four recommended steps below for answering open questions.

          *"WHAT WAS THE MOST SIGNIFICANT HISTORIC EVENT OF THE
          1960s?"*

Four steps to follow when answering an open question, i.e., specu-
   lation/divergent and evaluation:

1. CLARIFY THE QUESTION: Explain what you understand the question
       to mean.
2. PROPOSE SOLUTIONS: Identify at least three different ways to
       answer the question.
3. EXAMINE CONSEQUENCES: List the good and bad points for each of
       your possible answers.
4. MAKE PERSONAL CHOICE AND JUSTIFY IT: Choose the answer you
       think is best and give your reasons.

NOTE: The activity "Answering Open Questions" in Chapter I deals
       more fully with the four steps used in answering an open
       question. The teacher may want to review these steps with
       the students.

SPECIFIC OBJECTIVE: Historical events will be critically evaluated through
a speculation/divergent questioning process.

5.   What If . . . .?

when: two class periods

what: textbook and resource materials on slavery and the Civil War

how: Post the question: "What if there had been no Civil War,
would slavery have died out sooner or later? When and why?

(1) Have students research events, movements, decisions, etc.
that would have affected slavery. What are their conclusions and the data that support their conclusions?

(2) Hold class discussion on proposed question.

NOTE: This activity can be applied to many topics being
studied. Since most textbooks try to recall events
as they took place and do not speculate on possible
alternatives that MIGHT have happened, this type of
question forces the student to speculate.

For example:

What if the South had won the Civil War?

What if there had never been an American Revolution?

What if the British had won the Revolutionary War?

What if Napoleon had not been willing to sell the land
encompassed in the Louisiana Purchase?

What if the U.S. had not entered World War I?

What if . . . (as an illustration) Hitler's Germany had
won World War II? (The following are some interesting speculations.)

a. England was invaded and occupied by German troops.

b. Russia agreed to German demands for a part of
Russian territory and sued for peace.

c. The U.S. elected an isolationist President and
negotiated a peace treaty with a United Europe
under Hitler.

d. Japan attacks English, French, Dutch, and American
possessions in Asia.

e. Germany, now the center of Europe, declares war on
on Japan and is allied with the United States.

6. <u>Processing Ideas Through Word Association</u>

when: one class period; use this activity before reading the
        assigned key words or after reading as a review

what: butcher paper and magic markers, or assigned space to place
        list of words

how: (1) Divide the class into groups. Since there are "winners"
            in this activity, separate the groups so there will be no
            opportunity to overhear another group and thereby cheat.
            Give each group paper and a marker.

        (2) Write first key word on the board and have groups list as
            many associations as they can in a stated time period
            (perhaps five mintues). For example:

            FIRST KEY WORD: <u>Imperialism</u>
              Associations: internationalism
                             interventionism
                             military power
                             force
                             etc.

        Have groups display lists. The one with the most associ-
        ation words is the winner of this round.

        (3) Write second key word on the board and again have groups
            list associations (use the same time period as for first
            list). For example:

            SECOND KEY WORD: <u>War</u>
               Associations: invasion
                              peace conference
                              aggression
                              national interest
                              etc.

        Have groups display lists; the one with the most associa-
        tion words is the winner of this second round.

        (4) Now, using the two word association lists, have groups
            see how many pairs they can list by matching one word
            from the first list to one word from the second list.
            For example:

                internationalism / peace conference
                   military power / invasion

        The group with the most matches is the winner.

        It is quite possible that this activity will stir controversy
        and it should be made clear that groups may have to defend
        their choice of "association" words. This activity is particu-
        larly appropriate in those lessons where new and confusing
        words are introduced. Word association activities will help
        the reader to identify and define key words.

SPECIFIC OBJECTIVE: Learn to identify bias and analyze historical materials for their possible bias.

7. Is History Literature?

when: two to four class periods

what: resource materials on chosen topic

how: (1) Discuss with the class how each person must view an event, ponder a problem, take part in an experience, etc., from his/her own individual point of view. How each person "sees a thing" is affected by his knowledge, background, previous experiences, feelings, etc. The classic example is the dissimilarities of two eyewitness accounts of the same accident.

One of the most popular ways to demonstrate this is through the activity "Pass It On." Prepare a brief statement such as the one below. Whisper it to the first student, who in turn whispers it to the next student, and so on until the last student repeats the story aloud. How drastically has the statement changed in the repeated tellings?

A sample statement to whisper:

> "The President of the United States is meeting with the President of Mexico to discuss the price of natural gas and the potential threat of Cuban subversion."

(2) The same, of course, is true of historians, no matter how objective they claim to be. No two reports of the same event will be identical. Discuss with the class what factors might influence how a historian writes about an event. See activity "Your Title Is Your Point of View II" in this chapter. Historians as everyone else are born with three givens: a time in history, a place, and a set of parents. These givens do affect one's perception.

(3) Pick an event in U.S. history and have students locate sources dealing with the event, i.e., different history texts, old history texts, eyewitness accounts, etc.

(4) Discuss the different sources, how they differ, and what may be the causes for the differences. Can any generalizations be drawn on the writing of history? Some authorities have said that history texts are no more than a sequencing of answers to the author's questions. If it is true that the questions the author asks are really answers in the form of content, then can students by reading selected pages of text speculate on what the question is the author is trying to answer? What would be a valid alternative to the author's text answer? If I give you the answer, can you give me the question?

8. <u>Fact or Opinion II</u>[21]

when: two class periods

what: newspapers

how: (1) Teacher should find two editorials on the same subject
            but with different points of view. Sometimes "letters
            to the editor" in the newspaper will carry letters with
            opposing points of view about a controversial topic.
            Rival newspapers often have editorials with opposing
            points of view.
        (2) Reproduce the two articles or letters so that each stu-
            dent can have a copy. Can students separate fact from
            opinion? During class discussion, list facts on the
            board and on each side list words or phrases that slant
            the topic toward a particular point of view.
        (3) Have students find reports of a speech or event from two
            sources or have students write their own from two points
            of view. Have students compare the two accounts and
            decide what is fact and what is opinion. This is par-
            ticularly appropriate to use on a speech if the actual
            text of the speech can be obtained. For example:

Report of the President's News
Conference:

The President held his monthly
news conference this week. At
the conference he spoke about
inflation. "For the past ten
years inflation has eaten away
at the dollar to the point
where America's money is in
trouble around the world. The
American dollar is still respected and will remain the
base for world trade."

VS.

Editorial Comment:

The President held another rather
useless, mostly ineffective news
conference this week. As usual
the President started the conference with an oft repeated, dull
and uninspiring lecture on inflation. In his lecture he said that
America's money is no longer respected anywhere in the world and
is losing its value as the base of
world trade.

Report of Labor Sec'y Speech:

The Secretary of Labor, in
speaking before the Press Club,
announced that the number of
unemployed workers was down to
10.2%, and all indications
suggested that the improving
economy would bring this percentage down substantially over
the next six months. The
Secretary pointed to the in-
dicators of economic growth
as favorable by suggesting
that profits are up this year
for most industries.

VS.

Editorial Comment:

The Secretary of Labor today once
again recalled for the press corps
the dismal record of the administration by announcing that unemployment was still above 10%. That
percentage represents the failure
of the richest, most powerful,
democratic country in the world to
manage its economy successfully.
The Secretary suggested that there
was an improving economy; however,
this improvement has yet to reach
those who are in real economic
distress but rather has lined the
pockets of the rich.

9. Understanding Bias II[22]

    when: two class periods

    what: newspapers, magazines

    how: The New College Edition of the American Heritage Dictionary (1979), p. 128, defines the word bias this way:

    bi·as (bi´as) n. Preference or inclination that inhibits impartial judgment; prejudice.

    People who wish to persuade us have a bias, a preference for some product or value or action. Most written materials, movies, advertisements, and other forms of media are written and produced with a bias, persuasion as their objective.

    (1) Discuss bias with students.
        What is bias? Define?
        Do you suppose most people are biased? Are students biased?
        Should we be able to recognize bias?
        How does bias affect one?
        Is it natural to be biased? Is it good to be biased? Can it be bad?

    (2) Divide the class into groups. Have each group establish a checklist of ways to test for bias. In other words, what should students look for in checking for bias? Two questions to help in preparing checklist are:

        How is the item reported?
        Is emotion involved?

    (3) Have groups report on their checklists. Through class discussion combine and refine the checklists to make a basic checklist students can use to check for bias. (One of the best places to check for bias is the social studies text.) Have students identify a sample of bias from a newspaper, magazine, or other media.

    Example of what bias to look for:

    sex (male, female)
    age (too young, too old)
    size (too small, too fat, too tall)
    handicapped (blind, deaf, disabled)
    experience (must have previous experience OR no experience needed- will train)

    Sources for bias:

    newspapers: editorials, letters to the editor, movie ads, movie reviews, want ads, comics, sports, etc.
    TV: bias toward certain audience or product

10. Bias and Opposing Points of View

when: two class periods

what: excerpts from two separate sources, preferably secondary
sources, on the same subject or topic. Some historical events
will be discussed from different points of view in different
textbooks.

how: (1) Have students read the two excerpts that differ markedly
from each other on the same event.
(2) On the board list (from class discussion) the points on
which the authors agree. What are the authors' major
differences?
(3) Have students read other accounts of the same event.
Write an account that covers only the facts on which all
accounts agree.
(4) One favorite example of a clear difference of opinion was
the War of 1812. Much has been written about reasons
for that war from different points of view. Most historic controversial issues can be treated as opposing
points of view. The following activity is a simple but
effective way to not only illustrate bias but also to
illuminate a controversial issue which generated strong
differences of opinion.
The following quotes are from persons who corresponded
with the House Foreign Affairs Committee in 1812. The
question was, "Should the Congress support a declaration
of war against Great Britain?"

The West is seeking war so that the United States might acquire rich Canadian lands. The West intends to use the threat of English control of Canada as an excuse to seize the great reserves of agricultural land in Canada.

If the Western War Hawk has his way, the administration will be bullied into a declaration of war. The West intends to have a war whether this nation wills it or not. War with England is the order of the day, and Canada is the prize.

Louis M. Hacker
Congressman

As you know from an earlier report, we fought a part of that army at Tippecanoe Creek. We were attacked by at least 5,000 savages. Al- though caught by surprise in a vicious dawn attack, we inflicted heavy casualties among them. By the day's end we had decisively defeated them. An inventory of Indian equipment was taken from their dead and wounded on the field. We found over 500 new English trade muskets and over a ton of the finest grade of English powder. [Harrison is writing about the Battle of Tippecanoe in Battle Ground, Indiana.]

Gentlemen, to be blunt: we must have a preventative war against Tecumseh's followers. To success- fully defeat him we must drive the English from Canada. We must act quickly, for the survival of the West hangs in the balance.
William Henry Harrison
Governor, Northwest Territory

Much of the Indian problem can be attributed to the attitudes of the pioneer. He regards the Indian as an inferior creature no better than a beast of the thickets. He refuses to extend to him the rights of English Common Law, nor will he allow the Indian to obtain citizenship or buy land. In many parts of the Northwest, Indians are hunted down and cruelly slain. In my opinion, the Indian is more sinned against than sinning.

> Winthrop Wainwright
> Director
> Bureau of the Census

We cannot allow attacks of this type to go unpunished. The integrity of our flag, our people and our country are at stake. Honorable Sirs, must we submit to having our territorial boundaries violated? Must we submit to attacks on our citizens? Must we allow these crimes to go unpunished? I urge each one of you to consider the consequences of allowing these attacks to continue unanswered by our government.

> Commodore Barron
> U.S.S. Chesapeake

HIS MAJESTY DOES NOT WANT WAR, BUT YOU SEEM TO BE INTENT ON DRIVING US TO IT. YOU TRADE WITH OUR ENEMIES [FRANCE], YOU PROVIDE A HAVEN FOR OUR DESERTERS, YOU THREATEN TO INVADE CANADA AND YOU DISCUSS A DECLARATION OF WAR IN YOUR CONGRESS. FOR THE SAKE OF ALL ENGLISH SPEAKING PEOPLE LET US HOPE COOLER HEADS PREVAIL IN YOUR CONGRESS.

> GEORGE CRANFIELD
> HIS BRITANNIC
> MAJESTY'S NAVY

British cruisers have continually violated the American flag on every sea. They have carried off thousands of persons sailing under the protection of our flag. Now they hover off our coast and harass our entering and departing commerce. They have wantonly spilt American blood within our territorial waters. How long must we be plundered before we are allowed to stand and fight?

> Stephen Decatur, Commander
> U.S.S. Constitution

Questions to ask the class:

1. Do you know of any contemporary world event that sounds similar to the events suggested above? Do the language and arguments sound familiar?

2. If the arguments are biased, how do you know they are biased?

3. Can you explain, having read the arguments, why the War of 1812 was controversial?

4. Suppose a world organization such as the United Nations was functioning in 1812, would that fact have made any difference, assuming, of course, that the United States, Britain, and France had belonged to that organization?

11. Tolerance/Intolerance[23]

    when: one class period

    what: paragraph and question on the Ku Klux Klan

    how: The question raised below is an open question. Students should read the paragraph on the Klan and then answer the question using the four steps used in answering open questions (see activity "Answering Open Questions" in Chapter I and activity "Review on Answering Open Questions" in this chapter).

THE KLAN

The period after World War I saw a revival of the Ku Klux Klan. The Klan offered its members a means of expressing feelings of hatred against those people and ideas believed to threaten "true" American ideals. The Klan opposed labor organizations, believing that they were un-American and Communist inspired. The Klan opposed foreign immigration. Foreigners were considered threats to the basic Protestant, Anglo-Saxon values. The Klan opposed any movement of Negroes away from the unskilled, low-paying jobs which they had held prior to the war. They opposed the sharing of political power with any of these groups and used threats, terrorism, and violence to discourage opponents. They believed women should stay at home and care for their children. The Klan's influence spread across the nation, made itself felt in local and state elections, and altered the fair administration of justice in many communities.

Twice in our history (after the Civil War and during the 1920s), the Ku Klux Klan has become a powerful force in America and it exists today in several parts of the country.

Write a one-page essay answer to the following question:

       How do you explain the fact that a group based so strongly on INTOLERANCE would prosper so in a country founded in large part upon the principle of TOLERANCE?

Remember, in answering the question you need to: 1) clarify the question; 2) suggest a number of possible answers; 3) explain the consequences of each; and, finally, 4) make a personal choice of what you believe and support it.

We will help you get started by providing some dictionary definitions:

    tolerance - the capacity for or practice of recognizing and respecting the opinions, practices, or behaviors of others.

    intolerance - bigoted, unable to accept opinions or behaviors different from your own.

12. <u>Doves and Hawks</u>[24]

 when: one class period

 what: statements to be labeled below

 how: (1) Students should be familiar with the terms doves (peace)
        and hawks (war) because they are so much in the news.
        Have students read the following statements and label the
        statements appropriately.

DOVES AND HAWKS

During the long years of the Vietnam conflict, a number of divisions
appeared in how America thought about the war. There were those who
strongly supported the war effort (HAWKS), those who were strongly
against the war (DOVES), and a lot of folks in the middle (MODERATES)
who just wanted the whole mess to end.

Read the seven quotations and classify each person on the basis of what
they are saying by writing either HAWK, DOVE, or MODERATE after each.

1. "It became necessary to destroy the town to save it."   _____
   - American officer at Ben Tre, February 1968

2. "We have never been in a better relative position."   _____
   - General Westmoreland, April 1968

3. "Probably the most serious liability which we must off-
   set is the illusion that the United States is deeply
   divided over Vietnam, and in the long run, will abandon
   its present policy."   _____
   - Maxwell Taylor in 1967

4. "We, the Government, wage the war in Vietnam for our
   security, but will permit your protest provided it is
   only a little bit disorderly. (We) the demonstrators
   will consider the war outrageous and will therefore
   break the law, but not by much."   _____
   - Norman Mailer in 1967

5. "If we ever let the Communists win this war, we are in
   great danger of fighting for the rest of our lives and
   losing a million kids."   _____
   - Bob Hope, Co-chairman, National Unity Week

6. "I suppose the protesters have a right to their point
   of view, but I just think they're wrong. There just
   isn't any way of winning this war militarily. That's
   why President Nixon is trying to get us out with some
   degree of honor. But the only way he can do that is
   if we present a united front."   _____
   - California housewife at Veterans' Day Parade

7. "They've been hit by napalm bombs, hand grenades,
   mortars (not all by VC either--many are hit by mistake
   by friendly forces) ...wrinkled old men and women who
   appear to have aged with the earth itself; younger
   people, old before their time ... children and tiny
   babies who lose limbs or become otherwise scarred
   before their lives have really begun."
   - U.S. Civilian Nurse, April 1966

Suggested answers: 1 - Hawk; 2 - Hawk; 3 - Hawk; 4 - Dove; 5 - Hawk;
                    6 - Moderate; 7 - Dove

>   (2) In class discussion go over the statements and examine
>   reasons for the labels chosen. Remember the answers
>   above are just _suggested_, they are not absolute and
>   students may have firm and logical reasons for choosing
>   another label.

13. Reports About the War

     when: one class period

     what: excerpts from reports

     how: When reading reports about wars and battles, one is often
            struck by how similar those reports are even though they may
            be separated by centuries. For example, the war in Viet Nam
            has some similarity to reports written during the American
            Revolution. In some cases both of those wars had some of the
            same characteristics, i.e., civil war between loyalists and
            revolutionaries, foreign troops that eventually entered the
            battle, and guerilla warfare tactics particularly employed by
            one side.

            Paragraphs have been selected from General Gage's reports to
            the British War Department on the battles of Lexington and
            Concord and some paragraphs were selected from contemporary
            reports on the Viet Nam war. Laying aside for the moment the
            moral questions which both wars raise, would you please label
            each paragraph as to which war the paragraph refers--American
            Revolution or Viet Nam.

1.   An Overview of the War   (This passage refers to _____)

     War is one of the least exact and predictable of human endeavors.
More often than not, a nation caught up in war cannot be sure whether it
is winning or losing until the fighting finally ends. And rarely in ...
history has this been more true than it is of ... this [war]. "The war,"
confesses General _____, "is the foggiest war in my own personal experience."

2.   The Field Officers Report to   (This passage refers to _____)
     the General

     But attended with a long list of killed and wounded on our side, so
many of the latter that the hospital has hardly hands sufficient to take

care of them. These people show a spirit and conduct against us they never showed [before] ... They are now spirited up by a rage and enthusiasm as great as ever people were possessed of, and you must proceed in earnest or give the business up. A small body acting in one spot will not avail. You must have large armies, making diversions on different sides, to divide their force.

3.   The Officers' Account of the   (This passage refers to _____)
       Ambush

The rest of the column tried to fight back, but their situation was desperate. The ..., well concealed in the bush and the towering trees, gave ... few targets. "We could not see them."

4.   An Officer's Account of an   (This passage refers to _____)
       Ambush

Our men had very few opportunities of getting good shots at them, as they hardly ever fired but under cover ... from behind a tree, and the moment they had fired, they lay down out of sight until the column had passed. In the road, indeed in our rear, they were most numerous and came on pretty close ... but when the column had passed, numbers [came] out from some place in which they had lain concealed, fired at our rear guard and augmented the numbers which followed us. If we had had time to set fire to those houses, many [of them would] have perished in them, but as [it got dark our commander] thought it best to continue to march.

5.   A Civilian Report   (This passage refers to _____)

The road [was] filled with frightened women and children, some in carts with their tattered furniture, others on foot fleeing into the woods. But what added greatly to the horror ... was our passing through the bloody field at ..., which was strewed with the mangled bodies. We met one affectionate father with a cart looking for his murdered son and picking up his neighbors who had fallen in battle in order for their burial.

6.   A Report on Differences of   (This passage refers to _____)
       Opinion About the War

This, of course, does not prevent either partisans or critic ... from passing verdict on it with utter confidence. There is, for example, General ..., who declares: "I see not a single unfavorable trend." At the other extreme are the ... who argue ... that the [military] is doing nothing right ... And standing somewhere between these two positions is ... "The war, it would seem, is unwinnable in a much deeper sense than is commonly realized. It is not that our forces cannot defeat the enemy's forces in battle. It is that the battles they fight cannot decide the war."

7.   A Report on Differences of   (This passage refers to _____)
       Opinion About the War

The government was alarmed at the unexpected success of the enemy and [was] at a loss what lies to fabricate which would destroy the force of the qualifications which accompanied the intelligence. [Reports] were sent ... [out that] were authorized to deny the authenticity of the facts, and so distressed was the Government that they officially requested a suspension of belief until dispatches were received from the General ....

Answers: 1. Viet Nam   5. American Revolution
          2. American Revolution   6. Viet Nam
          3. Viet Nam   7. American Revolution
          4. American Revolution

Questions to ask once the students know the correct label:

(a) Did you identify accurately which report belonged to
    which war?
(b) If you did have trouble, then can you account for the
    fact that these reports were written on two distinctly
    different wars almost 200 years apart?
(c) What were some of the similarities between the reports?
    And what were some of the differences?
(d) Select a country which is now fighting a revolution or a
    civil war. Could these same reports be filed on that
    war? Some sources of evidence for answering this ques-
    tion would be TV news, popular magazines such as Newsweek
    and Time and daily newspapers--be alert for biased re-
    porting. Can you find articles which are similar to the
    seven cited?

SPECIFIC OBJECTIVE: Learn research techniques and how to process the in-
                      formation that results from the research.

  14. Using the Library

       when: one class period

       what: illustration of cards from the card catalogue

       how: (1) Review briefly with students (or have school librarian do
                  it) the use of the card catalogue and the three types of
                  cards: author card, title card, and subject card. Use
                  either the illustration below or a selection of your own
                  or the librarian's.
              (2) Prepare a number of questions that will require the use
                  of the card catalogue. Students need not answer the
                  question, but they must identify the card that would
                  help them find the answer; check whether it is a title,
                  author, or subject card and briefly state what information
                  on the card would help them find the answer. For example:

| | cards | | | helpful information from card |
	author	title	subject	
1. Who wrote The Winds of War?				
2. What book did Arthur Schles-inger, Jr. write about the Kennedy administration?				
3. Where could one find a com-prehensive history of Lin-coln's prairie years and war years?				

```
        United Nations

341.23  Buckley, William Frank, Jr.
B           United Nations Journal:  A
        Delegate's Odyssey, by
        William F. Buckley, Jr.
        Putnam, 1974

           1. United Nations  2. Journalists-
        Corres., remin., etc.  I.T.
```

Subject card:

topic or subject is on
the first line followed
by author and title of
book

notes on contents of
book

```
341.23  Buckley, William Frank Jr.
B           United Nations Journal:  A
        Delegate's Odyssey, by William
        Buckley, Jr.
        Putnam, 1974


           1. United Nations  2. Journalists-
        Corres., remin., etc.  I.T.
```

Author card:

author is on first line
followed by title of
book

```
        United Nations Journal

341.23  Buckley, William Frank, Jr.
B           United Nations Journal:  A
        Delegate's Odyssey, by William
        F. Buckley, Jr.
        Putnam, 1974


           1. United Nations  2. Journalists-
        Corres., remin., etc.  I.T.
```

Title card:

title of book is on top
line followed by author

15. <u>Procedure for Researching a Topic or Issue</u>

when: as needed

what: brief Researching a Topic or Issue form below

how: When researching a topic or issue, some students are helped
       by having a form to follow. The following simplified form
       will help to direct attention to a systematic approach which
       reliable and valid research requires. The form offers a good
       outline from which to report results of research, i.e.,
       papers, oral presentations.

Researching a Topic or Issue Form

1. Issue or topic: _____

2. Hypothesis--what do you hope research will prove: _____

   _____

   _____

3. List of pertinent information from research: _____

   _____

   _____

   _____

4. Organize by separating those facts which support your hypothesis from those that disprove it and discarding those facts that
   have no bearing on your issue or topic.

   Supporting Facts   Disproving Facts

   _____   _____

   _____   _____

   _____   _____

   _____   _____

5. Analyze, synthesize, generalize. Do the majority of the facts
   support your hypothesis or are you going to have to change your
   hypothesis to fit the facts?

   _____

   _____

   _____

6. Evaluate. What did you learn about your issue or topic?

   _____

   _____

   _____

16. <u>Primary Sources Research</u>[25]

    when: one class period

    what: yearbooks from the 1950s. Students' families may have year-
           books from the 1950s that they would let the class borrow.
           The school library may also have copies of the school year-
           book for those years that could be used as primary sources.

    how: (1) Divide the class into groups and give each a selection of
               yearbooks or a single one depending on your "collection."
               Keep the yearbooks close in years for each particular
               group. For example, give one group years 1950, 1951,
               and 1952; a second group 1953 and 1954, etc.
           (2) Have students examine the books and answer the following
               questions.

USING THE PICTURES:

A. LIST THREE FASHIONS OR STYLES THAT WERE POPULAR FOR GIRLS IN THE 1950s.

    1.   2.   3.

B. BASED ON THE AMOUNT OF YEARBOOK SPACE USED, WHAT WERE THE THREE MOST
IMPORTANT SCHOOL ACTIVITIES?

    1.   2.   3.

C. FROM THE WILLS, PROPHESIES, JOKES, AUTOGRAPHS, ETC., WHAT WERE SOME OF
THE SLANG EXPRESSIONS THAT WERE POPULAR?

D. IN WHAT KINDS OF ROLES DO BOYS APPEAR IN THE PICTURES?

E. WHAT MAJOR DIFFERENCES DO YOU FIND IN THE 50S YEARBOOK THAN FROM YOUR
SCHOOL'S RECENT YEARBOOK?

           (3) Hold class discussion on comparison between early and
               late 1950s and 1960s and the current year in terms of
               the questions above. Be sure to point out that the
               class is using primary (firsthand) sources to conduct
               their research.

17. <u>Short Oral Report--Outline</u>

when: as needed

what: short oral report outline below

how: Good oral reports do not just happen; they are planned. A successful oral report provides new information to one's listeners in an interesting way. The following outline should help students plan an oral report that will hold the attention of the other students.

ORAL REPORT OUTLINE

1. Introduction

This opening should contain the topic, the point one wishes to make, and how it concerns the listeners. It is important that the introduction "grabs" the attention of the other students immediately. A controversial statement, a visual, humor, a question, or a quote are all good for an opening.

2. Main points to be made:

State each point separately, simply, and concisely. Follow each point stated with the facts that support the point. (Remember this is a short oral report; do not try to squeeze in too many facts into it.)

3. Closure:

The conclusion of one's report should be a logical result from the main points. As in the introduction, it can contain a visual, a quote, humor, the answer to a question asked earlier, etc. (See oral report forms, Chapter II, pp. 127 and 128.)

Hints for preparing a short oral report:
 a. select topic
 b. read up on topic and take notes
 c. choose points you wish to make and put each on a file card with its supporting facts
 d. select opening and closing statements and write on separate file cards
 e. practice report but do not memorize it word for word

 f. CHECK TOPIC AND OUTLINE WITH TEACHER

18.   Read Any Good Books Lately?

when: one class period

what: Book Review outline form

how: Discuss with class the difference between a book review and a
summary of the book. A book review is a critical analysis of
what has been read; it is not a description of the events or
plot of the book. The following form will give students an
outline of the important points to be covered when reviewing
a book.

BOOK REVIEW

Preparation and presentation:

1.   Teacher approval of book selection
2.   Date due
3.   Number of words (set by teacher)
4.   Presentation: typed double-spaced, one side of paper only
handwritten in ink, one side of paper only
mechanics (spelling, punctuation, sentence
structure) will be graded

- -

Cover page:

1.   Title of book
2.   Author
3.   Publisher and date
4.   Student's name
5.   Class

- -

Review content:

1.   Brief description of what book is about; not a summary of
the plot.

2.   What author is trying to say; author's point of view, what
author wants to prove.

3.   Facts used by author to substantiate point of view.

4.   Background information on author if it relates to the book.

5.   Evaluation of book:
a.   strong points
b.   weak points
c.   interesting points
d.   did student learn anything new or have a change of
attitude after reading the book
e.   significance of the book
f.   student's opinion of style

C.   General Objective: To develop the skills to examine <u>values</u> and beliefs

SPECIFIC OBJECTIVE: Learn to identify personal and national values and beliefs and critically examine these changing values.

1.   <u>Nationalism and Traditional Values</u>

when: two class periods

what: Pledge of Allegiance, Preamble to the Constitution, chart below

how: (1) Have students examine these two documents for the <u>stated</u> and <u>implied</u> rights, responsibilities, values, and <u>goals</u>. Have students use the chart below to help them clarify their thinking.
(2) Hold a class discussion. Put large chart (using form below) on the board and fill in the various categories with the students using their individual charts for reference.
(a) How do students feel about the ideals (rights, responsibilities, values, and goals) they have listed? Are they basic values that apply to the world we live in today?
(b) Do most Americans make some sort of effort to live up to what is stated in the documents?
(c) What about the federal government, how closely is it aligned with what is suggested by the Preamble to the Constitution and the Pledge of Allegiance?
(d) Are the symbols of nationalism, i.e., flag, national anthem, etc., as respected as they once were? How many of the students in the class can recite the first verse of the "Star Spangled Banner" without any prompting? Is patriotism "out of style"? Because one uses the symbols of nationalism, does that mean the person is patriotic? Are rituals that feature national symbols necessary in a free and open democracy?

	Rights of Citizens	Responsibilities of citizens and government	Values	Goals
PLEDGE OF ALLEGIANCE				
PREAMBLE TO THE CONSTITUTION				

2. A Question of Personal and National Values II[26]

when: one class period

what: charts below

how: (1) Have students fill out the first chart on "What I Do For Others, For Myself, And For Both."

WHAT I DO FOR OTHERS, MYSELF, AND BOTH

(example)

for others	for myself	for both
1. share class notes	1. study for test	1. make batch of pop-corn
2. give friends a ride home	2. scrounge food at lunchtime	2. participate in team sport
		3. attend school sports and social events

---

(2) In class discuss examples cited by students. What do students think is a motivating factor for most people: "taking care of number one first" or being responsible for others, or do actions even out fairly equally between what one does for oneself and what one does for others?

(3) Now expand this idea to the country as a whole and have students fill out chart of "What Country Does For Others, For Itself, And For Both."

WHAT COUNTRY DOES FOR OTHERS, ITSELF, AND BOTH

(example)

for others	for itself	for both
1. send medical supplies to earthquake victims	1. restrict imported goods	1. get rid of food surpluses by sending food to needy in foreign countries
2. promote peace accords among third world nations	2. strict immigration laws	2. sale of arms and training armies to discourage invasion and civil war
		3. cultural exchanges

---

(4) Hold class discussion on students' examples. Do the actions of the country reflect the personal charts of the students? Do the students and the country share similar values? Is there a feeling of obligation to others? Should citizens in the real world of power politics expect their country to practice values which are consistent with their values? If one practices "dirty tricks" must all other countries practice those tricks if it is a question of survival? If you practice "dirty tricks" because "they" did it to you, then have you become "them"?

3. <u>Pick Your Favorite Big Five</u>[27]

when: one class period

what: prepared list of athletes or athletes suggested by students and listed on board

how: (1) Divide the class into groups and have each group list whom they believe are the five greatest male and five greatest female athletes in the 20th Century. Make the cut-off date five years ago because of the problem of judging the "greatness" of current athletes.

What do students need to know to prepare their lists?
(a) different categories of sports
(b) performance levels
(c) names
(d) other criteria

(2) Have students rank the athletes in order of importance, 1 - first choice, 2 - second choice, etc., after the athletes' name and other criteria have been identified and listed on the board.

(3) Have groups compare lists and then have them compare their choices with the list below. The names on the lists are people who <u>made</u> history. To study and compare lists is the study of history. The difference between athletes is <u>time in history</u>, <u>performance</u>, and <u>the sport</u>. The athletes chosen, of course, will most likely represent the values of the person choosing.

(The following list is a result of a poll of 35 sportswriters and editors for <u>The People's Almanac</u> #2, 1978.)

MALE ATHLETES

1. Jim Thorpe, U.S. track and field, football, baseball

2. Babe Ruth, U.S. baseball

3. Muhammed Ali, U.S. boxing

4. Jack Dempsey, U.S. boxing

5. Jack Nicklaus, U.S. golf

FEMALE ATHLETES

1. Babe Didriksen Zaharias, U.S. golf, track and field

2. Chris Evert Lloyd, U.S. tennis

3. Helen Wills Moody, U.S. tennis

4. Billie Jean King, U.S. tennis

5. Wilma Rudolph, U.S. track and field

(4) Discuss with class the fact that most Americans, as well as people from other cultures, admire good athletes. But athletes are not the only people we admire. What other famous Americans do we admire?
(a) What traits do these people have that are admirable?
(b) How many of these traits do they hold in common?

(c) Brainstorm a list of characteristics which they
might think are ideal.
(d) Can the class narrow the list to five characteristics or traits that will satisfy the majority of
the students?

Alternative:

Have students fill out the following questions on "Who Do You
'Idol-Eyes'?" Teacher may want to use class discussion to
answer questions 1 and 2, and then have students answer questions 3 and 4 individually. Have students share their answers to questions 3 and 4 in class discussion.

WHO DO YOU 'IDOL-EYES'?

1. MAKE A LIST OF FIVE (5) PEOPLE LIVING IN AMERICA TODAY THAT YOU
THINK MOST YOUNG PEOPLE WOULD CONSIDER TO BE HEROES.

    1. _____

    2. _____

    3. _____

    4. _____

    5. _____

2. MAKE A LIST OF FIVE (5) PEOPLE LIVING IN AMERICA TODAY THAT YOU
THINK YOUR PARENTS WOULD CONSIDER TO BE HEROES.

    1. _____

    2. _____

    3. _____

    4. _____

    5. _____

3. WHEN PEOPLE IN THE YEAR 2000 LOOK BACK AT THE 1970S AND 80S,
WHICH OF YOUR HEROES WILL THEY REMEMBER?

4. LIST THE REASONS FOR YOUR CHOICES, REMEMBERING THAT THE QUESTION
IS REALLY ASKING, "WHAT DETERMINES WHETHER OR NOT A HERO HAS
LASTING FAME?"

4.   <u>The Music Is the Message</u>

   when: two class periods

   what: old sheet music or records of popular songs

   how: (1) Give copies of the lyrics from the sheet music or records
              to the students. After the students have read the
              lyrics, discuss with the class the values and customs
              revealed in the lyrics.

          (2) Divide the class into groups. Have each group identify
              a current popular record or song and analyze the lyrics.
              How do the values expressed in the modern music compare
              with those in the old songs? Have the groups compare
              findings.

          (3) If values have changed, what do students think caused
              that change?

       <u>Alternative or extended activity</u>:

          (1) Have foreign language teachers supply popular foreign
              songs with translations of the lyrics (or have your stu-
              dents who are taking a foreign language supply the song
              and lyrics).

          (2) Have groups identify the values and customs expressed
              in the lyrics of the foreign songs.

          (3) Have groups compare findings. Are there wide differences
              between the countries or are there similarities? Does
              environment play any role in the values and customs ex-
              pressed in the lyrics?

Some lyrics from old popular songs. What is the message?

"You're the Top" (1934)

At words poetic I'm so pathetic that I always have found it best--
Instead of getting 'em off my chest, to let 'em rest unexpressed--
I hate parading my serenading as I'll probably miss a bar,
But if this ditty is not so pretty
At least it'll tell you how great you are.

REFRAIN
You're the top! You're the Coliseum.
You're the top! You're the Louvre Museum.
You're a melody--from a symphony--by Strauss.
You're a Bendel bonnet, a Shakespeare sonnet,
You're Mickey Mouse.
You're the Nile, You're the Tow'r of Pisa.
You're the smile on the Mona Lisa.
I'm a worthless check, a total wreck, a flop,
But if Baby I'm the bottom, You're the top!

"Jeepers Creepers" (1938)

I don't care what the weather man says.
When the weatherman says it's raining,
You'll never hear me complaining.
I'm certain the sun will shine.
I don't care how the weathervane points,
When the weathervane points to gloomy,
It's gotta be sunny to me,
When your eyes look into mine.

REFRAIN
Jeepers Creepers! Where'd you get those peepers?
Jeepers Creepers! Where'd you get those eyes?
Gosh all git up! How'd they get so lit up?
Gosh all git up! How'd they get that size?
Golly gee! When you turn those heaters on,
Woe is me! Got to put my cheaters on.
Jeepers Creepers! Where'd you get those peepers?
Oh those weepers! How they hypnotize!
Where'd you get those eyes?

"Goody Goody" (1935)

So you met someone who set you back on your heels, goody goody!
So you met someone and now you know how it feels, goody goody!
So you gave him your heart, too, just as I gave mine to you--
And he broke it in little pieces, now how do you do?
So you lie awake just singin' the blues all night, goody goody!
So you think that love's a barrel of dynamite--
Hooray and hallelujah! You had it comin' to you.
Goody goody for him, Goody goody for me,
And I hope you're satisfied you rascal you.

Think about these questions:

   (a) Does the musical message change as does the generation?

   (b) Can you identify when these songs were probably written?

   (c) Would these songs fit contemporary popular music trends;
       in other words, could these songs be popular now?

   (d) How is it that you know that it either could or could
       not be popular now? Does contemporary music carry a
       message that is somewhat different from these songs?

   (e) What would you suppose might be the musical message a
       year or two from now?

5.   Working Wives and Mothers[28]

    when: one class period

    what: background paragraph and strength of feeling ratings below

    how: (1) Have students read the background paragraph and then identify their strength of feeling on each of the four following statements.
        (2) Hold a class discussion on the question, What do you think is the impact of working women on the American family?
           (a) Before World War II, very few women worked outside the home. Why?
           (b) In today's society there are many wives and mothers (over 50%) pursuing careers outside the home. What has brought about this change?

Napoleon said that an army travels on its stomach but WW II demonstrated that wars are won in factories. American industry responded in an unprecedented manner to the challenge of producing war material for the allied forces. Firms that had been making vacuum cleaners before the war began to make machine guns. Automobile plants produced airplanes, engines, and tanks. The Canadians also made an amazing conversion. For example, before the war they were making about 14 airplanes a year and by the end of the war they were making over 4,000.

American war production was aided tremendously by the 3,000,000 women who went to work in 21 key industries where it was found that they could successfully do 8 out of 10 jobs normally done by men.

World War II brought some very significant changes to the American family. In addition to removing millions of fathers, sons, brothers, and uncles, the war also called many women to work outside of their homes.

Before we begin to discuss the impact this had on American families, think about your own feelings concerning working women, and mark your positions on the following statements: (circle one)

1.   Most men would prefer their wives not work outside the home.

        disagree -1 -2 -3 -4 -5 0 +1 +2 +3 +4 +5 agree

2.   Most wives would like to work outside the home.

        disagree -1 -2 -3 -4 -5 0 +1 +2 +3 +4 +5 agree

3.   The chances of having a good marriage are better if the wife does not work outside of the home.

        disagree -1 -2 -3 -4 -5 0 +1 +2 +3 +4 +5 agree

4.   Children of working mothers have more problems than those whose mothers are at home.

        disagree -1 -2 -3 -4 -5 0 +1 +2 +3 +4 +5 agree

Now let's consider this question:

"What do you think is the impact of working women on the American family?"

6.   <u>Should We Be Paid for Not Working?</u>[29]

    when: one class period

    what: background paragraph and ranking below

    how: (1) Have students read the background paragraphs below and
                then rank the ways people are paid not to work.
            (2) Divide the class into groups and have group members dis-
                cuss their ranking and their reasons to reach some con-
                sensus on the circumstances under which it would be
                justifiable to pay a person not to work.
            (3) May wish to compare group results.

Historian David Muzzey describes the <u>1930s</u> by saying . . .

"surpluses of both manufactured and agricultural products piled up
in the U.S. Owing to hard times and the growing number of the unemployed, Americans were unable to purchase these. They were
threatened with being smothered by their own plenty. They had
millions of surplus bushels of wheat and millions of men hungry;
millions of extra pairs of shoes and men going barefoot; billions
of dollars lying in the banks and industry was paralyzed."

On May 12, 1933, Roosevelt created the Agricultural Adjustment Agency
(AAA). Recognizing that the surplus of farm products was the number one
cause of low farm prices, the AAA set about reducing that surplus by
limiting the production of wheat, corn, cotton, hogs, tobacco, and milk.
In addition, they ordered existing crops plowed under, livestock killed,
potatoes dumped in the ocean, and milk poured on the ground.

The AAA plan brought to the attention of the American people two ideas
that were relatively new to our way of thinking at that time.

First, THAT WE SHOULD NOT PRODUCE UP TO OUR CAPACITY and,

secondly, THAT WE SHOULD PAY PEOPLE FOR NOT WORKING.

The following are examples of some ways today in which people are paid
for <u>not</u> working. Rank them in order from what you think is most justified (#1) to the one that is least justified (#9) to do.

_____ unemployment compensation   _____ sick leave

_____ college scholarships   _____ job training

_____ social security   _____ maternity leave

_____ welfare payments   _____ Payment in Kind

_____ paid vacations

7. Defining Human Dignity

when: one class period

what: no materials necessary

how: (1) Have each student compose a definition of human dignity.

(2) Divide class into groups. Each group should identify a consensus definition of human dignity by combining the individual definitions of its members.

(3) Have groups decide how human dignity is affected by the following statements or situations.

(a) School busing to achieve racial balance in schools.

(b) Forced retirement at age 67 or younger.

(c) Laws calling for capital punishment for certain crimes.

(d) Unscheduled locker searches for drugs.

(e) Mandatory dress and appearance codes for schools.

(f) Strict censorship of books in school library; in public library.

(4) Hold a class discussion on differences between groups' definitions and decisions on the above situations.

(5) Can the class as a whole arrive at a definition of human dignity that will satisfy most of the students? Why is the question of the meaning of human dignity even raised? Is it a problem or issue for the students or for anyone else?

8. Code of Conduct[30]

when: one class period

what: background paragraph and strength of feeling rating

how: (1) Have students read the paragraph and then mark their strength of feeling about the following statements.

(2) Divide the class into groups. Group members should share their ratings and attempt to compose a code of conduct for a soldier, spelling out when to fight, when to surrender, when to obey and disobey orders, etc. Can they reach a consensus on this?

(3) Have groups share code with the class.

Since the 1700s warfare has changed drastically. Where military careers were once thought of as a profession that required lengthy training and long-term service (a soldier in the 1700s in Europe would have a 10 to 20-year enlistment), modern nations have developed the notion of the citizen-soldier who would rally to his country's defense in times of need and return home as soon as the crisis passed.

Voluntary service has sometimes provided enough soldiers, but most nations have found it necessary to resort to conscription, that is, a draft. When a country requires citizens to serve in the army it raises some tough questions about what they can be expected to do. (World War II saw the creation of huge armies on all sides made up of drafted citizens who had to meet the expectations of their respective governments.) In this activity you will be asked to consider some questions that are raised when a citizen becomes a soldier. As you consider the following, keep in mind the words: duty, citizen-soldier, honor, and responsibility.

CIRCLE THE NUMBER THAT EXPRESSES HOW YOU FEEL ABOUT THE STATEMENT

(+5 means you strongly agree, -5 means you strongly disagree)

1. It would be cowardly for a soldier to surrender in combat.

     disagree -5 -4 -3 -2 -1 0 +1 +2 +3 +4 +5 agree

2. A soldier should resist the enemy with every means available.

     disagree -5 -4 -3 -2 -1 0 +1 +2 +3 +4 +5 agree

3. Committing suicide in combat would be better than surrendering.

     disagree -5 -4 -3 -2 -1 0 +1 +2 +3 +4 +5 agree

4. If a soldier becomes a prisoner, he should not give the enemy any information that would harm his country even if this results in torture or death.

     disagree -5 -4 -3 -2 -1 0 +1 +2 +3 +4 +5 agree

5. A person should consider it an honor to serve his country and defend it against its enemies.

     disagree -5 -4 -3 -2 -1 0 +1 +2 +3 +4 +5 agree

6. A soldier should be willing to do anything against the enemy that would shorten the war.

     disagree -5 -4 -3 -2 -1 0 +1 +2 +3 +4 +5 agree

D. General Objective: To apply knowledge through active participation

SPECIFIC OBJECTIVE: Learn to participate through generating data, generalizing and sharing ideas and beliefs.

1. <u>Slogans Carry a Message</u>

when: one class period

what: definition of the word slogan and list of slogans

> slo-gan (slō´gan) n. 1. Originally a battle cry of the Scottish clans. 2. The catchword or motto of a political party, fraternity, school, or other group. 3. A catch phrase used in advertising or promotions.

List of slogans:

Put Your John Hancock There
No Irish Need Apply
Fifty-Four Forty or Fight
Tippecanoe and Tyler Too
Old Rough and Ready
Vote Early and Often
The Union Forever
Pike's Peak or Bust
Remember the Maine
Give Until It Hurts
Happy Days Are Here Again
Roosevelt and Repeal
Better a Third Term Than a Third Rater
Win With Willkie
Zip the Lip and Save a Ship
Praise the Lord and Pass the Ammunition
Join the Navy and See the World
Give-em-Hell Harry
The Buck Stops Here
There's a Ford in Your Future
We Shall Overcome
America, Love It or Leave It
Every Litter Bit Hurts
Keep America Beautiful
Save the Whales

how: (1) Have students examine slogans. Reading the slogans and identifying the time and circumstances that produced the slogan give insight into history. Have students speculate on when and why the slogan appeared.

(2) Have students choose an event, a time period, or document (see activities "Is the Declaration of Independence a Guide to Behavior?" and "Creating a Data Bank" from Chapter I for examples), or the teacher can assign specific events, i.e., political campaigns.

(3) Have students develop an ad or slogan concerning their events. The students should keep these brief. (One good source of slogans is bumper stickers.) List students' slogans on board.

(4) Hold a class discussion on slogans. Is it clear what each refers to? Are they accurate? Why have slogans? What is a slogan for and what do slogans have to do with American History?

2. <u>A Language All Our Own</u>[31]

when: two class periods

what: questionnaire about slang below

how: (1) Distribute slang questionnaire to students and through class discussion make sure they know what each of the 15 words in the first column really meant.
(2) Have them take questionnaire home and question parents (or someone their parents' age) to find out what term the parents would have used when they were in high school.
(3) List the 15 terms on the board or on transparency for overhead. Through class discussion find out what words parents used for each specific term. List those on the board after each term. If there are differences in slang terms used by parents, point this out and ask why. The area of the country where they lived is one possible explanation; education is another.
(4) Have students fill out last column, then examine the changes in language from the 20s to the 80s. What do these changes suggest about American culture, about language? Is the study of changing language history?

IN THE 1920s A:	REALLY MEANT A:	MY PARENTS WOULD SAY:	TODAY WE SAY:
1. FLIVVER			
2. PIKER			
3. BUNGALOW			
4. STICKS			
5. FLAPPER			
6. TIN-LIZZIE			
7. HOTCH			
8. SPORT			
9. RUBBED-OUT			
10. "IT"			
11. PETTING			
12. SMART			
13. BOBBED			
14. FLIRT			
15. VICTROLA			

1920s answers: automobile, cheapskate, home, small towns, young lady, Ford, illegal liquor, young man, murdered, sex appeal, kissing, fashionable, short haircut, an immoral person, record player

3. <u>Values: Past, Present, and Future II[32]</u>

    when: two class periods

    what: student-prepared questionnaire

    how: (1) Brainstorm with the class the issues that seem to be of
              concern in our world today. List these quickly on the
              board as they are suggested by the students, i.e., war,
              hunger, ecology problems, etc.
          (2) Make three columns on the board under the titles of Social,
              Political, and Economic. Briefly discuss each of the
              issues suggested by the students and list them under
              one of the columns.
          (3) Divide the class into three groups. Give each group one
              of the columns. The group must write at least five
              questions on the issues listed in its column. The
              questions must be worded so that they can be included in
              a questionnaire that students will eventually administer
              to others.
          (4) When the groups have completed their questions, combine
              them into a questionnaire.
          (5) Give three copies of the questionnaire to each student.
              The student must administer the questionnaires to some-
              one their own age outside the class, their parents or
              someone their parents' age, and their grandparents or
              someone their grandparents' age--in other words, three
              generations.
          (6) Have each group tally the results of their questions and
              present them to the class for discussion.
              (a) Do people in one age group have similar answers to
                  a specific question?
              (b) Are there specific events or causes that would lead
                  one generation to answer a question in a particular
                  way?
              (c) What values seem to be expressed in the answers?
                  Do they differ for the three generations?
              (d) How will the questions be answered in the next
                  generation? What values will influence future
                  answers?

4. <u>Local History</u>

    when: two weeks

    what: materials as needed

    how: Students may have a choice of several activities described
          below or teacher can assign one specific activity for the
          entire class, or groups can undertake different activities.

          (1) History of the local community: Students can research
              the history of the local community including talking to
              people whose families have been long-time residents. By
              making this an oral history using a tape recorder, the

students can return to school and transcribe the conversations and present them in booklet form, or simply play the significant part of the audio tape to the class.

(2) Students should select a historic site such as a historic home, preferably in the local community, but at least within the state. Students should research this site and detail their findings using the following questions.

(a) Who was the principal individual involved and what do you know about that person? (For example, the home owner and where he/she came from and was educated.)

(b) What was the prevailing architecture of the time and how well did it fit the local environment?

(c) What were the needs of the individual? What could be obtained locally? What needed to be brought from some distance away?

(d) What kind of influence did this individual have locally, regionally, or nationally?

(e) Compare the house and furnishings to those of today.

(f) Describe the forms of travel and communication and the leisure time activities of the era.

(3) Visit a cemetery and select a family. Using the information on the grave stones, produce a possible family tree. Describe what life would have been like for the various family members.

(4) Produce your own family tree, branching off as far back as you have information for.

Your Name
Date of Birth
Place of Birth

Father   Mother

Grandfather   Grandmother   Grandfather   Grandmother

Great-   Great-
Grandfather   Grandmother   etc.   etc.

(5) Student-developed activity approved by teacher. The following are some suggestions on where students can seek out and develop their own activities:

- Historical societies
- Buildings on National Preservation list
- Commercial firms that have been in the community for some time often have histories which recount the changes of the industry and the community
- Commemorative monuments and historic markers put up by local, state, or national agencies

A particularly appropriate activity for study in U.S. History is the activity "Community Study and Social Action" found in Chapter I. That activity encourages students to apply history through the study of their own community past, present, and future. Also, many of the activities in Chapter IV of this book, specifically in the section on Values and Issues, would be appropriate content for the last third of a senior high U.S. History course.

Notes

1 Barth, J. L. Advanced social studies education (Washington, DC: University Press of America, 1977), p. 23.

2 This activity was originally published in Elementary and junior high/middle school social studies curriculum, activities, and materials (2nd ed.) by J. L. Barth (Washington, DC: University Press of America, 1983), p. 264. It has been revised for publication in this text.

3 This activity was originally developed in 1980 for "Questions Social Studies Students Ask," a Division of Innovative Education ESPA Title IV-C Research Project of the North Montgomery School Corporation, Linden, IN. In particular the author wishes to recognize the contribution of James Spencer and David Horney in the development of this project. This activity has been revised for publication in this book.

4 Ibid.

5 Ibid.

6 Barth, Elementary and junior high, p. 151. This activity has been modified for publication in this text.

7 Ibid., p. 270.

8 Ibid., p. 271.

9 Ibid.

10 This activity was first presented as a paper at the "Teaching About the Holocaust in Indiana" pre-convention, 1981 Indiana Council for the Social Studies clinic by Professor S. Samuel Shermis of Purdue University. It has been modified for publication in this text.

11 Barth, Elementary and junior high, p. 273. This activity has been modified for publication in this text.

12 "Questions Social Studies Students Ask." This activity has been revised for publication in this text.

13 Barth, Elementary and junior high, p. 276. This activity has been modified for publication in this text.

14 "Questions Social Studies Students Ask." This activity has been revised for publication in this text.

15 Barth, Elementary and junior high, p. 274. This activity has been modified for publication in this text.

16 Ibid., p. 283.

17 Ibid., p. 286.

18 Ibid., p. 266.

[19]This section on questioning was first published in Barth, J. L., Methods of instruction in social studies education (Washington, DC: University Press of America, 1979), Chapter VII, pp. 149-165. The activities have been modified for publication in this text.

[20]"Questions Social Studies Students Ask." This activity has been revised for publication in this text.

[21]Barth, Elementary and junior high, p. 202. This activity has been modified for publication in this text.

[22]Ibid., p. 164.

[23]"Questions Social Studies Students Ask." This activity has been revised for publication in this text.

[24]Ibid.

[25]Ibid.

[26]Barth, Elementary and junior high, p. 284. This activity has been modified for publication in this text.

[27]Wallechinsky, D., & Wallace, I. The people's almanac #2 (New York: Bantam Books, 1978), pp. 1057-1058.

[28]"Questions Social Studies Students Ask." This activity has been revised for publication in this text.

[29]Ibid.

[30]Ibid.

[31]Ibid.

[32]Barth, Elementary and junior high, p. 286. This activity has been modified for publication in this text.

INTEREST FORM

You have just completed the Chapter U.S. History. In an effort to have you identify activities and materials that seem most promising to you in this subject area, please fill out the following interest form.

Instructions:

Identify two activities from this chapter. Name the activities and briefly describe why these particular activities are of interest to you.

ACTIVITY 1

ACTIVITY 2

NOTES

CHAPTER IV

SENIOR PROBLEMS, VALUES/ISSUES, FUTURES, AND CAREERS
(TWELFTH GRADE SOCIAL STUDIES)

ACTIVITIES AND MATERIALS FOR
SENIOR PROBLEMS, VALUES/ISSUES, FUTURES, AND CAREERS

CHAPTER IV

SENIOR PROBLEMS, VALUES/ISSUES, FUTURES, AND CAREERS

Organization of the Chapter

Each chapter represents a particular subject area, in this case twelfth grade social studies. Each chapter consists of three parts: the first part is a brief discussion on courses, topics, and national trends in teaching this subject area throughout the United States; the second part is an example of a state subject area program; the third part has activities and materials categorized by the four objectives of teaching social studies--gaining knowledge, processing, valuing, and participating.

I. Topics Taught and National Trends in Teaching Twelfth Grade Social Studies

Twelfth grade social studies usually includes a senior problems course (World Problems, Modern Problems, Problems of Democracy, Values and Issues, etc.). Depending on the state, the course is either required or offered as an elective. Occasionally the problems course is a full year, but most often the course is one semester combined with U.S. government or one of the social sciences or in some instances with U.S. history. U.S. government (see Chapter I, "Civics and U.S. Government") is the second most frequently offered social studies course in twelfth grade.

Courses, Topics, and Themes Frequently Covered in Twelfth Grade Social Studies

Objective of the Course

The traditional problems course as taught by Citizenship Transmission (CT) teachers provides an opportunity for organized study of major societal problems and issues of the present day. The objective is to enhance the skills and attitudes needed for citizenship by encouraging students' commitment to democratic institutions. This commitment is encouraged through the study of controversial problems. The objective of those who teach social studies as social science differs from the traditional (CT) because the problems studied and the methods of analysis are those of the social scientist, the objective being to encourage students to identify problems and seek solutions as a social scientist might. The objective of the Reflective Inquiry (RI) teacher in a problems course would be to encourage students to identify personal/social problems which are based on the needs and interests of students and are processed through a reflective thinking method.

The general objective of the Problems of Democracy or Senior Problems course has been to integrate the separate social science--history--and the students' social/personal problems into a course that capstoned (pulled together) the K-12 social studies curriculum. The goal of the social studies curriculum is to encourage graduates to be effective citizen participants in a democratic society. The educators who originally suggested the integrated course in 1916 felt that training in citizenship was not to be left to chance, but rather should be an important capstone subject in preparation for the full participation of seniors as thoughtful decision-makers in the community.

To summarize, some educators identify the twelfth grade social studies curriculum as a final opportunity to provide a general capstone course aimed at preparation for citizenship responsibilities. Also, a second course during the senior year is recommended, and in some cases required, which fits the students' career goals. Students who are in a college preparatory track are normally encouraged to elect introductory social science courses such as economics, psychology, sociology, anthropology, and perhaps world history. Students who are in the general or commercial track are advised to take such courses as consumer economics, values and issues, and current problems. Though the goal of the social studies curriculum may be citizenship education, the purpose of twelfth grade social studies is that of providing a similar capstone for all seniors and a variety of elective courses to meet their different career goals.

Basic Content of the Course

Of course the content of a problems course will vary according to the different objectives noted above. However, the following would be character-istic of such a course. Both domestic and international problems are usually treated. Some courses also include a unit on personal adjustment that draws heavily on psychology and sociology with topics such as heredity and environ-ment, mental health, motivations in individual behavior, etc. Typical units are: the family; education; religion in our society; crime and delinquency; political parties and elections; propaganda and public opinion; intergroup relations; civil rights; the American economic system with emphasis on con-sumer economics and careers education; using resources wisely (this may in-clude world resources); communism; comparative economic systems; international relations (or the U.N. system of maintaining world peace); world trade; population (treated in both domestic and world aspects); underdeveloped (or "developing") countries; and future studies.

Trends in Teaching Twelfth Grade Social Studies

Trends in teaching senior problems and values and issues courses are towards increased attention to topics such as civil rights and intergroup relations with emphasis on the American economic system and contemporary/ consumer economic problems. Also there is increased attention to future studies and world problems. The following are typical examples of topics covered in problems courses:

1. Career planning

2.   Comparative economic systems and consumer economics

3.   Communism as a political, social, economic system

4.   Technology and future studies

5.   International relations

6.   Intercultural relations

7.   Rights and responsibilities

8.   Social problems

9.   Worldwide issues

10.   Underdeveloped countries

A consistent trend for the past century has been to identify and teach basic concepts and generalizations from the various social sciences. Social scientists have generally promoted this trend. Their recommendations tend to follow cycles. At times their recommendations are seriously considered, and at other times a social studies integrated approach is practiced. For example, the Problems of Democracy or Values and Issues course is an attempt at integration of the social sciences and humanities, whereas the teaching of separate social science courses, i.e., economics, sociology, and psychology, is an attempt to preserve the integrity of a specific social science field. As one might anticipate, proposals for improving the K-12 social studies curriculum move in quite differing directions. One proposal is to throw out all social studies which emphasizes integration of the social sciences and humanities and teach separate disciplines from the first grade through senior high school. Another proposal is to teach at each grade level a series of units each of which is focused on a separate discipline. Another proposal is to retain the expanding environment or expanding horizons approach which is now the most popular K-12 approach to social studies. Suggestions to improve this latter approach have been to emphasize concepts and generalizations of the social sciences and comparative studies between cultures. This final proposal to improve the

expanding horizons seems to be the most popular among educators, though it
continues to be criticized by historians and social scientists as inadequate
citizenship training.

II. Illustrations of a State's
Twelfth Grade Social Studies Course Offerings

There is no one prescribed social studies program throughout the United
States. However, one state's description of its twelfth grade social studies
offerings will illustrate the content which the state expects to be taught.
These illustrations identify a state's suggested social studies curriculum for
the following subject areas: anthropology, citizenship, current problems,
economics, ethnic studies, introduction to social science, psychology,
sociology, urban affairs, and values and issues.

Anthropology
This course provides an opportunity for students to broaden
their perspective concerning life styles or patterns of
culture among peoples. The study also introduces students
to the anthropologist's processes of observation and
analysis of human behavior. The study should include the
theories and principles of culture formation, growth,
functioning, and change, the relationship of culture to
environment, and the relationship between cultural background and personality.

Citizenship
The course in citizenship is designed to facilitate the
student's development into an independent thinker and a
conscientious citizen. To accomplish this, it is necessary
for the course to deal with political behavior problems
which students and citizens consider to be relevant or
most pressing of the day. The course is to provide students with experiences in developing attitudes toward
their role as citizens within a framework of identified
democratic ideology. The content should center on the
process of public policymaking, methods and means of public
participation in policymaking, on the citizenship rights
and responsibilities as they relate to the individual in a
changing society, and on the relationship between modern
society and government.

Current Problems
The problems course is to give students an opportunity to
apply techniques of investigation and inquiry to the study

of significant problems or issues. Students should be expected to develop competence in recognizing cause and effect relationships, recognizing fallacies in reasoning and propaganda devices, synthesizing knowledge acquired into a useful pattern, generalizing for factual evidence, and stating and testing hypotheses. The content of the course may vary from school to school and from year to year to take advantage of the most relevant problem areas. Problems or issues selected should have both contemporary significance and historical perspective, and should be studied from the viewpoint or within the framework of any one or more of the social science disciplines.

Economics

This course is designed to provide an opportunity for students to study basic principles concerning production, distribution, and consumption of wealth and income. The study is also concerned with such problems as the conflict between man's unlimited wants and limited resources that results in scarcity. Other areas of consideration are problems and public policy connected with such concepts as interdependence, exchange, markets, price, costs, and economic stability and growth. The economic concepts developed in the course should be both personal and consumer economic approaches.

Ethnic Studies

This course provides an opportunity for students to broaden their perspectives concerning life styles or patterns of sub-culture among the various ethnic groups in the United States. The course should accurately depict the multi-ethnic society which exists in the United States. Emphasis should be on how the contribution, heritage, and cultural aspects of minority groups have added to the richness of the American scene.

Introduction to Social Science

The purpose of this course is to develop an understanding of the nature of the social sciences and present the reasons for studying them. This involves consideration of the social sciences as the study of man; of the reasons for dividing this study into separate fields or disciplines; of the objectives, materials, and methods used in each discipline; and of the difficulties encountered by the social scientist in applying the scientific method to the study of man. Content would include groups, individual behavior and education, society, and the role of the social sciences.

Psychology

This course provides an opportunity for students to study some elements of individual and social psychology and how the knowledge and methods of psychologists are applied to the solution of human problems. Content for the course is designed to give students some insight to behavior patterns and adjustment to social environment. Students

should be encouraged to develop critical attitudes toward
superficial generalizations about human behavior, to
recognize the difficulty of establishing the truth of a
proposition, and to develop a heightened sensitivity to
the feelings of others and to an understanding of their
needs.

Sociology

Sociology at the secondary level provides an opportunity
for students to study Man and his basic institutions.
Broad areas of content include study of institutions found
in all societies, such as the family, religion, and community organizations, political and social activities, and
the use of leisure time. Also covered will be the role of
moral values, traditions, folkways, and the mobility of
people and the factors in society which influence human
personality.

Urban Affairs

This course is designed to explore those unique problems
and life styles created by the urban world. Students
should examine common problems of city life and examine
various alternative solutions. Background studies should
include topics such as the migration to the cities, industrialization, city governments, and race relations.

Values and Issues

This course is designed to illuminate the basic values of
our society. The course is based on the belief that values
and commitment are the most important outcomes of social
studies teaching and on the belief that an understanding
of values and personal commitment is best obtained by an
honest and rigorous examination of the value, how it has
developed, and the problems which holding to the value may
entail. The following recommended units will allow young
people to examine basic values of the American society,
the education of our citizens, the extension of individual
liberty, the challenge of competing ideologies, population
and food, the American family, and citizen control of
government.

Summary and Final Thoughts

"Senior Problems, Values/Issues, Futures, and Careers" is different from

other chapters in this book. The other chapters had a common theme such as

government, world history, or American history, whereas this chapter will con-

centrate on a twelfth grade social studies curriculum. And this curriculum

includes not only a capstone to a general citizenship education but also numerous electives. The activities that follow are designed, in part, to account for the senior problems course and also to apply to all other electives. No single secondary social studies activity book could claim to even begin an adequate coverage of all of the courses, subjects, topics, and content that could possibly be offered during twelfth grade social studies.

No attempt has been made to include topics and content that would specifically apply to any one single course. An effort has been made to identify activities that would be appropriate to many of the possible courses listed under "II. Illustrations of a State's Twelfth Grade Social Studies Course Offerings."

Because of the nature of this chapter, the four objectives which have been the source of organization of this book no longer clearly offer a classification under which activities fit. Many of the activities in this chapter could be classified under several of the objectives, if not all four, at one time. This multi-objective classification ought to be looked upon as a positive good, for the activities carry with them all of the objectives of gaining knowledge, processing, valuing, and participating. The growing complexity of the activities, in fact, reflects more closely the real world of adult problems and decision-making. The activities focus on processing, valuing, and participating, which again is consistent with the role of adults in a democratic society. In summary, the following activities reflect both the complex problems of the society and the processes by which citizens learn to make effective decisions.

III. Activities and Materials

SENIOR PROBLEMS

A. General Objective: To develop skills necessary to process information

SPECIFIC OBJECTIVE: Compare quality and quantity of work with grade achievement as identified in three different student-teacher contracts: contracting by objectives, levels of performance, and projects completed.

1. <u>Contracting by Objectives</u>

    when: depends on time allotted by teacher

    what: contract for completing activities; list of objectives and activities

    how: This contracting is not for a grade. The student is contracting for activities that will fulfill objectives set by the teacher for the unit being studied.

    (1) Write on the board the knowledge and skill objectives you (the teacher) expect the students to have mastered by the end of the unit study currently being undertaken.

    (2) Brainstorm with the class (or prepare your own list) for suggestions of a wide range of activities students might undertake to accomplish the objectives. For example:

poster	bulletin board display	wall hanging
cartoon	poetry	TV show
graph	play	movie
chart	essay	photo essay
collage	song	audio tape
diorama	speech	etc.

    (3) Give each objective a number or letter and place that number or letter next to the activities that would possibly accomplish the objective. Estimate the time needed to complete each activity and write that next to the activity.

    (4) Have students fill out contract form below. Each objective must be covered by at least one activity. Check to see that contracts are filled out correctly. At end of unit check contracts to make sure work has been completed.

	CONTRACT	
Objectives for unit	Activity	Approximate time needed
	Total	

I, _____ contract to complete the above activities to the best of my ability by the
    (student's name)   end of this unit on
                      (date) _____

_____   _____
(teacher signature)   (student signature)

    (contract date) _____

2. Contracting Level of Performance

   when: depends on topic, subject, or unit being studied

   what: contract form

   how: The following is one type of contract form that can be used
         to contract for a grade. The topics and projects are not
         listed here but rather the level of performance. All reading,
         papers, projects, and activities will have to be done at a
         particular level of performance.

CONTRACT

_____ is contracting for a grade of _____ .
(student's name)

_____ may contract for a different grade after con-
(student's name)   sultation with the teacher.

                                All work is due on the date it is to be
                                handed in.

      Student's Signature _____

I will give the grade of _____ if all work planned is completed to that
level of quality.

      Teacher's Signature _____

- -

To earn a grade of C you will be required to turn in all written work at an
average pass level. If papers and class presentations are not of a pass
quality, you will be asked to re-do the written work and quizzes until pass-
able, up to three times. You need not attend all classes. You need to participate in some class activities but you need not necessarily attend field
trips. You are required to complete all work to reach a pass average level.
You will have the opportunity to repeat quizzes and re-do written work up to
three times, after which that work will receive a failing grade.

To earn a grade of B all written work must be at a very good level which
means that you will have proofread with care all papers and demonstrate that
you have thoughtfully considered your response on the required papers and
quizzes. If papers are not thoughtfully prepared, you will be asked to re-
do the papers until they are judged to be at a very good level. If written
work is repeatedly unacceptable and must be redone more than twice to reach
a B level, you are not performing B work. Also you will be asked to attend
most class sessions and participate in most class activities including field
trips.

To earn a grade of A all written work must be at a superior level which means
that your work demonstrates that you are giving a serious and thoughtful response. You will be scrupulous in your proofreading. If papers are not at a
superior level, you will be asked to re-do them until they are judged to be
at a superior level. If written work is repeatedly unacceptable and must be
redone to reach a pass level, you are not performing A work. You will attend
all classes and participate in all the activities and field trips.

3. Contracting by Projects Completed

when: recurring

what: contract form

how: Student participates by entering into a contract with teacher.

CONTRACT

_____ is contracting for a grade of _____ .
(student's name)

may contract for a higher grade at any time
_____ but never for a lower grade.
(student's name)

(Twenty points will be subtracted for each
_____ day work is overdue.)
(due date)

_____   _____
(teacher's name)   (date)

Activities selected from the list below to fulfill contract obligations:

Activity selected (describe) _____

possible points _____   grade _____

- -

Contract Activities for Egypt
(example)

Points

 50 1. Prepare a chart of the foreign countries that ruled Egypt and the
        dates of their rule.
100 2. Create maps of Egypt: 2000 BC, 10 AD, current.
100 3. Write an essay on power structure and government in the time of the
        Pharoahs.
 60 4. Prepare a chart on foods and export crops grown in Egypt.
 75 5. Read text _____, pages _____ to _____. Answer
        questions _____ on page _____.
100 6. Write essay on construction of Aswan High Dam and the result of the
        prevention of the annual Nile flood.
100 7. Write an essay comparing Egypt to another Middle East country.
 50 8. Learn to speak a few words (greetings, phrases) in Arabic.
200 9. Write a biography of any Egyptian political leader from the time
        Egypt gained independence to the present.
 60 10. Make a chart of wildlife and domestic animals native to Egypt.
 25 11. Prepare native Egyptian food and serve to class.
100 12. Write essay on Muslim religion and customs.
 50 13. Write a summary of the Egypt/Israel Camp David Peace Accords.
  ? 14. Student-identified activity with teacher approval. Teacher sets
        possible points.

_____points = A _____points = B _____points = C

_____   _____
(student's signature)   (teacher's signature)

SPECIFIC OBJECTIVE: Identify and apply the five different types of grouping.

4. <u>Grouping as a Discussion Technique</u>

when: one class period

what: listing of group techniques below[2]

how: Many of the activities suggested in this text encourage grouping as a technique to foster participation in classifying,
valuing, and interpreting. Because of the importance of this
technique it is essential that students know the different
types of grouping. Each type of group calls for different procedures and different kinds of responses from the students. A
copy of the following list of five different types of groups
should be given to all students so that they will identify
their responsibilities in group discussions. Hopefully, when
instructions are given to form a certain type of group, students will know what is expected of them.

<u>TASK-ORIENTED</u> SMALL GROUP
   Purpose: to bring the various members of the small group together to focus
      on a specific project or proposal.
   Guidelines: (1) clearly define your task so that all members understand and
      agree; (2) sharply delineate roles and assignments for the individual mem-
      bers of the group.

<u>BRAINSTORMING</u> SMALL GROUP
   Purpose: to bring the various members of the small group together to discuss
      freely and uninhibitedly a topic which is problem centered or solution
      centered.
   Guidelines: (1) the ideal number for a "Brainstorming" group is about 12;
      (2) the topic should be relatively simple, familiar, and talkable; (3)
      criticism is ruled out--judgment of ideas is done at a later time; (4)
      quantity of participation is wanted.

<u>TUTORIAL</u> SMALL GROUP
   Purpose: to emphasize individual instruction usually of a remedial nature
      or to evaluate an independent study project of an advanced nature.
   Guidelines: (1) remedial work should be of a type that is general enough to
      benefit all members of a small group; (2) the emphasis is on the teacher
      dealing with each member of the group in turn; (3) no attempt is made
      here for group dynamics and interaction between students.

<u>DISCURSIVE</u> SMALL GROUP
   Purpose: to encourage free and uninhibited discussion by students of a topic
      which has some previous structure and relevance to material under study.
   Guidelines: (1) structure of topic should be presented to students prior to
      coming to class; (2) teacher acts primarily as an interested observer--
      listens attentively, notices who participates, watches for student reaction.

<u>SOCRATIC</u> SMALL GROUP
   Purpose: to bring students and instructors together to discuss a problem
      posed by the teacher for which an answer can best be determined through
      the open and honest exchange of informed opinion.
   Guidelines: (1) begins in Stage 1 with teacher challenging, disturbing, de-
      manding definitions, driving the discussants back into a corner to examine
      their prejudices, to defend their positions; (2) during the second stage
      the teacher does a lot of good hard listening, then becomes a leader and
      participant--probing, directing, stimulating, enticing, responding, chal-
      lenging, and synthesizing.

SPECIFIC OBJECTIVE: Identify different techniques that students could use to report inquiry and other project type assignments.

5. Techniques to Report an Inquiry Project

when: flexible

what: materials as needed; list of projects or activities

how: Some teachers tend to limit classroom activity to lecturing, question and answer sessions, group discussions, or individual research/written paper projects. Perhaps they feel this is the best way to accomplish the objectives they have set for the particular topic or unit being studied. Occasionally, however, it might be worthwhile to give the students an opportunity to use creative expression to accomplish the objectives. What follows is a partial list of activities students might undertake.[3]

Potential Activities or Projects
bulletin board display
crossword puzzle construction
food preparation
presenting native dance
creating maps
model
drama (write a play)
photographic essay
posters
puppets
movie
slides
collage
interview
develop a game
debate
assemble a collection
diary
costume (dressing a doll)
mobile
music
modeling in various media
cartoons
construction of charts, graphs, diagrams
tape recordings
TV show
filmstrips
conduct a survey
create a mural or montage
writing (poetry, short story, etc.)

NOTE: Creative expression activities, including those listed above, can be incorporated in contracts and used as a means of presentation in inquiry. Problems studied through the inquiry method often lend themselves to visual display as well as other forms of expression.

SPECIFIC OBJECTIVE: Use a mode of research to focus thought on an issue or problem.

6. Research Outline

when: two weeks

what: research outline

how: Research without direction is wasted effort. What follows is a research outline that will help students focus their thinking and make their research efforts more efficient.

Researching

A. Identify the problem

B. Hypothesize (give a tentative solution to the problem)

C. Research (collect information from available sources)

D. Organize and evaluate research findings

E. Conclusion (what you infer or deduce from findings)

F. Form or Method of presentation of research and conclusion (this may previously have been determined by the teacher)

   1. research paper
   2. oral report
   3. debate
   4. panel discussion
   5. visual presentation (charts, graphs, mobiles, collage, etc.)
   6. role play
   (See activity "Techniques to Report an Inquiry Project," previous page in this chapter.)

G. Letter to congressman expressing your concern about the problem and your research findings and conclusion.

Note to teacher: Brainstorm with the class possible social problems for students to research and list their suggestions on the board. They need not choose one of the topics on the board, but the topic they ultimately identify should have your approval.

Examples: nuclear arms proliferation
hazardous waste disposal
minority rights
military involvement in foreign affairs
child abuse/parental abuse (old people)
rights of crime victims

SPECIFIC OBJECTIVE: Use a mode of inquiry to investigate an issue; include the process of stating a hypothesis, locating and gathering information, revising the hypothesis based on the data, and stating and supporting a conclusion.

7. Inquiry: A Method of Proof

when: three class periods or as needed

what: inquiry steps (below); resource materials

how: (1) Student selects issue to investigate.
(2) Student follows Inquiry Form while investigating issue.
(3) Individualized instruction--teacher gives help only when needed.
(4) Students report generalizations (conclusions) to class.

INQUIRY FORM

1. EXPERIENCING: What issue are you investigating and what experience have you had with this issue that has caused you to be interested in or curious about it?

_____

_____

2. UNCERTAINTY AND DOUBT: The issue can become a personal as well as a social problem if you feel the need to know. Express as best you can the uncertainty you feel about the issue. What confuses you?

_____

_____

3. FRAMING THE PROBLEM:

What do you know for sure about the issue? What are the facts?

_____

_____

What do you think you know about the issue? (Your bias, prejudice, gossip, unverified information, rumors--anything you think might be true but are uncertain about)

_____

_____

What is it you do not know about the issue? What do you need to know?

_____

4. FORMULATING A HYPOTHESIS: The hypothesis is a proposed point of view on the issue. That view needs to be proved or disproved. In other words, what do you think about the issue before you have studied it? Try to state this in one simple sentence. Hypothesize means to infer, specu-late, or predict.

_____

5. EXPLORING AND EVIDENCING: Gather and evaluate sources of evidence on the issue. List the sources you plan to use to find information about your issue:

        books   filmstrips   personal observation   pictures
        interviews   newspapers   magazines   etc.

_____

_____

List specific pieces of information that deal with your hypothesis. Organize the information. One way to do this is to put a plus (+) sign by evidence that supports your hypothesis, a minus (-) by evi-dence that disproves it, and a question mark (?) by evidence that seems neutral or may have nothing to do with your hypothesis.

_____

_____

_____

6. GENERALIZATION: How does your information prove or disprove your hypothesis? In other words, briefly analyze it (How accurate is the information? Fact, opinion, bias?). Can you draw a conclusion based on the evidence you gathered?

_____

_____

7. EVALUATING THE INQUIRY: What have you learned? Has the inquiry into the issue provided you with an accurate point of view on the issue? Explain:

_____

_____

NOTE: An important point is that the inquiry method starts with a personal concern. This method is not successful if problems or issues are identified for the student. The motivation to complete an inquiry is intrinsic; that is, the method is one way to study and perhaps develop an appropriate response to life's problems. Inquiry offers citizens in a democratic, complex, indepen-dent society one method by which to rationally think through problems and issues. Those teachers who use inquiry believe that the proper place to prac-tice inquiry decision-making is in the schools.

SPECIFIC OBJECTIVE: Develop the ability to communicate effectively in groups, analyze group roles, and assume roles which help maintain the group and which help accomplish the task.

8. Identifying Group Behavior and Consensus Procedures

when: one class period

what: list of statements; consensus

how: (1) Divide the class into groups and tell the groups they must reach a consensus on the value statements listed below. Explain that consensus is not a majority. Consensus means a decision reached is a decision agreed to by every member of the group (a position they can live with). Give groups a specific amount of time to reach a consensus, possibly 15-20 minutes.
(2) Allow groups to work for a limited period of time (half of the time allotted for the consensus to be reached). Stop the groups.
(3) Hold a class discussion on group behavior and procedure.
(a) Does the group have a plan on how to reach a consensus?
(b) Does the group need a leader?
(c) Are all ideas being heard?
(d) What actions would help the groups perform better?
(4) Allow groups to return to trying to reach a consensus. Stop them after the allotted time. Did they work better the second time? What did they learn about the group and its behavior?

List of Value Statements[4]

(circle the number that represents your feeling for each of the statements)	strongly agree	agree	neutral	disagree	strongly disagree
1. I believe discrimination against minorities is perfectly all right.	1	2	3	4	5
2. I believe in equal opportunity for all citizens.	1	2	3	4	5
3. To be biased is to be a good American citizen.	1	2	3	4	5
4. I believe in equality before the law.	1	2	3	4	5
5. I believe races in this country should be segregated.	1	2	3	4	5
6. Promoting achievement for all students is important.	1	2	3	4	5
7. Prejudice against minorities is deserved because the majority should rule.	1	2	3	4	5

9. Group Evaluation

when: one class period

what: group evaluation form

how: Have students individually fill out the group evaluation form after they have spent extended time in one group with the same members. Do not require students to put their names on the papers so they will not feel inhibited in filling out the evaluation. The results may help the teacher divide the class into more harmonious and efficient groups the next time group work is required.

GROUP EVALUATION

1. This group was   effective / ineffective   because:
   (circle one)

2. Who were the most influential group members?

3. Which of the influential members influenced you the most?

4. Did any influential member arouse antagonistic feelings?

5. Did the leader make sure everyone's ideas were considered courteously?

6. Did the group members really cooperate, or did several of the members do all the "work"?

7. Did the group "stick" to the project or task assigned to it?

8. Were the group members relaxed and friendly or was the situation tense?

9. Could you suggest anything that would help the group function more effectively?

10. Would you be   happy / unhappy   remaining in this same group?
    (circle one)

SPECIFIC OBJECTIVE: Establish a process by which to examine a historical or contemporary issue.

10. <u>Categorizing the Qualities of a Presidential Candidate</u>

when: three class periods

what: descriptions (see below)

how: (1) Hold a class discussion on the qualifications needed to be President. Start with the Constitution:
  a natural born citizen of the United States
  35 years of age or older
  been a resident <u>within</u> the United States at least 14 years
(2) The Constitution enumerates a minimal set of requirements. Over the years people have developed ideas of the qualities they would prefer the President to have--desired but not necessary or demanded qualities. Through class discussion have students suggest those qualities they think are important for an individual seeking the Presidency. List their suggestions on the board. Discuss each quality as it is suggested, having students defend the suggestion and note how other class members feel about it.
(3) When the teacher feels the students have a concrete idea of the qualities the students want in a President and the qualities are listed and classified on the board, give the descriptions below to the class and see how well they fit the class's desired qualifications.
(4) Having considered the sample candidate cards below, have students individually draw up their own descriptions. What categories do they choose: age, sex, experience, looks, education, charisma, etc.? Do any of the students' descriptions fit possible presidential candidates?

NOTE: If this is an election year, this is an appropriate time to examine candidates using the categories emphasized by the students.

Male Age: 47 Catholic	Female Age: 55 Presbyterian
Occupation: Astronaut; Test Pilot; State Governor	Occupation: Teacher; State Senator; U.N. Representative
Education: B.S. and M.S. in Aeronautical Engineering	Education: B.A. Humanities M.A. History Ph.D. Social Studies Ed.
Divorced, no children	Unmarried
Male Age: 75 Quaker	Male Age: 35 Methodist
Occupation: Lawyer; International Ambassador to Egypt	Occupation: Accountant; Labor Union Treasurer; U.S. House Representative
Education: B.S. Business Adminis. LLD International Law	Education: B.S. Accounting
Married, 2 children	Widower

SPECIFIC OBJECTIVE: Identify American values as reflected in such areas as federal, state, and local government, and observe ways in which the government affects our personal life.

11. Liberty, Freedom, and Regulation

when: two class periods

what: chart below

how: (1) Have students make a record of all the activities they take part in during the course of one day from the time they get up until they go to bed. Students should identify how many of these activities were in some way connected to laws or regulations enacted by the local, state, or national government.

TIME CHART

(example)

TIME	ACTIVITY	CONNECTION TO LAWS OR REGULATIONS
Morning		
7:00	Wake up to music on clock-radio	FCC regulations
7:15	Shower	Water continually tested and treated by municipal water treatment plant
7:30	Breakfast: cereal, milk, toast, juice	Food and Drug Administration rules on additives and preservatives in food
7:50	Get on school bus	Bus inspected by state; driver licensed by state
8:25	Get to school	School building inspected by local building inspector
8:30	Go to classroom--principal and teacher talking in hall	Both licensed by state
Afternoon		
.		
.		
.		
Evening		
.		
.		
.		

(2) Hold a class discussion. Most students will be surprised at the amount of regulation in their lives.
   (a) Did the students do anything they believed was free of laws or regulations? What were they? Perhaps another student can see a connection to laws or regulations.
   (b) Do the students believe our lives are too regulated?
   (c) What would be the effect of less regulation? No

(cont.)

regulation?
(d) If, in fact, the items we use, as illustrated in the "Time Chart," are regulated, does that mean that we citizens in reality are without liberty and freedom?
(e) Do citizens' liberty and freedom have anything to do with regulation of things? Do we citizens have greater or lesser freedom because of regulations such as FCC, water treatment, Food and Drug Administration, and state licensing?

12. The Government Acts on Values

when: two class periods

what: local newspaper

how: (1) Divide the class into three groups. Assign each group to one type of news: local, state, or national.

(2) Have each group search one issue of the local newspaper to identify all the articles they can find that deal with their assigned level of government. Have each group record the number of articles and identify what values, according to the article, are expressed in the government's actions. For example:
Local police set up road block--value is safety from drunk drivers.

The state legislature passes a bill to license retirement homes for the elderly--the state values the proper care of older citizens.

The President of the U.S. meets with other heads of nations to plan for the storage of grains against world hunger caused by drought along the equator--the concern is for those who are starving.

(3) Hold a class discussion. List on the board the three headings of local, state, and national. Under each write the number of articles each group collected. Then under each heading list the values that the groups identified as being expressed or implied by the articles.

(a) What type of news appears to get the most coverage by the newspaper?

(b) How do the values compare? Do we have the same values locally that appear to be held statewide or nationally? What might be reasons for differences?

(c) Do the students agree with all the values expressed?

(d) Are any of the values in conflict with others?

SPECIFIC OBJECTIVE: Identify social issues and speculate on the effect of those issues in the present and future times.

13. <u>Is Holocaust Coming?</u>[5]

   when: four class periods

   what: source readings on immigration just prior to World War II, specifically on Jews who left Germany in the 1930s

   how: Although most Jews remained in Germany during the 1930s, hoping that Hitler and his repression would prove to be just one more historical experience which they would have to survive, a few, afraid of what the future would bring in Germany, emigrated, many to the U.S.

   (1) Have the students research the following questions:
       (a) Why did the Jews who emigrated feel a Holocaust was coming, while many others turned a blind eye to Hitler's anti-Semitism and what it might hold for the future?
       (b) What reasons did the Jews who remained give for staying in an increasingly hostile Germany?
       (c) What kind of Jews immigrated to the U.S. in the 1930s? Can some generalizations be drawn on this question? Who are some famous people who immigrated at this time and what are their contributions to U.S. life?
       (d) Where did the Jews tend to settle when they got to the U.S. and why?
   (2) Have students interview Jews whose families immigrated in the 1930s. What were conditions in Germany like when they left and what conditions awaited them when they entered the U.S.? Have students either take notes or tape the interviews and then report back to the class.
   (3) Hold class discussion on issues raised by the research or the interviews.
       (a) Have there been immigrants from foreign lands to the U.S. since World War II because of a "Holocaust" in their country?
       (b) Should the United States be open for settlement by Holocaust victims anywhere in the world?
       (c) Is Holocaust coming?

14. <u>Possible Future World Government</u>[6]

   when: two class periods

   what: no materials necessary, but presupposes some knowledge on students' part of current world history and current affairs

   how: Hold a class discussion:
   (1) By now students should know the term Holocaust, which was the word used to describe the planned annihilation of the Jews by the Nazis during World War II. Has there been anything like the Holocaust since that time? Where?

Students should give specific evidence and data to support their answers. To encourage thought the teacher may have to remind students of the destruction of Cambodians--in numbers now known to be possibly in the millions--as a consequence of political conflict between the Vietnamese and Kampucheans in the late 1970s; the mass killing by Protestant Lebanese, with passive consent of Israeli military, of Muslim Palestinian refugees in Beirut; genocide practiced by Idi Amin in Uganda.

(2) Is there any possible connection between scattered terrorist incidents in which innocent individuals (Spanish, French, Basque, Protestant, Catholic) are killed deliberately or accidentially and the officially sanctioned murder of a large number of individuals by those in authority? What is the similarity, if any? What, if any, are the differences?

(3) If you think that (a) genocide is a potentially serious problem, and (b) genocide may be prevented, the task is to create a series of international legal structures that might prevent a future Holocaust from happening.

Instructions: All of the above questions are higher level ones which require real thinking. The real problem, of course, is the last question which calls for the creation of legal structures which do not now exist. This question calls for speculation and evaluation--both higher levels of thinking-- for it requires not only imagination but criteria which students themselves create. The fact that it is an abstract question, however, should not deter one. Some possible ways of evaluating students' answers:

(1) Brainstorming or ideational fluency. How many different ideas can students come up with that would preserve world peace? (At the first stage of this exercise, be completely permissive; indeed, do not let other students comment negatively, saying, "That's dumb!" or "Aw, that would never work.") The idea is to fill the board with possibilities.

(2) When teachers reach the point of categorizing and analyzing the various recommendations, they will need to ask two kinds of questions:
(a) What would that mean? Or similar sorts of questions such as: "How would that work in practice?" "What would that look like?" "How would that work if it were tried?" These are implication type questions. Thus, if for instance, a student says, "We should have officers from the United Nations free to visit any spot in the world to check up on the status of minorities," this suggestion for a structure should be met with a variety of probing questions from teacher or students:

"How many officers ought there be?"

"What kinds of authority should they have? Merely persuasive? or ought they have some authority to compel governments to, say, disband a potential concentration camp?"

(b) How do you evaluate this suggestion? These judgment questions are designed to elicit a value judgment from students BUT each of the value judgments must be backed up with something more than an assertion. Consider the example in (a) above:

"Yes, but if there were U.N. officers, as you suggest, would this not be perceived by some as a threat to national sovereignty?"

"How would you prevent nations from intimidating or bribing the U.N. officers?

"You might get a country like the U.S. or Canada to agree to this, but how about one like Libya or Vietnam or Iraq? These countries already have a long history of committing genocide against some of their own minority groups. Do you think that they would willingly give up this practice?"

Thus, evaluation of creative ideas ought to be in terms of whether one can demonstrate that they are, in some sense, feasible, workable, or possible. They cannot obviously be judged in terms of whether a proposition is already "right," "wrong," "correct," or "incorrect."

SPECIFIC OBJECTIVE: Identify the role of selected words and distinguish between words and the reality they represent.

15. The Potency of Words to Stereotype and Bias

when: two class periods

what: no materials necessary

how: (1) Discuss with students our reliance on the spoken or written word as our major means of communication. It is well known that different English-speaking countries use different words for the same object. We say "elevator," the English say "lift." We say "gas," the Nigerians say "petrol." When Nigerians say "gas" they mean "bottled gas" for cooking. These differences in meaning can, of course lead to problems. Words also can create emotion, and this is probably when they are most potent. Words make us laugh and cry; they make us angry. How many of us have been in a situation where something has been said that offended us, and only later, after some time has passed, could we think of a quick reply or "put down." We were reacting to the words as symbols of things or

feelings. That is the distinction we must make--words
are just symbols, they are not the reality itself.

(2) For a specified number of days have students write down
words (or phrases) that evoked some emotion, what the
emotion was, and why the word was potent enough to
create that emotion.

(3) Divide class into groups and have group members share
some of the words that evoked emotion.
(a) Do some words evoke the same emotion in everyone?
(b) Are there words that cause emotion in some students
and not in others? Why?
(c) What words seemed to bring forth the strongest
emotion? Why?
(d) Were students reacting to the words or the "reality"
the words symbolized?

(4) Have groups share some of their discussions with the
class.

(5) Students might also be encouraged to identify words or
phrases in the media that are meant to elicit emotion
and bring these to class to discuss how effective they
are. Do the students think most people are reacting to
the words or the reality they represent? For example,
the following list of words, when put in a proper context, might well elicit strong emotional feeling. Can
the students categorize groups of words in terms of
their attempts to emotionally arouse feelings about an
individual, the family of an individual, the ethnic or
racial origin of an individual?

Preface the following words with the stem "You dirty . . ."

Mick
Gook
Kraut   for example:
Honky
Greaser   "You dirty Kraut thief!"
Slopehead
Liar   "You dirty Greaser cheat!"
Cheat
Thief   "You dirty Honky liar!"

Some adjectives that might elicit emotion:

indecent	modest	attractive
obscene	honest	beautiful
prude	decent	radiant
corrupt	refined	gorgeous
coward	wholesome	well-built
innocent	charming	sexy
virtuous	elegant	handsome

16. <u>Language of War</u>[7]

    when: one class period

    what: lists of historical events and terms below

    how: Most of us tend to be less than careful with the words we use.
            Because our peers know us and understand our language patterns
            they understand us. If there is doubt, we usually continue
            to explain until understanding occurs. Usually this is
            sufficient in our everyday life. However, when people are
            making policy about important social matters and when they
            are making decisions and choices about what is of value, the
            language one uses does matter. The language of law is very
            precise, for example. Robbery with a deadly weapon is quite
            different from robbery without. Premeditated murder and man-
            slaughter are quite obviously not the same thing.

            When we discuss war and the killing that occurs during or as
            a result of war, the terms we use to classify events matter
            greatly. Some words can arouse strong feeling just by their
            use alone.

            Have students complete the exercise below by trying to "class-
            ify" the event with a word or phrase that conveys the proper
            meaning of that event, and then discuss the different choices
            of words or phrases.

Match the letter for a descriptive term with the historical event it best
fits.

    a. genocide

    b. Holocaust

    c. mass murder

    d. accidental destruction

    e. violence in which the death of humans was a by-product and not
        intended

    f. justified defense, appropriate to any war situation

    g. simple retaliation which is to be expected during a war

    h. homocide

    i. a conflict that simply got out of control

    j. accidental deaths

    k. killed them to save them

    l. (students may have other word choices) _____

_____ 1. After many long years of war in which the cry was "Delendo est Carthago" ("Carthage must be destroyed"), the Romans finally did destroy the entire city, killed all of its inhabitants or enslaved them, and sowed the soil with salt.

_____ 2. In the year 1572, in what is called the St. Bartholomew's Day Massacre, 20,000 Huguenots or French Protestants were killed.

_____ 3. On a number of occasions, American colonists traded or gave the American Indians blankets which they knew were used by sufferers of smallpox. Smallpox wiped out many tribes.

_____ 4. In 1915, conflicts between Turks and Armenians (who wished to be free from Turkish domination) resulted in the expulsion of well over a million Armenians and the death of 600,000.

_____ 5. Beginning in 1928, the Soviet government decided that kulaks, well-to-do peasants, would form the backbone of opposition to the new government. Accordingly, in a variety of ways, the government "wiped out" the kulaks.

_____ 6. In the year 1943, over 4,000 Polish writers, engineers, physicians, army officers, professors, and teachers were taken into the Katyn Forest and shot in the back of the head.

_____ 7. An unknown number of German civilians were killed in a systematic "fire bombing" of the German city of Dresden during World War II in retaliation for similar bombing in Britain.

_____ 8. Within one week in 1945, two Japanese cities, Nagasaki and Hiroshima, were destroyed and several hundred thousand persons were immediately burned to death by an atomic bomb; many thousands died weeks, months, or years later of the effects of radiation.

_____ 9. An unknown number--doubtless in the thousands--of Irish Catholics and Protestants continue to be assassinated by terrorist gangs in continuing conflict in Northern Ireland.

_____ 10. Ethnic groups within the country of Lebanon have for over 10 years killed each other in a continuing series of battles.

_____ 11. In the late 1970s, in a conflict between the Vietnamese and the Cambodians, both of whom were supported by Soviets and Chinese who were in conflict with each other, an estimated million persons died of disease, starvation, and neglect.

SPECIFIC OBJECTIVE: Learn to recognize propaganda techniques, stereotypes, and bias, and their effect on how decisions are made.

17. Propaganda

   when: one or two class periods

   what: list of propaganda techniques; Identifying Propaganda Techniques Form how: The most common definition of propaganda that comes to mind is persuasion; in other words, trying to sway someone's thinking to another desired point of view. The word propaganda came from the same word spelled with a capital P meaning to preach the gospel and establish the church in non-Christian countries. And that is exactly what propagandists do--they preach their views until we become "believers."

Advertising is perhaps the most obvious field where propaganda can readily be observed. The following is a list of effective and common propaganda techniques.

a. BANDWAGON - everyone has one! etc.
b. CARD STACKING - stressing the good or unique features
c. GLITTERING GENERALITIES - all pretty girls are dumb
d. NAME CALLING - purposefully using negative words to describe or label someone
e. OVERSIMPLIFICATION - distorting by giving too simple a reason
f. PREJUDICE - using preconceived adverse opinions or judgments
g. PLAIN FOLKS - "good 'ol boy," in tune with the majority
h. OUT OF CONTEXT - lifting a statement out of entirety in order to suggest a different meaning
i. SLOGANS - catchy words or phrases that grab our attention
j. TESTIMONIAL - using a well-known person to promote an idea or product
k. TRANSFER - shift positive thoughts from one person or idea or product to another
l. VAGUENESS - using positive but general (unspecific) words
m. WISHFUL THINKING - false identification of wishes with reality
n. AROUSING FEELINGS - appealing to emotion
o. SALES PROMOTION - appeal to the saving of money by purchasing an item at a reduced rate
p. APPEAL TO RANK AND STATUS - appealing to ego, "you deserve this"
q. REPETITION - repeating over and over again an idea or word so it will be easily recognized and recalled

(1) Discuss the techniques with the class. They can probably recall immediately examples from TV, radio, newspaper, or magazine ads.

(2) Have each student collect three examples of propaganda to bring to class to share.

(3) Check the school newspaper for propaganda techniques.

(4) Have each student try to correctly fill out the following form. Discussion on the different items in the form will help to clarify the "meaning" of each of the techniques.

IDENTIFYING PROPAGANDA TECHNIQUES FORM

Place the letter of the propaganda technique (previous page) next to the statement which best represents the technique.

p ___ 1. The Madison Hotel: A Renaissance of Graciousness.

o ___ 2. Half price sale for the next 30 days only.

j ___ 3. Governor Victor Atiyeh: Governor of Oregon, Former State Legislator, Senator, and Businessman, said, "I'm the NRA!"

q ___ 4. The Pork Avenue Collection, including world famous Pig Shirt, Hogwash laundry bag, and Pig Mints chocolate. . . . You'll love our friendly service too. It's faster than a greased pig.

e ___ 5. Speak Spanish like a Native with Linguaphone. You could easily be speaking Spanish in 2 or 3 months.

i ___ 6. Delta is ready when you are.

m ___ 7. What your home could have in common with the Met, the Tate, and the Louvre.

b ___ 8. Renault Alliance . . . Independent suspension with unique twin coaxial torsion bars for a quiet, smooth ride. Sedan comfort for five, with Renault's exclusive pedestal seats for extra rear seat leg room.

k ___ 9. A taste of Vermont for Christmas.

n ___ 10. The bridge between two cultures can be built by a child. Won't you help?

c ___ 11. All the politicians in this state are corrupt.

d ___ 12. That Senator is a liar and a fraud.

f ___ 13. That group of people will never be accepted until they clean up their act.

l ___ 14. ITT announces the biggest advance in television since color.

a ___ 15. Everyone has jeans with that label, it's the only one to buy.

h ___ 16. "The President is a simpleton," said the general. He really said, "The President would be a simpleton to consider the course of action suggested by the Secretary."

g ___ 17. "I'm just a farm boy from Iowa," said the candidate.

18. Collecting Stereotypes

> when: intermittently over a period of time
>
> what: materials as collected by students
>
> how: (1) Have students examine magazines, etc. to find pictures
>   that represent a common stereotype, i.e., woman as nurse,
>   woman as housewife/mother, man as business executive,
>   man as dentist, woman as dental technician/hygienist.
>   Have students collect these examples and mount each
>   example separately for display.
>   (2) Occasionally choose one of the stereotyped examples and
>   have students bring in examples that dispute the stereo-
>   type. For example: men as nurses and secretaries,
>   women as doctors and dentists--depending on the stereo-
>   type being disputed.
>   (3) Discuss with class different stereotypes that seem to be
>   breaking down. List these on the board as they are
>   suggested by students. Have them bring in magazine
>   picture examples to support the theory that a specific
>   stereotype is breaking down. (They may find examples of
>   other stereotypes breaking down not listed on the board
>   to bring in.) Of course, one of the best sources of
>   stereotype roles is TV. Identify which roles are stereo-
>   typed and which are anti-stereotype, i.e., women who are
>   president of the company, men who are domestics, etc.

19. Social Stereotype

> when: one class period
>
> what: 3" x 5" cards or other similar pieces of paper
>
> how: (1) Print the name of a common stereotype status on each card
>   or sheet of paper.
>
>   (2) Mix up the cards or sheets. Have a student draw a card
>   and role play the status until the class identifies the
>   stereotype being portrayed--similar to the game of
>   charades.
>
>   (3) Before going on to next "charade," have students discuss
>   what mannerism or behavior revealed the stereotype to
>   them and why this mannerism or behavior is so identified
>   with the stereotype.
>
>   Alternative: Have a job or role card which is pinned to the
>   back of each student, i.e., busdriver, principal, police officer,
>   dog catcher, banker, etc. Give the class five minutes to mix
>   and to treat people in terms of the job or role pinned to
>   their back. After five minutes, have the students guess the
>   role pinned to their back by interpreting how people acted
>   towards them. The point being that the social order has
>   built in roles and attitudes which at times become stereotypes.

20. <u>Preference for: No Pets, No Children!</u>

when: one class period

what: the classified ads section from several issues of the local newspaper

how: This can be either an individual or a group activity.

(1) Have students examine the classified ads and identify those which emphasize a specific value or bias. For example: "mature woman as baby sitter; married man for farm work; retired teacher would like to tutor in math and science; pretty girls to work in massage parlor; bartender--male or female--over 21; apartment for rent--no pets or children."
What preference or bias is being expressed in the following ads?

1 Babysitter needed for 5-month old. Days 30 hr/wk. Nonsmoker. References required. Call 555-xxxx.	4 Need married couple 6-8 hrs. Cleaning on weekends. Clean More Co. Call 555-xxxx.
2 Want a bargain? Female needed for 2nd semester. Brownstone sublease. Sign early and save 20% on rent. Only $127/month and ¼ util. Call 555-xxxx.	5 Female nonsmoker needs to share 2-bedroom, 2-bath at Peppermill. Call 555-xxxx.
3 *To protect your body use your head. Security Escort Services, 9 pm to 1 am. A safe walk to or from home. Call 555-xxxx.*	6 Chemical Technician. Do you have 18 hours of college chemistry, good mechanical aptitude? If you are self-motivated, industrious, and a team player, contact Mr. Hall at xxxxxxx Industries.

(2) Have students select a place, person, or object that most people think of as solely American, i.e., the Statue of Liberty or Mt. Rushmore, something most people value as being American either past or present, and have them write an appropriate ad. They must be economical with words, phrasing their ads similar to those in the classified section of the paper. For example: put the White House up for sale; Speaker of the House of Representatives needs a job; Betsy Ross needs some suggestions for a flag; wanted--appropriate national anthem, etc.

(3) Have students share ads with the class. Divide the ads into appropriate categories, i.e., homes for rent or sale, employment opportunities, job wanted, services offered, etc., and display on bulletin board or poster.

21. Biased vs. Unbiased

when: two class periods

what: editorial and Letters to the Editor pages from the local newspaper

how: (1) Save the editorial page and the Letters to the Editor page from several issues of the local newspaper. Pick out the best or most obvious examples of emotion or bias and reproduce these so that all students can have a copy.
      (2) Have students underline those statements which they think represent emotion or bias.
      (3) Have class discussion on student choices. Discuss with students the fact that the emotion and bias they identified was fairly obvious. However, this is not always the case and often emotion or bias can be very subtle. (If there is an example of that in teacher's collected editorials or letters, show it to the students.)
      (4) Have each student bring in one example of subtle emotional or biased statements to share with the class. Biased oral statements that one could hear in conversations are also fair game for class discussion.

      EXAMPLES of emotional or biased statements and those that are not.

BIASED

But some legislators do their most effective work for the private interests of their law clients.

. . . we don't have criminal justice, we have "a criminal joke." Law officials' hands are tied so many times on account of the so-called "rights" of criminals.

Probably the most timeless example of appalling madness is the legend of Emperor Nero fiddling while Rome burned. But it is rivaled by the spending of a President and Congress confronted by monumental deficits and debt.

And this is what prompted the outcry against the casual witless and promiscuous lumping of women, blacks, Jews, and "cripples"--precisely those who have been dehumanized in the past in our society.

UNBIASED

The court system is a delicate interrelationship between the adversary advocates and the sitting judge under the application of law and procedures, sometimes before juries.

Informed, responsible decisions, however, are such a vital part of the public process that there must be hope that the public is maturing in this role, as indications in the poll suggest, boding well henceforth for better considered public policy.

It is customary for governmental units to clean out the money drawers on the last day of the fiscal year.

Political difference is wholesome. It is political indifference that hurts. Failure to emphasize the differences leads to the indifference.

SPECIFIC OBJECTIVE: Learn to identify differences between fact and opinion, primary and secondary sources.

22. Recognizing Primary and Secondary Sources

when: one class period

what: list of primary and secondary sources for students to identify

how: Discuss with students the terms primary and secondary as they refer to sources. Primary means firsthand, as it actually happened. Secondary means secondhand, someone's account or interpretation. (For a more complete explanation of primary and secondary sources, see the activity "Identifying Differences Between Primary and Secondary Sources" in Chapter I of this text.)

The following is a list of sources for students to identify as either primary or secondary. The items below are examples; teachers should create their own items to fit the topic under consideration.

TOPIC: Rights and Responsibilities

Write P in front of the source if it is primary.
Write S in front of the source if it is secondary.

____ 1. The Declaration of Independence by Thomas Jefferson

____ 2. The Bill of Rights as described by a Ku Klux Klan pamphlet

____ 3. The Mayflower Compact as commented on by Cotton Mather

____ 4. The Alien Act of 1798 as published in Commanger's Documents of American History

____ 5. John Brown's last speech as reported by Robert E. Lee

____ 6. Dred Scott vs. Sanford, a Supreme Court case in 1857, as edited in Evans Cases Constitutional Law

____ 7. Emancipation Proclamation as interpreted by a Quaker elder

____ 8. Universal Declaration of Human Rights as published by the United Nations

(Numbers 1, 4, 6, and 8 are Primary sources.)

(Numbers 2, 3, 5, and 7 are Secondary sources.)

B. General Objective: To gain knowledge about the human condition which
includes past, present, and future

SPECIFIC OBJECTIVE: Learn to identify voting rights of citizens, the role
of political parties, and the process of political campaigns.

23. The Constitution on Voting[8]

when: one class period

what: excerpts from the Constitution and the Amendments to the
Constitution dealing with the right to vote

how: Realize that each state sets voting requirements; however, it
is important to note that the national government shares in
that exercise of power.

(1) Have students read the excerpts on voting below.

Article I, Section 2, states that, "The electors of each
state (voting for members of the House of Representatives) shall
have the qualifications requisite for electors of the most numerous
branch of the state legislature." It further provided for members
of the Electoral College to be selected in each state, "in such a
manner as the legislature thereof may direct." All states allow
people to choose the electors.

Eight amendments deal with voting. Amendment XII of the Constitution directs each elector to vote separately for President and
Vice-President.

The Fourteenth Amendment (1868) forbade unreasonable discrimination between people in election laws as in other laws. The same
amendment also threatens the states with loss of representatives in
Congress as a penalty for denying adult male citizens the right to
vote in state and national elections.

The Fifteenth Amendment (1870) forbade abridgment of the right
to vote "on account of race, color, or previous condition of servi-
tude." The purpose of this amendment was to give the Negro the right
to vote.

The Seventeenth Amendment (1913) provides for the direct
popular election of United States senators in repeating the language
of Article I, "The electors in each state shall have the qualifications requisite for electors of the most numerous branch of the state
legislature."

Amendment XIX (1920) guarantees that no person can be denied
the right to vote because of sex.

The Twenty-Third Amendment (1961) gave the residents of the
District of Columbia the right to vote in Presidential elections.

Amendment XXVI (1971) prohibits any state from denying the
right to vote to any person eighteen years or older.

(2) The students, having read the excerpts, might consider the following questions.

    (a) What do the Amendments suggest? Do they "permit" or "forbid" or do they do both?

    (b) Over the period of the Constitution and the Amendments can you identify a change in attitude toward citizens of the United States? Can you identify citizens who were not included under the Constitution in 1800? Why do you suppose they were not included? What did they do to deserve being included? Is there any evidence that the country is "better off" with the enlarged franchise?

    (c) From your point of view do the voting Amendments demonstrate that America is progressing in its stated belief about the worth and value of human beings or is it, as some suggest, admitting that historically the country did not actually believe in human worth?

24. Minor Political Parties[9]

when: two class periods

what: no materials necessary

how: Americans have traditionally thought of the United States as a two-party country. However, throughout our history there have been many movements which have given rise to minor political parties.

(1) Give students a list of the minor political parties and ask them to choose one party to research for answers to the following questions:

    (a) What movement or idea caused it to be created?

    (b) What were its major aims and objectives?

    (c) Is it still an active political force?

    (d) To what degree have the aims and objectives of the party been achieved?

    (e) If it is no longer an active political force, why did it come to an end?

(2) Have students place the date and party name on a time line denoting the beginning of various political parties in American history. Draw conclusions as to why it came into being, when it did, and reasons for its ending. Why have third parties tended to be unsuccessful in the United States?

25. <u>Straw Vote Election</u>[10]

when: three weeks

what: no materials necessary

how: (1) Make a list of all known party candidates running for
         Presidential office. Assign one candidate to each group
         of three students for research on platforms, positions,
         methods of campaigning, publicity, etc. In each group
         one student might serve as the candidate, one the cam-
         paign manager, and a third as publicity/advance person.
     (2) Allow the groups three weeks for research, development of
         campaign literature, and campaign activities.
     (3) Each group presents its candidate to the total class
         either through a campaign speech, slide tape presentation,
         panel interview, or video tape/film production.
     (4) On the basis of a pre-developed criteria for evaluation,
         have the class vote for the candidate of their choice on
         a straw ballot.
     (5) Consider such questions as:
         (a) the role of party organization in selling a candidate
         (b) the advantages/disadvantages for a candidate for the
             office to be sponsored by a party
         (c) the viability of having more than two parties in the
             United States
         (d) effects on American government of doing without parties
             as a means of promoting and electing candidates for
             office
         (e) Suppose there were only one party, how might that
             affect American politics?

C. General Objective: To apply knowledge through active <u>participation</u>

   SPECIFIC OBJECTIVE: Learn to participate by identifying and applying the
                        structure of a political party to an election.

★★★

26. <u>Political Parties Game</u>[11]

   when: three class periods

   what: participant descriptions (included)

   how: The objectives of this activity are to have students recognize
         differences in party platforms, introduce the role of party
         membership, and demonstrate the effect of competition on
         party activities and campaigns.

         (1) <u>Role Assignment</u>
             Appoint a party leader, two #1 workers, and two #2
             workers for each of the two major parties (Republican
             and Democrat). Allow the leaders and workers a 10-minute
             caucus. In the caucus, each party should (a) agree on
             a possible candidate for their party (to be recruited

from the remainder of the class), (b) list possible party
members in order of preference (to be recruited from remainder of class), and (c) list some arguments which
would support the party platform. While the party members caucus, the rest of the class should be given voter
forms. Each student should jot down his ideas on the
three topics listed on the forms.

(2) Recruitment
Allow a 5-minute recruitment period. Each party should
concentrate on recruiting a candidate and new party
members. Announce to voters that they do not have to
join a party and that they should investigate what each
party stands for before making a commitment.

(3) Campaign Planning
Allow a 10-minute caucus period. Supply each party with
newsprint and magic markers. Each party is to develop a
party slogan and to make signs which depict the slogan.

Each candidate and party leader are to work together to
develop a two-minute speech based on (a) the party platform, (b) the party slogan, and (c) some special appeal
which will gain votes from the class.

During the party caucus the teacher should discuss with
voters their views and ask if the voters can list differences between the parties.

(4) Campaign
Allow a 5-minute voter registration drive during which
each party attempts to get voters to register as Demo-
crats or Republicans. Allow each candidate to give a
2-minute speech.

(5) Voting
Using a secret ballot, each class member votes for the
candidate of his/her choice.

(6) Review and Evaluation
Ask the class to briefly review the activity with you.
Some helpful questions are:
(a) How and why were candidates chosen?

(b) Why were certain voters chosen as objects for recruitment?

(c) What was the main appeal of a party for a voter
during the initial recruitment period?

(d) What role did the campaign have on voter recruitment?

(e) How did the desire to be on the winning side influence voters?

(The teacher may wish to assign some reading on political
parties as an overnight assignment.)

(f) What role does the amount of <u>time</u> available play in party planning, in campaigning, and in making a decision as a voter?

(g) What role does <u>issue</u> play in recruiting party members and winning elections?

(h) What value is the <u>number of members</u> in a party in a campaign?

(i) What value is a <u>candidate</u> to a party?

(j) What are some considerations parties make in the development of campaign <u>strategy</u>?

(k) What are some of the <u>problems</u> parties face in attempting to <u>win</u> an election?

(l) What relationship is there between party activity and <u>representative democracy</u>? Between party activity and <u>good government</u>?

(m) Is there a better way?

Name _____

DEMOCRATIC PARTY LEADER

Your responsibilities are as follows:

1. Develop issues which will

    a. please your workers;

    b. attract enough voters to win election.

2. Organize the campaign

    a. Appoint a chairman to oversee the writing of a party platform.

    b. Appoint a chairman to oversee the recruitment of voters.

3. Select and recruit a candidate who will

    a. please your workers;

    b. attract enough voters to win election.

4. Your party must win the election.

Name _____

DEMOCRATIC PARTY WORKER #1

You may not switch parties.

You must have the following points introduced into the final party platform, and your candidate must endorse them.

1. The government must boost the economy by:

   a. creating new government jobs;
   b. sponsoring new government projects;
   c. placing tighter restrictions on business and fewer restrictions on labor.

2. The government must expand individual civil rights by:

   a. appointing judges who are particularly strong for human rights;
   b. increasing the enforcement powers of federal regulatory agencies;
   c. supporting the Equal Rights Amendment.

3. The government should take the lead in foreign affairs by:

   a. emphasizing the importance of reduction in nuclear weapons;
   b. expanding foreign aid to Third World countries, particularly in Africa;
   c. withdrawing support from countries with poor human rights records, i.e., South Africa, Argentina.

Your party must win the election.

Name _____

DEMOCRATIC PARTY WORKER #2

You may switch parties.

You do not care what the platform is as long as the party leader appoints you as either:

Chairman of the platform committee
or
Chairman of the voter recruitment drive.

Your party must win the election.

Name _____

REPUBLICAN PARTY LEADER

Your responsibilities are as follows:

1. Develop issues which will

   a. please your workers;
   b. attract enough workers to win election.

2. Organize the campaign.

   a. Appoint a chairman to oversee the writing of a party platform.
   b. Appoint a chairman to oversee the recruitment of voters.

3. Select and recruit a candidate who will

   a. please your workers;
   b. attract enough voters to win the election.

4. Your party must win the election.

Name _____

REPUBLICAN PARTY WORKER #1

You may not switch parties.

You must have the following points introduced into the final party platform, and your candidate must endorse them.

1. The government must initiate a responsible economic policy by:

   a. seeking to balance taxes and spending;
   b. cutting out unnecessary government jobs;
   c. encouraging business expansion and hold the line on wages.

2. The government must ensure the rights of law-abiding citizens by:

   a. appointing conservative judges;
   b. cracking down on importation of drugs;
   c. curbing the enforcement powers of the federal regulatory agencies to permit greater individual initiative.

3. The government must stabilize foreign relations by:

   a. increasing foreign involvement in the civil wars of friendly countries;
   b. increasing foreign aid to countries that purchase arms from the United States;
   c. increasing nuclear capabilities to have clear superiority.

Your party must win the election.

Name _____

REPUBLICAN PARTY WORKER #2

You may switch parties.

You do not care what the platform is as long as the party leader appoints you as either:

Chairman of the platform committee
or
Chairman of the voter recruitment drive.

Your party must win the election.

VOTER

Party _____   Student's name _____

Part I: Below are the issues in the campaign. Write a brief state-
         ment of how you feel on each. Place an asterisk (*) to the
         left of the issue which is most important to you.

A. The Economy -

B. Civil Rights -

C. Foreign Policy -

- -

Part II: In the space below give your reasons for your vote.

SPECIFIC OBJECTIVE: Participate by defining a school or community problem and identifying an action to deal with the problem.

27.   Senior Campaign: You Can Make a Difference

when: one week (depends on time available)

what: materials as needed for activity

how: The purpose of this activity is to involve the students in a community or school "campaign" where hopefully they can observe how their involvement makes a difference, results in a visible change, etc.

(1) Brainstorm with the students possible school or community problems where the influence of a class effort might be felt. Try to reach a class consensus on the problem the students would be interested in pursuing.
(2) Divide the students into groups and have each group determine what step or angle of the problem they wish to investigate.
(3) Have groups contact the involved officials (school administrators, city officials, etc.) to find out background and what has already been attempted to solve the problem.
(4) Have groups prepare their campaigns. They should use whatever techniques they feel will get people's attention and influence them.
(5) Have groups present their campaigns to the class.
(6) The next step is to implement the campaigns. How will they be carried out? In what order? When?
(7) Hold a class discussion on how well the campaigns succeeded.

SPECIFIC OBJECTIVE: Participate by applying a legal trial procedure to examine and evaluate issues.

28.   Trial by Jury

when: two weeks to allow for planning

what: research materials about issue to be placed on trial; general trial procedures

how: Although a trial usually means the trial of an individual, the trial system would be just as effective if an issue were put on trial. What is suggested below is just a general trial procedure. Factors such as class size, issue on trial, etc. will make modifications necessary.

TRIAL PARTICIPANTS:

Judge: preferably a teacher
Jury: part of the class or another class
Chief Prosecutor: should be responsible student with leadership qualities
Assistant Prosecutor: should also be a responsible student

Chief Defense Counsel: should be responsible student with leadership qualities
Assistant Defense Counsel: should also be a responsible student

The chief prosecutor and chief defense counsel will be the
leaders of their groups with responsibility for preparing
the case: research, writing statements, selecting and re-
hearsing witnesses, etc.

TRIAL PROCEDURE:

Opening statements by both Prosecution and Defense in that order.

Prosecution presents its case and introduces evidence.
Prosecution   examination
Defense   cross-examination

Prosecution   re-examination
Defense   re-cross-examination

Defense presents its case and introduces evidence.
Defense   examination
Prosecution   cross-examination

Defense   re-examination
Prosecution   re-cross-examination

Rebuttal witness for Prosecution and Defense in that order.

Closing arguments for Prosecution and Defense in that order.

Instructions to the Jury

Deliberation of Jury

Verdict of Jury

SPECIFIC OBJECTIVE: Learn to participate in identifying community problem
situations.

29. Setting the Scene for Problem Situations

when: one week

what: no materials necessary

how: (1) Divide the class into groups. Each group is to create
(outline) a fictitious city, providing size, location,
population, background, etc.
(2) Have groups prepare up to five possible problem situations
that might confront the mayor, city manager, or highest
ranking city official in their fictitious city. These
situations should be arranged in the order they might
possibly happen in any given day.
(3) Have groups select one of their members to play the role
of the city official.
(4) Have groups role play their own problem situations before
another group's city official. One of the group members
should act as the city official's secretary. The city
official should not know the problems in advance and he
must settle the problems without leaving his desk.

(5) Hold class discussion after each one of these "scenes" is played in front of the class. Some heated debate may arise.

Alternative: This same type of activity could be used substituting company executives, political bosses, presidents of countries, etc. for the city official, and, of course, creating appropriate settings.

SPECIFIC OBJECTIVE: Student and teacher identify their roles in evaluating achievement.

30. Shared Evaluation by Student and Teacher

when: depends on activity being evaluated

what: evaluation form

how: This evaluation form is used both at the beginning and end of the activity or project being evaluated. Both the students and the teacher take part.

EVALUATION

Student Evaluation

I. Beginning of activity:

   A. Subject being studied -

   B. Brief description of project or activity -

II. Completion of activity:

   C. Steps undertaken -

   D. Sources consulted -
      (authors and titles)

   E. What was learned -

   F. I think I deserve a grade of _____ because

   G. Suggested changes for project or activity -

Teacher Evaluation

   Comments:

evaluation of:

project _____

research _____

cooperation _____

if group work _____

time spent _____

Final Grade _____

SPECIFIC OBJECTIVE: Practice an activity by identifying a group plan for producing a documentary.

31.   Planning and Producing a Documentary

      when: one week

      what: planning and producing guides

      how: Producing a TV show requires planning and cooperation. The following outlines and guides should help a student group that wishes to produce a show. This is an excellent project.

PLANNING GUIDE

Proposed Title _____

Synopsis _____

Style (circle one): Documentary, Animation, Biography, Storytelling, School Film, Impressionistic, Collage

Type (circle one): Black and White, Color, Combination

Location: Inside, outside, studio, etc. _____

Length: _____ hours, _____ minutes, _____ seconds

Proposed Audience: _____

Other factors to be considered: cost, number of actors needed, props, special effects, lighting, sets, type of action, etc. _____

STORY BOARD GUIDE

Title _____   scene # _____

shot # _____

Length: minutes _____ , seconds _____

Location: _____   Time of day _____

Type of lighting _____

Background (set):

Actors Needed:

Type of Action:

Production Notes:

SHOOTING SCHEDULE				
SCENE #	SHOT #	LOCATION	TIME & DAY	COMPLETED

SPECIFIC OBJECTIVE: Identify and evaluate group behavior.

32. Checking on How the Group Functions

when: one class period

what: materials as needed

how: (1) Divide the class into groups, setting aside enough stu-
             dents so that each group can be observed by at least one
             student.

         (2) The observer's task is to observe the assigned group to
             check on how the group functions. In other words, to
             keep track of those statements that are supportive, those
             statements or actions that are disruptive, and those
             statements that are related to the topic being discussed
             by the group.

         (3) Assign a controversial current event topic to the groups
             for discussion, and have groups discuss and observers
             observe for a long enough time for observers to collect
             evidence on how the groups function.

         (4) Hold a class discussion and have observers report on
             their findings either individually or after they have
             combined their results. According to what the observers
             witnessed, what would help the groups perform more effec-
             tively?

         (5) Allow groups to give a brief report on their discussions.

NOTE: Observers may want to make a small chart to keep track of
       statements said by group. For example:

Put a check in appropriate column for statements made by group members.			
Supportive	Disruptive	Related	Sample Comments:

VALUES AND ISSUES

General Objective: To develop the skills to examine values and beliefs

Prologue to Values and Issues

A constant theme throughout the social studies curriculum, kindergarten to grade 12, has been knowing yourself by identifying your beliefs, values, and culture, and comparing that identified self with others in your community, state, nation, and around the world. One of the skills of rational decision-making is being able to identify what one believes and does as a base from which to think of appropriate responses. This in a democracy would seem to be a fundamental requirement. The assumption of most social studies educators is that identifying and applying one's values and beliefs is a learned skill that requires attention over the period of one's educational life. The following activities are, then, the culmination of a social studies curriculum that has stressed the importance of knowing thyself.

SPECIFIC OBJECTIVE: Learn to identify and compare and contrast one's own values and beliefs with those of the community as a basis for decision making.

1.   What Do I Value?

when: one class period

what: What Do I Value Chart below

how: As a beginning to understanding your own values, fill out the chart below; add categories to the chart that would be particularly appropriate for you.

WHAT DO I VALUE?

WHAT I WISH WOULD BE TRUE FOR ME

Instructions: For each value listed across the top, check the items that apply to it in the list below.

	others need me	time to reflect	care about things	be like others	own things	be generous	be hateful	be loved	be healthy
1. solitary activity									
2. family activity									
3. with friends									
4. now									
5. future									

6. free										
7. costly										
8. dangerous										
9. unrealistic										
10. probable										
11. unimportant										
12.										
13.										
14.										
15.										

SPECIFIC OBJECTIVE: Compare and contrast social values of the past with those of the present as a basis for predicting future changes.

> 2.   Equal Dignity and the Feminine Soul
>
>   when: one class period
>
>   what: statements to mark below
>
>   how: This is a gaining knowledge and valuing activity designed to stimulate a class response to historic attitudes on the status of women.
>
>   (1) Have students complete form below.

REACTING TO HISTORIC ATTITUDES ABOUT WOMEN

Instructions: Circle A for Agree or D for Disagree in front of each statement.   At the end of each statement, briefly give the reason you agreed or disagreed.

A D 1.   In childhood a woman must be subject to her father; in youth to her husband; when her husband is dead, to her sons. A woman must never be free from subjugation. (The Hindu Code of Manu, V.)

_____

A D 2.   Take my word for it, the silliest woman can manage a clever man, but it needs a clever woman to manage a fool. (Kipling)

_____

A D 3. The five worst infirmities that afflict the female are indolcili-ty, discontent, slander, jealousy, and silliness . . . Such is the stupidity of woman's character, that it is incumbent upon her in every particular to distrust herself and to obey her husband. (Confucian Marriage Manual)

_____

A D 4. Choose in marriage only a woman whom you would choose as a friend if she were a man. (Joubert)

_____

A D 5. Nature intended women to be our slaves--they are our property; we are not theirs. They belong to us, just as a tree that bears fruit belongs to a gardener. What a mad idea to demand equality for women! . . . women are nothing but machines for producing children. (Napoleon Bonaparte)

_____

A D 6. I will not say that women have no character; rather, they have a new one every day. (Heine)

_____

A D 7. Women in general, want to be loved for what they are and men for what they accomplish. The first for their looks and charm; the latter for their action. (Theodore Reik)

_____

A D 8. Women better understand spending a fortune than making one. (Balzac)

_____

A D 9. Being a woman is a terribly difficult trade, since it consists principally of dealing with men. (Conrad)

_____

A D 10. I would gladly raise my voice in praise of women, only they won't let me. (Winkle)

_____

A D 11. Woman as a person enjoys equal dignity with men, but she was given different tasks by God and Nature which perfect and complete the work entrusted to men. (Pope John XXIII)

_____

A D 12. Talk to women as much as you can. This is the best school. This is the way to gain fluency, because you need not care what you say, and had better not be sensible. (Disraeli)

A D 13. The great question that has never been answered, and which I have
not been able to answer despite my thirty years of research into
the feminine soul is: What does a woman want? (Sigmund Freud)

A D 14. When God saw how faulty was man He tried again and made woman. As
to why He stopped there are two opinions. One of them is woman's.
(DeGourmont)

---

(2) Quickly tally the responses by a show of hands. Identify
those statements which students most agree with and those
they least agree with. Hold a class discussion.

(a) Are there differences between the male and female
responses in the class and what are the reasons for
their responses?

(b) Are the attitudes expressed in the items above changing? Can the class identify why they might be changing?

(c) Taking into consideration the statements above and
the present attitude of the class, what might one
predict about the status of women 100 years from now?

Additional Activity:

As can be seen by the activity above, attitudes about the
status of women and the roles women play have changed consid-
erably over the last few decades. Divide the class into
groups. Have each group consider the role of women in American life, and list five ways in which the role of women has
changed since the time the students' grandparents were the
age of the students, and five ways the role of women has remained the same. Have each group present what they identified
as the major changes through a visual such as a poster, chart,
etc. Do most groups agree on women's role changes and the
ways those roles have remained the same? Is the ad right when
it says, "You've come a long way, Baby!"?

SPECIFIC OBJECTIVE: Learn to define one's personal/social values and how they relate to consensus decision-making in a group.

3. Ranking Your Social/Personal Priorities

when: one class period

what: list of priorities

how: (1) Have students individually rate priorities in order of importance (1 being highest, etc.). Priorities may be the examples below or those arrived at through class discussion.

(2) Separate students into groups and have each group try to reach a consensus on the rating of the priorities.

(3) Compare listings of groups for class discussion. If there is much variation, how might the class account for that?

SOCIAL/PERSONAL PRIORITIES

_____ A. drug control

_____ B. inflation

_____ C. unemployment

_____ D. crime prevention

_____ E. air pollution control

_____ F. nuclear waste disposal

_____ G. improving education

_____ H. cancer cure

_____ I. explore low cost, efficient, safe energy

_____ J. improved manufactured organs for transplant

_____ K. etc.

_____ L.

_____ M.

_____ N.

SPECIFIC OBJECTIVE: Learn to identify conflict between one's values and
possible future goals.

4.   Identifying Goals, Values, and Conflicts

   when: two class periods

   what: copies of rating values (goals)

   how: (1) Have students pick what they feel are the three most im-
              portant goals from each list. Can they see any conflicts
              among their choices (does the reaching of one of their
              choices negate or make difficult the possibility of reach-
              ing another goal)?

          (2) Divide the class into groups. After group discussion did
              the students make any changes in their choices?

WHAT DO YOU VALUE?

Rate the following items 1 - 10 (most to least important to you) in
each category.

INTERNATIONAL:

___ detente
___ population control
___ maintaining peace in the
      Middle East
___ reduce starvation
___ encourage growth of democratic
      governments
___ encourage countries to respect
      human rights
___ reduce barriers to trade
      between nations
___ encourage nations to become
      self-sufficient in production
      of food

___
___
___

NATIONAL:

___ reduce taxes
___ increase military spending
___ pollution control
___ increase drug control
___ decrease dependence on raw
      materials from other
      countries
___ protect our industries from
      foreign imports
___ increase our exports to
      other countries

___
___
___

PERSONAL:

___ earn a lot of money
___ increased leisure time
___ a successful marriage and family
___ a wide circle of friends
___ improve the community environment
___ participate in the political process

___
___
___

5. <u>Identify Value Differences and Attain Group Consensus</u>

when: one class period

what: list of value statements

how: (1) Have each student mark the list of value statements according to the instructions below.

(2) After the students have marked their lists, divide them into groups. The groups are to reach a consensus, a unanimous agreement, on the marking of each statement. Group members should discuss reasons why they cannot agree on specific markings. If necessary they may change the wording of the statement to reach a consensus.

(3) Have groups share markings for each statement and any wording change they may have made and why.

INSTRUCTIONS: Read each statement and mark whether you agree (A) or disagree (D).

_____ 1. Social, political, and economic problems became critical in this country only after the 1930s.

_____ 2. We Americans should be looking to a future where most problems and issues will be solved.

_____ 3. Life is just a series of problems and issues which we citizens will probably always be working on throughout the history of our country.

_____ 4. When you think about it, almost every problem that the U.S. has ever had from its beginnings is still with us today.

_____ 5. Actually, most of our nation's problems would be solved now if the Congress and President had limited immigration to the right people after the Civil War.

_____ 6. The only thing we Americans need fear is the fear of not having the power to persuade other people about the value of our "American Way."

_____ 7. If history tells us anything, it is that we must stand manfully and heroically for those ideas that we believe.

_____ 8. There is no substitute for victory; we must win. We must be number one; anything less would betray our forefathers.

_____ 9. The myths that we learn about our country are necessary and important, for we need to believe in heroes, we need people who are good examples to be thought of as "larger than life."

SPECIFIC OBJECTIVE: Define the duties and rights of citizens and establish a criterion by which to judge one's performance of those duties.

6. Citizenship

when: one class period

what: strength of feeling exercise

how: The American Heritage Dictionary defines "citizenship" as:

> cit·i·zen·ship. n. The status of a citizen with its attendant duties, rights, and privileges.

The point is that a citizen of the United States has certain rights and privileges, but that individual also has certain duties. Citizenship implies a two-way street--carrying out responsibilities and duties in exchange for rights and privileges.

(1) Have students complete the following exercise to pretest students' attitudes and opinions concerning citizenship.

(2) After the students have completed the exercise, use it as a basis for discussion. The objective of the discussion is to establish a criterion for citizenship that is acceptable to the class. The task may require rewording or editing some of the items in the strength of feeling exercise.

(3) Use the exercise as a posttest after studying the Bill of Rights, etc. to determine if students have changed their opinions or attitudes about the duties, rights, and privileges of citizens.

INSTRUCTIONS: Rank order the ten items (in the place provided before each item) with 1 being the first choice and 10 being the least important. Also mark your strength of feeling for each item by circling the appropriate number after each item: 1 = strongly agree; 2 = agree; 3 = neutral; 4 = disagree; 5 = strongly disagree. Remember there are no right or wrong answers; your rank order and strength of feeling are personal choices.

DUTIES OF CITIZENS

_____ Obeying the laws established by the government or suffering the consequences.   1   2   3   4   5

_____ Working to contribute to one's own self-sufficiency.   1   2   3   4   5

_____ Serving one's country in a time of need (war, economic crisis, natural disaster, etc.).   1   2   3   4   5

_____ Participating actively in the decision-making process of government by voting, petitioning, peaceful demonstration, etc.   1 2 3 4 5

_____ Contributing a portion of one's wealth to the government for the public good, i.e., services, etc.   1 2 3 4 5

_____ Opposing violence as a means to an end.   1 2 3 4 5

_____ Preserving natural resources and protecting the environment.   1 2 3 4 5

_____ Refusing to discriminate on the basis of race, religion, sex, or social class.   1 2 3 4 5

_____ Taking an active part in politics by belonging to a political party and participating in its activities, a way to achieve results.   1 2 3 4 5

_____ Providing for the needy.   1 2 3 4 5

RIGHTS OF CITIZENS

_____ Ownership of private property   1 2 3 4 5

_____ A decent education.   1 2 3 4 5

_____ Freedom to live as one chooses, unless one violates the rights of others.   1 2 3 4 5

_____ Protection from violators of law.   1 2 3 4 5

_____ To affect how one is governed by voting, writing, speaking out, petitioning, and assembling to protest.   1 2 3 4 5

_____ Expecting a government that works toward equal political and economic opportunities for all citizens.   1 2 3 4 5

_____ Life and liberty.   1 2 3 4 5

_____ Freedom from cruel and unusual punishment, including torture and extreme penalties.   1 2 3 4 5

_____ Freedom from discrimination on the basis of race, religion, sex, or social class.   1 2 3 4 5

_____ Freedom from hunger, disease, and poverty.   1 2 3 4 5

7. <u>They Are Known By What They Did</u>

    when: one week

    what: resource and research materials; criteria of duties and
           rights of citizenship established in the activity "Citizen-
           ship"

    how: (1) Have students each choose one of the following individuals
               for a research project:

               (a) Martin Luther King, Jr.

               (b) Barry Goldwater, Sr.

               (c) Jesse Jackson

               (d) Claire Booth Luce

               (e) (another woman)

               (f) etc. (teacher or students choose as many or as few
                    as needed)

           (2) Students must do an in-depth study of their selected indi-
               vidual using research techniques suggested in the activity
               "Inquiry: A Method of Proof" or "Research Outline" in
               this chapter or those techniques suggested in other chap-
               ters in the text.

           (3) Students must apply the citizenship criteria (established
               in previous activity) to the individual they are research-
               ing to determine how the individual exercised his/her
               rights and carried out his/her duties.

           (4) The results of the students' research should be presented
               in some creative manner approved by the teacher. (See
               activity "Techniques to Report an Inquiry Project" in
               this chapter for presentation ideas.)

8. <u>When Is Citizenship Loyalty?</u>

    when: one or two class periods

    what: Pledge of Allegiance to the Flag and quotes (included)

    how: (1) Have students write down the words to the Pledge of
               Allegiance. (Teacher may have to write it on the board
               if students are unable to.) Seeing the written words will
               help in the following discussion; also, a recording will
               do.

               (a) What does the Pledge call for? Does it call for
                   loyalty?

(b) How does the Pledge involve the speaker?

(c) In summoning loyalty and support for one's country, does the Pledge recall a sense of pride and belonging?

(d) Introduce the case of the teacher in Connecticut who refused to recite the Pledge. She claimed that the phrase "liberty and justice for all" was not a fact in our country. She was suspended from teaching shortly thereafter. Was the dismissal justified? Have students briefly debate the issue giving reasons supporting their opinions.

(2) Now have students examine traditional nationalism.

(a) What purpose do the following serve in the pattern of traditional national loyalty: flags, heroes, holidays, parades, pledges, anthems?

(b) Do the above "symbols" affect the students? Do those symbols mean loyalty to America?

List on the board all suggestions students have on when loyalty is a form of citizenship.

(3) Consider with the class the following quotes. Do the students agree with some of the quotes but not others? Be sure students explain why they might prefer one quote over another.

"Our country, right or wrong. When right, to be kept right; when wrong, to be put right."

C. Schurz, 1872

"There can be no fifty-fifty Americanism in this country. There is room for only 100 percent Americanism, only for those who are Americans and nothing else."

T. Roosevelt, 1902

". . . build an America which shall fulfill the aspirations and justify the heroism of the men who made the nation . . . a definite crusade for Americanism!"

H. W. Evans, Imperial Wizard, Ku Klux Klan, 1926

"Why do people speak of great men in terms of nationality? Great Germans, great Englishmen?. . . Great men are simply men."

A. Einstein, 1926

SPECIFIC OBJECTIVE: Examine and explain the effect of legislation and court
decisions on the public welfare.

9.   Legislation, Court Decisions, and Values

when: three class periods

what: chart below; list of court decisions and legislation

how: (1) Compile a list of legislation and court decisions for
students to examine. For example:

Medicaid/Medicare	Income tax
Prohibition	Social Security
Lowering voting age to 18	Desegregation

Court decisions to dissolve monopolies such as Standard
Oil, American Telephone and Telegraph (AT&T), etc.

(2) Divide the class into several groups and give each group
several pieces of legislation or court decisions to research in order to fill out the chart below. For example:

*In 1982-83 the federal court ruled that AT&T (Ma Bell) was in violation
of antitrust laws. Bell was accused of monopolistic practices because of
its ownership of long distance phone lines and other public communication systems. AT&T was forced to divide its national operations into
various independent companies. The desired effect of breaking up any
monopoly is, of course, to allow competition and thus keep costs down.
However, as a near monopoly AT&T was able to spread its profits and losses
over a wide range of services. Because the services are now broken up into
separate companies, long distance rates go down and local service rates go
up in price. Congress may have to pass legislation to control the cost
of service. Expensive phone service may be out of the reach of those
people who may need it the most such as old people, the handicapped, those
on a fixed income or confined to their homes, etc. It is not yet clear
what the consequences of breaking up Ma Bell will be; yet the federal
government is following a set of values that requires Ma Bell to act in a
particular way. It may be important that students identify just what
those federal values are.*

LEGISLATION AND COURT DECISIONS				
Date	Brief description of legislation or Court decision	Desired results	Actual results	Who is affected? (special age, sex, or race group)
Values expressed by legislation/Court decision:				

con't.

(3) Hold class discussion on group charts. (An opaque projector would be a good way to display each chart to the whole class.)
 (a) Does the class agree with or hold the values expressed by each piece of legislation or Court decision?
 (b) In terms of the final outcome was it a wise decision or legislation?
 (c) Have values changed since the time of the legislation?

SPECIFIC OBJECTIVE: Learn to identify social problems and choose among alternative responses those which correspond to one's values.

10. Social Problem: Patriotism

when: two class periods

what: strength of feeling chart (next page)

how: (1) Have each student question three people (excluding class members) about patriotism:

- Do they think they are patriotic?
- How do they display their patriotism?
- How would they define patriotism?

(2) Hold a class discussion.

(a) By a show of hands get a rough tally of how many of the people interviewed thought they were patriotic.

(b) List on the board the ways that people show their patriotism.

(c) Discuss how people defined patriotism. List some of the common elements on the board. Can the class arrive at a general definition of patriotism?

(d) Did the class as a whole achieve a sense of the strength of patriotism in today's society? Is there some reluctance for people to openly display patriotism? How do the students themselves feel about patriotism?

(3) To stimulate thought, give each student a copy of the chart. Ask them to fill it out, then discuss each of the items.

(4) Questions to ask:
 (a) Are there common strong agreements among the students?
 (b) Do the agreements or disagreements suggest a pattern of responses?
 (c) Does that pattern, if there is one, help the class define the meaning of patriotism?
 (d) Is there a universally understood meaning of patriotism in America or is the meaning an individual's own

(personal) definition? Does the strength chart and the interviews with three people provide evidence to support an opinion on this question?

PATRIOTISM CHART

INSTRUCTIONS: Circle the number that represents your feeling about each item (1 = strongly agree; 2 = agree; 3 = neutral; 4 = disagree; 5 = strongly disagree).

1.	Display the flag on the Fourth of July	1 2 3 4 5
2.	Pay taxes, not just some but all that is owed	1 2 3 4 5
3.	Join the military	1 2 3 4 5
4.	Support the President	1 2 3 4 5
5.	Protest against involvement in war	1 2 3 4 5
6.	Protest the importation of foreign cars	1 2 3 4 5
7.	Obey all laws	1 2 3 4 5
8.	Vote in all elections	1 2 3 4 5
9.	Stand respectfully during the playing of the national anthem	1 2 3 4 5
10.	Love, support, and defend one's country	1 2 3 4 5

---

11. Social Problem: Uncle Sam Wants You![12]

when: one class period

what: copy of "call to service" notice, description of three potential draftees; plus list of draft board classifications (following pages)

how: This activity requires role-playing by six students and a written paper by each member of the class agreeing or disagreeing with the outcome of the role-playing.

   (1) Give three students each a copy of the invitation to appear at the draft board for induction and the descriptions of the three young men hoping to be deferred. The three students will role-play these young men.
   (2) Give three students who are role-playing the draft board members the brief descriptive paragraph about the draft board and the list of possible Selective Service classifications.
   (3) Give all role-playing students a few moments to prepare. At the same time explain to rest of class that at the conclusion of the role-playing they must write a short paper either agreeing or disagreeing with the decision of the "draft board" and their reasons for their decision.
   (4) Have each of the three "young men" appear one at a time to plead his case. Only one of the men can be deferred. Give the "draft board" time to discuss and make its

decision based on the list of draft board classifications.
(5) Have students write papers.
(6) Students may want to discuss draft and current registration of 18-year-olds at the end of this activity.

Greetings:

Having submitted yourself to a local board composed of your neighbors for the purpose of determining your availability for training and service in the land or naval forces of the United States, you are hereby notified that you have now been selected for training and service therein. This local board will furnish transportation to an induction station. You will there be examined, and, if accepted...you will then be inducted into the land or naval forces. If you are employed, you should advise your employer of this notice. Your employer can then be prepared to replace you if you are accepted, or to continue your employment if you are rejected. Willful failure to report promptly to this local board at the hour and on the day named...is a violation of the Selective Training and Service Act of 1940, as amended, and subjects the violator to fine and imprisonment...

POTENTIAL DRAFTEES

1. CHARLES is 18 years old, one of three children whose father died two years ago. His two sisters are married and live in other parts of the country. Although his mother is only 45, she is not well and unable to work outside the home. Charles works at the gas station where he is chief mechanic. He is asking to be reclassified III-A because he is his mother's sole support.

2. HOMER is the youngest son, 19, of an area farmer whose other son has been in the army for one year. It would be very difficult for his father to put out the crops (180 acres) by himself. They also farrow about 200 pigs a year. He is asking to be reclassified II-C so that his father can continue to farm at capacity.

3. At age 20, BILL is a very serious and quiet young man who opposes the idea of killing another human. He works at the drug store and hopes to be a pharmacist some day. He is married, but has no children. He is asking to be reclassified I-O as a conscientious objector.

DRAFT BOARD:

In order to raise an army for World War II, America passed a Selective Service Act which required men to register for military service. Six separate registrations were conducted for men between the ages of 18 and 64 with a total of 50 million men being registered. Of these about 36 million were liable for service. About 20 million men were examined by the services of whom more than one-third were rejected. All together 10,021,279 were inducted into the military services during World War II.

The obvious problem with a military draft was that no sooner do you set the rules for who must go until you are faced with an exception. Determining those exceptions was the responsibility of the local draft board. Each local board was given a monthly quota by the government to supply a certain number of men. A man could not be drafted unless he was classified I-A. If a man received the I-A classification, he could appear before his draft board and ask to be reclassified.

Suppose you are a member of a local draft board. You are about to hear from three young men, each asking to be reclassified. You may ask questions, take notes, and then you will briefly discuss with each other before choosing who goes.

Following is a list of the 20 different classifications that the Selective Service System created, 17 of which would exempt a man from service. Students role-playing the draft board should use these classifications to help them decide which one of the three men to exempt.

I-A	Available for military service.
I-A-O	Conscientious objector available for non-combatant military service only.
I-C	Member of the Armed Forces of the United States, the Coast and Geodetic Survey or the Public Health Service.
I-D	Member of a Reserve component or student taking military training.
I-O	Conscientious objector available for civilian work contributing to the maintenance of the national health, safety or interest.
I-S	Student deferred by statute.
I-W	Conscientious objector performing civilian work contributing to the maintenance of the national health, safety, or interest.
II-A	Registrant deferred because of civilian occupation (except agriculture and activity in study).
I-CE	Registrants who have enlisted.
I-CI	Registrants who have been inducted.
II-C	Registrant deferred because of agricultural occupation.
II-S	Registrant deferred because of activity in study.
III-A	Registrant with child or children living with him in a bona fide family relationship; or registrant deferred by reason of extreme hardship to dependents.
IV-A	Registrant who has completed service or only surviving son.
IV-B	Officials deferred by law.
IV-C	Certain deferred aliens.
IV-D	Ministers of religion or divinity students.
IV-F	Registrant not qualified for military service.
V-A	Registrant over the age of liability for military service.

12. <u>Social Problem: Patterns of Dissent</u>[13]

    when: one class period

    what: attitude checklist

    how: (1) Have students read the background paragraph and then check <u>one</u> attitude statement with which they most completely agree.

           (2) Have students break up into groups according to which number they checked on the attitude checklist. For example, all those checking statement one are in one group, all those checking statement two in another group, and so on.

           (3) Have each group record each group member's reasons for selecting the group's specific attitude statement. Have the group then summarize these reasons and report to the class.

        NOTE: The purpose is to show that there is a <u>set of reasons</u> for each of the positions checked.

PATTERNS OF DISSENT

If you wanted to change something in our government, how would you go about doing it? The following may help you answer that question.

In 1846, Henry David Thoreau, a New England poet, refused to pay his poll-tax as a symbol of protest against a government that permitted slavery and waged what he considered an unjust war. The war was the Mexican-American War, which Thoreau felt was a case of "might makes right"—a strong country taking land from a weaker country simply because it had the means to do so. He was jailed for not paying his tax and, upon release, wrote an essay called "Civil Disobedience."

That essay called for all citizens to distinguish between good government and bad government and stated that it was a citizen's <u>duty</u> to resist evil in the state even to the point of open and deliberate <u>disobedience</u> to its laws. "Under a government which imprisons any unjustly, the true place for a just man is also in prison."

There seem to be three categories of dissent:

I. LAWFUL FORMS OF DISSENT	II. CIVIL DISOBEDIENCE	III. VIOLENCE AGAINST PEOPLE AND PROPERTY
includes free speech, free press, right of assembly and petition, political activity, boycotts and lawsuits.	*includes non-violent breaking of laws done in public to gain support. The protestor must be willing to suffer the consequences.*	*such as kidnapping, murder, arson, blackmail and other means taken to force change, including revolution.*

ATTITUDE CHECKLIST:

Now, thinking about those three patterns of dissent, mark the one item that you most agree with.

___ 1. Dissent seldom accomplishes much. Officials may change, but they still follow the same patterns. I would not waste my time.

___ 2. As citizens, I believe we have a duty to support our government officials and trust that they understand the larger picture. Dissent usually just causes trouble.

___ 3. I believe things that are wrong need to be changed and good citizens should use the lawful means open to them. That's what democracy is all about.

___ 4. I admire people who get involved in trying to change things. I would support using legal means and civil disobedience but would never use violence.

___ 5. Peaceful protest is not effective. It's only when something really drastic is done that things change.

13. Social Problem: TV's Impact on Family Life[14]

  when: one class period

  what: background paragraph and question

  how: (1) Have students read paragraph and answer the question, "If we had no television, our family would probably . . ."

Perhaps no single change had more impact on the way Americans lived than the invasion of almost every home by television in the 1950s. In 1950 there were only 3.1 million TV sets in America; by 1955 there were 32 million, and by 1959 the average U.S. family was watching television six hours a day, seven days a week. Oftentimes it is the small things that add up to really change the way in which we live. For example, television's impact on family routine was subtle but significant. Americans learned to eat their evening meal of frozen TV dinners from folding TV trays while watching the evening news by the indirect light of their TV lamp.

Bedtime was now determined by the 10:00 news, with millions of Americans falling asleep with their last hazy thoughts being tomorrow's weather forecast. Even our biological functions were rearranged--as evidenced by Toledo, Ohio's noticeable drop in water pressure on the hour and half hour.

Families played fewer games, read fewer books and in many cases, ceased talking to one another at least during 'prime time.' They visited less and relatives became someone you saw on Thanksgiving and Christmas or at weddings and funerals. Whether these changes were for the better or worse is up to you to decide, but they most certainly made life different in America.

  (2) Divide class into groups and see if group members can reach a consensus on this question, "Would family life be better or worse if there were no TV?"

  (3) Have groups share their decisions.

14. <u>Social Problem</u>: Reform--American as Apple Pie?[15]

    when: one class period

    what: background paragraph and list of reforms; attitude checklist

    how: (1) Have students read background paragraph and reforms and then complete attitude checklist.

REFORM: AMERICAN AS APPLE PIE?

Some argue that the American Revolution didn't end 200 years ago, but is, instead, a continuing process still happening today. This argument holds that the ideas set forth in 1776 have been a source of debate ever since. Periodically, throughout our history, Americans have had bursts of reform activity that either sought to correct the wrongs in our society or to spread our high ideals to other corners of the world. To some, reform movements have had a kind of rhythm that surfaces about every other generation. Below is a chart outlining areas of reform that were hotly debated in the decades shown.

<u>1840</u>	<u>1900</u>	<u>1960</u>
TEMPERANCE	PROHIBITION	DRUG LAWS
VOTES FOR WHITE MALES WITHOUT PROPERTY	VOTES FOR WOMEN	VOTE FOR 18-YEAR-OLDS
WOMEN'S RIGHTS	FEMALE SUFFRAGE	WOMEN'S LIBERATION
ABOLITION OF SLAVERY	NAACP DRIVE AGAINST JIM CROW LAWS/LYNCHINGS	BLACK CIVIL RIGHTS
LABOR UNIONS/10-HR DAY	LABOR UNIONS/ COLLECTIVE BARGAINING	LABOR UNIONS/ WAGE AND BENEFIT CONCERNS
COMMUNES	FREE PUBLIC SECONDARY EDUCATION	EQUAL ACCESS TO POST-SECONDARY EDUCATION
FREE PUBLIC ELEMENTARY EDUCATION	CONSERVATION	ECOLOGY

ATTITUDES TOWARDS REFORM: Put an X in the blank you most AGREE with.
Put an O in the blank you most DISAGREE with.

____ 1. Reform movements are useless because they are rarely successful.

____ 2. Reforms usually are started by radicals who just want to make trouble and/or get attention.

____ 3. Reform movements are a good example of what people uniting for a common cause can accomplish.

____ 4. Every so often, we need reform movements to keep corruption down and make government do what the people want.

____ 5. A "good citizen" is one who participates in reform.

____ 6. America is great as it is and doesn't need "kooks" trying to change things.

(2) Divide students into groups and have each group discuss the following question:

DO REFORMS REALLY ACCOMPLISH ANYTHING WORTHWHILE
OR DO THEY JUST CAUSE TENSION AND BITTERNESS?

(3) Have groups briefly discuss their feelings or conclusions (if there were any) on the question. Did groups vary widely in how they felt about the question, or do all students feel pretty much the same way?

(4) One way to encourage proper discussion techniques is to allow one group to fill out the evaluation forms while observing another group discussing. After ten minutes or so, it is helpful to have the observers share their comments (see discussion evaluation forms) with the participants. Do not anticipate that discussions need to go on for a long period of time. Often the real discussion lasts no more than 5 or 6 minutes.

SPECIFIC OBJECTIVE: Analyze organizations to identify the values expressed in their constitutions.

15. Many Constitutions

when: three class periods

what: constitutions from student council and other student or civic organizations

how: (1) Have students obtain and bring to class the constitutions or by-laws of the school's Student Council, and other student organizations such as Boy Scouts, Girl Scouts, Y-Teens, Honor Society, etc.
(2) Students should spend some time examining the constitutions and identifying the values expressed in these documents. The students should identify that many constitutions have "hidden" or implied values not specifically spelled out that may very well determine membership. Private organizations that have restricted membership such as country clubs and social fraternities and sororities all have constitutions or by-laws that usually carry implied values--perhaps a preference for certain types of people for members and restrictions against others.
(3) After students have identified the expressed and implied values they should examine the organizations to ascertain if they are actually operating according to their constitutions and upholding the values expressed in them.
(4) The organization most visible and easy for the students to examine is, of course, the school student council. After students have identified the values expressed by its constitution, hold a class discussion on these values and whether or not the student council's actions are consistent with its stated values. A member of the class might attend a student council meeting and report

back to the class on the actions taken during a meeting.
(It is quite possible that a member of the class is also
a student council representative and could make this
report.)
(5) For the most part, do organizations consistently act
according to their expressed values, their implied
values, or both?

SPECIFIC OBJECTIVE: Analyze the media to identify the values they express.

16.   What You See Is What You Get: Values For Sale

when: two class periods

what: pictures from magazines and newspapers collected by students;
collage materials

how: (1) Hold a class discussion:

What are "American" values, in other words, what are
the values that Americans generally hold? List suggestions on board.   For example:
sanctity and worth of individual
independence (women in the last decade or so; also
the Marlboro Man)
maximizing one's potential
favor having alternative choices
believe in justice through due process of law
etc.
Students need to see that these values are all around
us, particularly in ads, i.e., independence as suggested
by the Marlboro western cowboy and liberation of women
as suggested in the Virginia Slims cigarette ads,
"You've come a long way baby!"
(2) Have the students bring in pictures that represent the
values discussed in class or values they believe should
be added to the list. The students should build collages
using the pictures that they have collected to represent
American values. Do the students believe that the
collages represent values that square up with current
"American life"? Or do they believe Americans hold some
values but practice others?
(3) Have students share collages with the rest of the class,
then use for display.
(4) Was it a good decision to link a product to a particular
American value? Could candidates for political office
be sold to the voters by linking them to American values?
Alternative:
Reverse the process above. Have students bring in pictures they think represent American values, then hold a
class discussion on What are American Values. List suggestions on board. How well do the students' selection
of pictures apply to the values decided on by the class?
As a culmination, have students construct collages, having
classified the pictures according to their demonstration
of an American value.

SPECIFIC OBJECTIVE: Identify a concept of public good and measure against that criteria the freedom of action of selected individuals.

17. Do They Have the Right?

when: two class periods

what: checklist

how: (1) Hold a class discussion on the right to strike, who has the right, and for what reasons.
(2) Using a specific strike case (any strike that is in the news will do) examine the steps it took from what caused the strike to the outcome. List the steps on the board.
(3) Examine the case of a strike in progress either in the U.S. or abroad. Discuss its progress in terms of the steps listed above. Have students speculate on the probable outcome. What variables might enter the picture to vary the probable outcome?

Example of a strike in progress:

More than 6,900 McDonnell Douglas Corporation workers in three states were called out on strike today after last-minute talks between the company and the United Auto Workers stalled. Union negotiators voted unanimously for the walkout after talks were halted at 9:30 p.m. Sunday. McDonnell Douglas spokesmen said the company would try to operate the affected plants with supervisors and employees from other divisions. A union spokeswoman said there would be few people crossing the picket lines. The union had hoped to win a substantial pay and benefit increase from McDonnell Douglas while retaining periodic cost-of-living adjustments. McDonnell commercial aircraft division claimed it had not made a profit in several years. . . .

(4) Below is a checklist, "Who Has the Right to Strike?" Have students mark the checklist as a stimulant to start student thinking about who has the right to strike. Does everyone have the right? Should there be those whose occupation is so important that they cannot be permitted to strike?

WHO HAS THE RIGHT TO STRIKE?

Instructions: Circle YES for those you feel have a right to strike and NO for those you feel should not have the right to strike.

YES NO 1. President of the United States

YES NO 2. Superintendent of your school district

YES NO 3. Teachers

YES NO 4. Doctors/Dentists

YES NO 5. Supreme Court Justices

YES NO 6. Garbage collectors

YES NO 7. Engineers at a nuclear plant

YES NO 8. Military personnel

YES NO 9. Military who are in charge of atomic ICBM

YES NO 10. Parents on strike against their children

YES NO 11. Employees of the water works

YES NO 12. Other (list additional occupations)

(5) Tally the results by a show of hands. Select the individuals whom the students feel should not strike. Why should they not strike? What are means other than the strike to gain one's goal?

(6) Select the individuals on whom there is strong disagreement and have students debate the pros and cons of each individual's right to strike. Have any students changed their minds about who may strike as a result of the debate?

SPECIFIC OBJECTIVE: Learn to recognize how one's values are reflected in relationships with others.

18. <u>Men and Women Differ, But How Do They Differ?</u>

when: one class period

what: form

how: In recent years and currently at a number of universities, the differences between men and women are being identified and categorized. One of the arguments is that the differences in some categories may be those that are nurtured and fostered by the culture whereas others are innate. There was a time within memory of most adults that women were thought not to be able to participate in vigorous physical activity. This includes the assumption of many coaches up to the 1970s that girls were not physically capable of competing in track and field and were not physically capable of playing full-court basketball. Two interesting questions for consideration: What are the differences between men and women and What are the differences between men and women's brains and nervous systems?

(1) Have students complete the form on the next page.

(2) Hold a class discussion:
   (a) Were the students surprised about the results or was it what they had expected?
   (b) Were there any items which most of the students identified incorrectly? Can they explain why they may have missed that item?

(c) Raise the question once again about the difference between males and females: How much of those differences is encouraged by the culture and how much is natural or innate?

(d) Speculate on the future differences between males and females. Given the growth of technology and the development of new drugs, hormones, steroids, etc., what would the class think the differences between men and women would be 100 years from now?

MEN AND WOMEN DIFFER, BUT HOW DO THEY DIFFER?

Instructions: Mark each item M for male and F for female according to what you believe best describes males and females.

M/F

___ 1. More sensitive to taste and touch

___ 2. See better at night

___ 3. Have keener hearing

___ 4. Can tolerate sounds

___ 5. Better daytime vision

___ 6. Faster reaction times

___ 7. More easily distracted

___ 8. More willing to explore a new environment

___ 9. Less sensitive to extreme cold

M/F

___ 10. Make quicker decisions

___ 11. More skilled at expressing themselves verbally

___ 12. Better manual dexterity

___ 13. Better depth perception

___ 14. More interested in people than things

___ 15. More empathy in emotional and social situations

___ 16. Better able to remember names and faces

___ 17. Better able to pick up information

Answer code: Items 1, 2, 3, 7, 10, 11, 12, 14, 15, 16, and 17 are female. Items 4, 5, 6, 8, 9, and 13 are male.

The answers to the above items are suggested by the most recent research on male and female brain and nervous system functions.

19. <u>Choosing a Life Partner</u>

when: one class period

what: ranking survey

how: One of the persistent sources of discussion among senior high students is the identifying of characteristics they believe are most appropriate for choosing a life partner. It may be interesting to note in the activity "Men and Women Differ" that females and males seem to have different responses to life situations, and this, of course, is also true in choosing a life partner.

(1) Have students complete the following ranking form.

```
┌─────────────────────────────────────────────────────────────┐
│                    CHOOSING A LIFE PARTNER                    │
│                                                               │
│ Instructions:  In the first column rank the characteristics (1│
│ highest to 3 lowest) in terms of your gender.  In the second  │
│ column rank the characteristics according to how you believe  │
│ members of the opposite sex would rank the characteristics.   │
│                                                               │
│  FEMALE-MALE                                    MALE-FEMALE   │
│  (circle one)    ____     DEPENDABILITY    ____  (circle one) │
│                                                               │
│                  ____   EMOTIONAL STABILITY ____              │
│                                                               │
│                  ____    MUTUAL ATTRACTION  ____              │
└─────────────────────────────────────────────────────────────┘
```

Answer code (according to a nation-wide survey):
   Male -- 1 emotional stability, 2 mutual attraction, 3 dependability
   Female -- 1 mutual attraction, 2 emotional stability, 3 dependability

(2) Hold a class discussion:

(a) How accurate were the students in their rankings, as compared to the nation-wide survey?

(b) Would the students individually or as a class dispute the nation-wide survey?

(c) What other characteristics might the class suggest? Are any of those characteristics more important than the three identified in the nation-wide survey?

(c) The nation-wide survey identifies that males and females differ in their rankings. Does this suggest a potential problem for the future in that each is looking for different characteristics?

Alternative:

Brainstorm with the class to identify a list of characteristics including the three above. Develop a ranking form of the characteristics identified. Have students survey the other members of the senior class for their ranking. Tally the results to see how closely the males and females compare in their rankings.

FUTURES

A.   General Objective: To _gain_ _knowledge_ about the human condition which
              includes past, present, and future

   SPECIFIC OBJECTIVE: Identify the effect of technology on everyday life.

   1.   Count the Light Bulbs

        when: one week

        what: no materials necessary

        how: (1) Brainstorm with students and list on the board all the
                   electrical appliances and other electrical items, in-
                   cluding light bulbs and battery operated items, found in
                   the home. The list should be categorized under such
                   things as KITCHEN, BATH, LAUNDRY, ENTERTAINMENT, TOOLS,
                   and LIGHTS.

               (2) Turn the lists into a checklist that students may take
                   home to check off the appliances and electrical items in
                   their individual homes.

               (3) For one week students should make a concerted effort to
                   identify what they can do to cut down on their personal
                   use of electricity. For example:
                     turn out lights when not in use
                     less (or no) stereo
                     towel dry hair
                     do homework instead of watching TV
                     turn off radio when leaving the room
                     hand wash the dishes
                     count the light bulbs in the home (How many of the
                       total are turned on at any one time?)

               (4) After one week have students write a short paper or hold
                   a class discussion on how they cut down on the use of
                   electricity.

                   (a) Were some of the cutbacks on use of electricity just
                       common sense ideas that could be continued with
                       little effort (such as turning out lights when you
                       leave a room)?

                   (b) How many of the appliances really make life easier?
                       For example: the automatic washer and clothes
                       dryer are easy to use, but do we therefore spend
                       more time using them, compared to our great-
                       grandmothers who washed clothes once a week by hand?

                   (c) What single appliance would students miss the most if
                       they had to give it up?

                   (d) Do students' families make any effort to conserve energy?

                   (e) What were the students' families' reactions to this
                       activity?

2.   Identifying a Dependence on Technology

   when: three class periods

   what: sample chart below

   how: (1) Hold class discussion on modern society's dependency on
           technological devices and what life would be like without
           them.

           (2) Have students each pick a category of technology that the
           student will promise to do without for a 24-hour period,
           i.e., paper products, transportation, electrical (plug-in)
           devices, etc. Be sure students understand just what is
           encompassed in their categories.

(Sample Chart)

TECHNOLOGY CATEGORIES			
Paper Products	Transportation	Electrical (Plug-in)	Other Categories
paper towels kleenex toilet tissue food packaged in paper (milk, orange juice, etc.) writing paper word processor printout books tickets to events paper money etc.	car bus bike motorcycle etc.	blow dryer toaster TV/radio stereo can opener electric typewriter lamp blanket clock-radio stove refrigerator etc.	

           (3) After the 24-hour period, hold a class discussion on
           students' feelings, frustrations, possible sense of
           accomplishment. Suppose the technology that the student
           did not use for 24 hours was not going to be available
           for the next ten years, how would that change the stu-
           dent's life?

           (4) Can the students conceive of an invention or product
           that might completely eliminate an entire category of
           different items, i.e., the car eliminated the horse and
           other animals as a source of modern transportation;
           the electric light eliminated the need for candles and
           kerosene lamps.

B.   General Objective: To develop skills necessary to <u>process</u> information

SPECIFIC OBJECTIVE: Learn to apply a matrix to visualize the interrelationships of human need factors and global trends.

3.   <u>A Human Needs/Trend Matrix</u>[16]

when: two class periods

what: see matrix below

how: The cross-impact matrix is another useful tool for thinking
about the future, since it can enable one to visualize the
interrelatedness of a variety of factors. The matrix below
will help students determine the interrelationships of
universal human needs (listed down side of matrix) and some
global trends (listed across the top).

(1) Have students list what the relationships are, in other
words how one influences the other, for each of the boxes
in the matrix (either on a separate piece of paper or on
an enlarged matrix). For example, box 11 is asking,
"How are your esteem needs influenced by urbanization?

(2) After completing the 24 boxes, have students go back to
the matrix and identify how the global trends might be
modified to enhance the human need satisfaction.

	POPULATION	SCIENCE/ TECHNOLOGY	URBANIZATION	TRANSCIENCE
PHYSICAL	1	2	3	4
SAFETY	5	6	7	8
ESTEEM	9	10	11	12
LOVE AND BELONGINGNESS	13	14	15	16
SELF- ACTUALIZATION	17	18	19	20
AESTHETIC	21	22	23	24

SPECIFIC OBJECTIVE: Identify social, economic, and political values of the past and compare them with the present for the purpose of predicting about the future.

4. Impact of Technology on the Future

when: one class period

what: no materials necessary

how: (1) The following are factors or aspects of most any culture. Assign one factor or aspect to each student or group of students.

government	food	work
family life	reproduction	leisure
transportation	education	etc.

(2) Have students identify one scientific breakthrough or technological advance that would have the most impact on their factor or aspect of culture and describe that impact in a short written report. For example, some future technology to consider:

(a) solar-powered satellites (reality by 1992) - satellites will convert sunlight to low density radio waves which will be beamed to earth and converted to electricity

(b) mass drive motor - has capacity to accelerate from 0 to 300 mph in 7/1000 of a second (used to launch space ships)

Alternative:
Through class discussion select a specified number of electrical plug-in devices most commonly used around the home. Divide the class into groups. Through consensus, group members must choose what they believe are the three most important items and prepare a report on what life would be like without those items. Have any of the students lived abroad or someplace where one of the three important items was not available? What kind of adjustment was made?

5. Future Scientific Advances

when: one class period

what: both a list of topics and a list of possible scientific or technological advances

how: (1) Have students choose one topic and a scientific or technological advance, listed in one of the categories in the charts, that would bring about the most dramatic change in the life of humans under that topic.
(2) Either in a brief written outline or in class discussion, have students identify their topic and scientific or technological advance. The students should explain why they selected their advances as being those which would

create the most dramatic change.
(3) Can the students identify other future advances not
    listed which ought to be considered as a technological
    breakthrough?

TOPICS:

Selected Scientific or Technological Advance:
(note it here)

Quality of life   _____

Poverty   _____

Aging   _____

Population   _____

Disease   _____

ADVANCES

Future scientific advances in
Education:

1. widespread use of teaching
   machines
2. automatic libraries
3. evolution of universal language
   from automated communication
4. feasibility of education by
   direct information recorded on
   the brain
5. brain-computer link to enlarge
   man's intellect
6. _____
7. _____

Future scientific advances in
Medicine:

1. artificial and electronic organs
   for humans
2. hereditary defects controlled by
   altering genes
3. control of aging process
4. effective fertility control
5. automated interpretation of
   medical symptoms
6. _____
7. _____

Future scientific advances
Chemically Induced:

1. drugs to produce personality
   change
2. primitive forms of life created
   in the laboratory
3. commercially feasible synthetic
   protein food
4. biochemicals to aid growth of
   new organs and limbs
5. drugs to raise the level of
   intelligence
6. biochemical general immunization
   against bacterial and viral
   diseases
7. _____
8. _____
9. _____

Future scientific advances in
Industry:

1. directed-energy (lasers, particle
   beams)
2. commercial ocean-bottom mining
3. commercial/global ballistic
   transport
4. facsimile newspapers printed in
   the home
5. controlled thermonuclear power
6. direct link from stores to check
   credit and to record transac-
   tions
7. economically useful exploitation
   of ocean through farming with
   the effect of producing 20% of
   world's food
8. widespread use of automatic decision making at management level
9. regional weather control
10. _____

6. Future Machines and Social Change

when: two class periods

what: consensus chart below

how: (1) Hold class discussion on the evolution of tools and machines. Talk about some specific examples: i.e., washboard to washing machine, scythe to enormous harvesting machines, hand assembly of autos to robot assembly, radio to stereo, manual typewriter to word processor. The list can go on and on for the modern machine is one of the essential precursors of social change.

(2) Have students individually list on the chart below ten machines that students feel are basic or essential at the present time. Have them list five machines that make present day life enjoyable or pleasant, but are not essential.

CONSENSUS CHART

My ten essential machines

1 _____
2 _____
3 _____
4 _____
5 _____
6 _____
7 _____
8 _____
9 _____
10 _____

My five machines for enjoyment

1 _____
2 _____
3 _____
4 _____
5 _____

Group's essential machines

1 _____
2 _____
3 _____
4 _____
5 _____

Group's invention

_____

Group's machines for enjoyment

1 _____
2 _____
3 _____

---

(3) Divide class into groups. From individual lists have groups identify five machines that the group agrees are essential and three machines they agree make life more pleasant.

(4) Compare groups' lists for class discussion. Where do differences appear? What are the probable causes for the differences of opinion?

(5) Have students return to same groups again. They must conceive a machine (or tool) of the future. They must establish what machine's purpose would be and who it

would benefit--possibly to what extent the machine would
benefit mankind or the ecology of the world.

(6) Have groups share inventions with class, identifying how
new machines would affect the speed of social change.

(7) Can the class identify a correlation between technology,
machines, and social change? Are new machines a sign of
progress?

7. By the Year 2005

when: two class periods

what: To stimulate the process of speculating or hypothesizing,
start with the example of technology and its effect on a life
style (see "School, Learning, and the Learner, Year 2005"
below).

how: (1) Have students write a short paper predicting future
changes up to the year 2005. The students have several
choices for the content of their papers.

(a) Pick one aspect of current life style or society and
explore how technology might change it for the future.
For example: energy (oil, solar, etc.), transportation, entertainment, medicine, food production,
sports, minority rights, etc.

OR

(b) Students can project their immediate family into the
year 2005 and speculate on what life would be like.
For example: school for children, home and furnishings, employment for parents, clothes, food, transportation, entertainment, etc. See example below.

(2) Hold a class discussion on some of the changes suggested
by students. How probable are the changes? Do the
changes suggest a change in values and beliefs also?
Does the class think technological advances affect
society's values?

```
>              School, Learning, and the Learner, Year 2005          <
>                                                                    <
>School would not be a place as it is today, but a thing, an event.<
>No need for school buildings, buses, or extracurricular activi-    <
>ties.  The technology for learning is built into each home.  Each  <
>home is equipped with a learning station, including TV and a com-  <
>puter.  Learning is based upon the individual's needs and inter-   <
>ests.  Individualized instruction is delivered whenever the indi-  <
>vidual is willing, ready, and able.  All extracurricular activi-   <
>ties are organized by private/public associations sponsored by the<
>community . . .                                                    <
>                                                                    <
>                                                                    <
>                                                                    <
>                                                                    <
>                                                                    <
```

8. <u>What Would Life Be Like If . . .</u>[17]

   when: one class period

   what: list of future events below

   how: Students are asked to consider what their lives would be like
          if certain events took place in their futures.

          Have each student select one of the future events from the
          list below. Students must write a short paper on how that
          event would influence their lives. For example, if a student
          chooses the item "What would life be like if I became very
          wealthy someday?", he/she could examine his/her own beliefs
          about the desire to do hard work, friendship, respecting
          others, welfare for the poor, intellectual enrichment, self-
          reliance, etc.

   LIST OF FUTURE EVENTS

   What would life be like if . . .

   - . . . you could visit other planets as you visit other cities
     today?
   - . . . you retired at age 45, but lived to be 145 years old?
   - . . . you could communicate with others using E.S.P. (mental
     telepathy)?
   - . . . it was decided that 50 babies, the exact duplicate of
     you, would be artificially produced?
   - . . . you lived in a "raceless" society?
   - . . . cars were only available to rent or lease on long inter-
     regional trips?
   - . . . your job became obsolete every five years?
   - . . . it was necessary gradually to reduce the nation's
     economic growth rate?
   - . . . you were only allowed to fill one small garbage can per
     week?
   - . . . you lived in a domed city under the ocean?
   - . . . the personalities of your friends were constantly being
     artificially altered?
   - . . . you could read people's minds?
   - . . . you had a sophisticated computer implanted in your brain?

9. <u>Predicting Future Innovations</u>[18]

   when: one class period

   what: future predictions

   how: (1) The teacher reads aloud the questions listed below. After
              each question is read, those students who take an affir-
              mative position should raise their hands. The results
              can be tallied on the board.
          (2) After the list has been read, go back to each prediction
              question and have students defend the position they took.

(3) Have students discuss whether they think the predictions will happen and then whether they think they should happen. This shifts the activity to future values consideration.

Preface each of the following questions with, "Who believes that . .

. . . schools will consist almost totally of teaching machines and students will learn by themselves at their own speed?"
. . . the life span of human beings will be well over 100 years?"
. . . children will be raised more strictly than they are now?"
. . . life on other planets will be found?"
. . . babies who are exact facsimiles of another human being will be produced artificially?"
. . . people will be able to communicate through E.S.P.?"
. . . people will be able to alter their personalities in specific ways by taking a drug?"
. . . people in cities will walk around wearing pollution-protection masks?"
. . . enclosed cities will be built in outer space?"
. . . enclosed cities will exist at the bottom of the ocean?"

C. General Objective: To develop the skills to examine values and beliefs

SPECIFIC OBJECTIVE: Learn to identify one's own values and beliefs as a base from which to predict whether these values will change the future.

10. Predicting Future Change[19]

when: one class period

what: Predictions Checklist (next page)

how: (1) Have students complete the checklist according to the instructions.

(2) Tally the results of the checklist markings on the board by a show of hands. Discuss those statements over which there seems to be strong disagreement.
(a) What are the major reasons for the disagreement?
(b) Can any pattern be discerned?
(c) Is change in our lives directly related to technology? Do your checkmarks suggest how you feel about change?

(3) Discuss students' predictions. What in our society today makes a strong case for this coming true in the future? Are most students' predictions looked on as good or bad changes?

The purpose of the checklist is to stimulate thought on the future, to categorize experiences and opinions, and to examine the validity of those opinions.

PREDICTIONS OF CHANGE BY YEAR 2001

Instructions: Put a check (√) beside those items you think will happen.
Put a plus (+) if you believe it will be a good change and a
minus (-) if you believe it will be a change for the worse.

√ ±

1. Because of a lower birthrate and medical advances, the majority of the population will be over 50.

2. Retirement will be advanced to 70 because more people are living longer.

3. Parents will be able to choose the sex of their baby.

4. All companies will be forced to provide daycare centers for pre-school children because both parents will work.

5. Private cars will be banned from city centers and public transportation will bring people to work from vast parking lots outside the city limits.

6. The school year will be lengthened so that there will be only one month of summer vacation and more subject hours will be required for graduation.

7. Students who are handicapped or unable to attend school for some reason will be able to watch the class and participate by means of TV.

8. Research will have discovered a material from which to make artificial organs that will not be rejected by the body.

9. There will be a war "somewhere" in the world still being fought by conventional weapons because the nuclear war is unthinkable.

10. (student prediction)

11. (student prediction)

11. <u>Future Colony</u>[20]

when: one class period

what: list of individuals requesting opportunity to colonize the orbiting space station factories

how: This is a contemporary problem in selecting participants for a future colony. This activity involves selecting appropriate people for a factory colony. Students must keep in mind that the people chosen will be making their homes on the orbiting space station and working in the factory. The space station will be their permanent home. A judicious choice of settlers is essential.

Orbiting solar-powered factories have been built. They will mine the moon for metal, silicon, gas, etc. The staff colony will live in normal gravity and will regulate length of days, climate, and seasons. A national selection committee has been established to determine what people will colonize the space station.

(1) Divide the class into groups. Each group will represent the national selection committee with the responsibility of choosing seven people from the list below. Students should take care with their choices because they will have to defend their choices later in class discussion.

INDIVIDUALS REQUESTING SELECTION FOR COLONIZING

1. 45-year-old gay white minister with a 5-year-old adopted child

2. 33-year-old stewardess suspected of smuggling drugs

3. 25-year-old Chicano cleaning woman looking for a better life

4. 41-year-old black sanitation worker who volunteers his weekends to work with special children

5. 49-year-old white male dentist who has been charged with child abuse

6. 54-year-old female white pathologist with a dependent retarded child

7. 48-year-old white male insurance salesman who has filed twice for bankruptcy

8. 37-year-old gay white telephone operator who is continuing her education in night school

9. 18-year-old man who packages items for a mail order business

10. 28-year-old black female computer programmer with epilepsy

11. 32-year-old white male race car driver sidelined by a heart attack

12. 39-year-old machine operator convicted of inciting unlawful labor strikes

13. 24-year-old white female elementary teacher who wants to devote her life to education

14. 43-year-old Asian female refugee secretary whose entire family perished in a civil war

15. 60-year-old white male county coroner, retired and seeking new challenges

(2) Have groups share their choices with the class by listing on the board.

(3) Prepare a class list: first, list each name that appeared on all group list selections. For example, if three individuals appeared on all group lists, then that leaves four positions open for debate. Have groups defend their choices.
(a) Are groups categorizing without realizing it?
(b) Do group lists try to equalize between men and women?
(c) Are they trying for an equalized race mixture, or is that of no concern?
(d) Did the individuals who were gay make any difference?
(e) What were some of the criteria the groups used to make their selection?

con't.

(4) Can the students answer this primary question: What is the purpose of this futures activity? Students should identify some of the following purposes:

- to categorize people and occupations (age, sex, race, occupation, etc.)
- to identify what they think is important
- to note that when they made their choices they also demonstrated their values, beliefs, and cultural biases

D. General Objective: To apply knowledge through active <u>participation</u>

SPECIFIC OBJECTIVE: Learn to participate in a group concerned with identifying items that represent values.

12. <u>Senior Time Capsule</u>

when: one week

what: durable, non-biodegradable container

how: The object is to prepare a container of items that would in some way describe us or be representative of us to someone about the year 2090.

(1) Discuss with students categories of items (not items themselves) that should be considered for inclusion in the time capsule. List suggestions on the board as they are volunteered by the students.

(2) Divide the students into groups and divide the categories among the groups. The groups must collect and bring in objects representative of their categories to be included in the time capsule. The groups must keep in mind that size is limited by the size of the container. (Expense may also be a problem--the items will need to be fairly inexpensive.)

(3) The school authorities will have to be consulted about an appropriate place to bury the capsule if it is to be buried on school property. A map will need to be prepared of the capsule's location. It would be nice to mark the location by planting a tree nearby or otherwise marking the location. The map should be stored in a safe place.

<u>Alternative:</u>

Have students suggest time capsule idea to local community groups. The students could prepare a formal presentation concerning the preparation of the time capsule and present this at a meeting of the community or civic groups. Students could take the initiative in preparing the time capsule and collecting the items to be placed inside.

13. New Harmony Revisited

  when: three class periods

  what: symbolic map of future location

  how: This activity is designed to encourage students to consider the
        problems of establishing a utopian futurist society (this society
        could be on earth, a space station, or distant planet or moon).
        What factors should be taken into consideration when establishing
        a futurist society? How do you survive in an alien environment?
        Students, having first considered the problems of survival in a
        future environment which may be "alien and inhospitable," are more
        likely to identify with contemporary problems which they face today.

        The purpose of this activity is to encourage students to speculate
        about the organization and goals that would achieve the "good life"
        in a future society. This activity should encourage students to
        look ahead, identify, classify, and project goals which may be
        useful as a standard to compare with their own. In a sense, we
        are asking students to walk in the shoes of a future society
        person with the hope that they will compare those shoes with the
        ones they now wear in their present society. If the students
        identify a concern for ecology, politics, economics, and other
        quality of life concerns for a future society, ought they not also
        be concerned as citizens in their present society?

  Instructions:

        You, the student, have been elected to lead a group of 500 people
        to begin a new social order in the future town of New Harmony II.
        Your New Harmony II society has become disenchanted with the pre-
        sent social, political, economic. and ecological conditions in
        its present society and is looking forward to designing a physi-
        cal environment and a social order that is more compatible with
        the members' concept of a good life. Therefore, the New Harmony II
        society has separated itself from others into an isolated environ-
        ment on earth, or a space station, or a distant planet or moon.
        You intend to design a society that is self-sufficient. You will
        take with you the "state of the art" in advanced technology. Among
        your new social order are people who are skilled in every phase of
        technology.

        Assuming for the moment that the technology is at a level to deal
        with the present needs and wants of the society, you must decide
        what the "good life" is and ought to be for the New Harmony II
        members and establish the goals necessary to reach that good life.

        The goals of the society should be stated in a short preamble. It
        is your job to write the preamble. In addition, suggest in out-
        line form the social, political, and economic structures or organ-
        ization that will achieve the goals mentioned in the preamble.

NEW HARMONY II

Preamble:

_____

_____

_____

_____

_____

_____

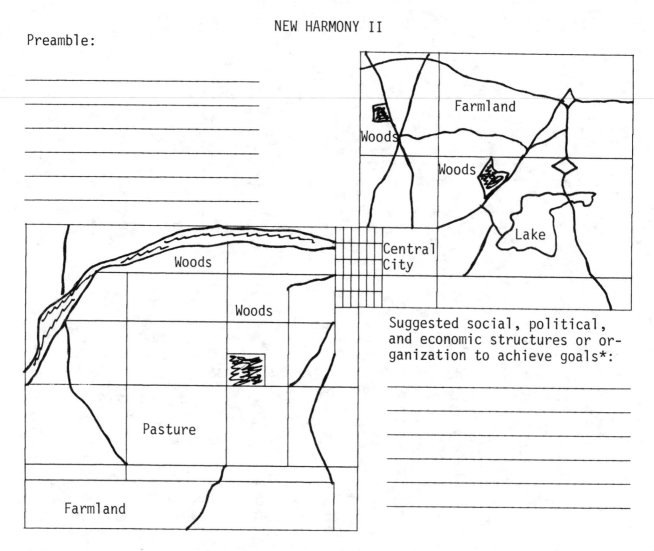

Suggested social, political,
and economic structures or organization to achieve goals*:

_____

_____

_____

_____

_____

_____

(1) Have students write individual preambles on the city map, keeping in mind
that they are dealing with a futuristic society.

(2) Divide the class into small groups and have each group develop a consensus
small group preamble and suggestions on how to achieve the goals set forth
in the preamble.

(3) Have each group present to the class its preamble and suggestions on how
the society will be structured or organized to accomplish the goals set in
the preamble. Have class reach a consensus on a class preamble.

(4) The class preamble can be used as a standard to compare with other preambles such as the Preamble to the Constitution, recalling of course that
the goals identified in the class preamble make up the class's vision of
the future.

* For example, what political system would further the goals (democracy, dictatorship, oligarchy, etc.), what economic system (capitalism, socialism,
communism, etc.), what social system (patriarchy, matriarchy, classless
society, etc.) would students choose for their New Harmony II?

CAREERS

A.   General Objective: To <u>gain knowledge</u> about the human condition which
                          includes past, present, and future

   SPECIFIC OBJECTIVE: Learn to identify duties, responsibilities, and rewards
                         of career choices.

   1.   Ask the Person Who Knows: Careers

        when: two class periods

        what: no materials necessary

        how: (1) Through class discussion select several occupations or
                   positions that carry a degree of responsibility or author-
                   ity, positions about which the class would wish to know
                   more.

               (2) Invite representatives of these occupations to speak to
                   the class about their duties, responsibilities, the re-
                   wards or possible drawbacks, and how that position influ-
                   ences their lives. Have students prepare questions
                   beforehand that they may want to ask the speaker.

               (3) May want to hold a "candid" class discussion on the occu-
                   pations after the speaker has gone.

               <u>Alternative:</u>
               Perhaps an even better way to find out about an occupation is
               to interview a person who is employed in that occupation at
               his place of work. Not only can the individual talk about
               his job but he can also show the student his working condi-
               tions, etc. Students could carry out the interview indi-
               vidually, or if more than one is interested in the occupation
               they could go as a group. Have interviewers report back to
               the class, offering a brief presentation on what they learned.
               Allow time for questions and class discussion.

   2.   Identifying Non-Traditional Jobs

        when: one class period

        what: no materials necessary

        how: (1) Have students identify persons who hold positions that a
                   few years ago were not open to them or not acceptable--
                   non-traditional jobs. For example:

                   female fire-fighter   female construction worker
                   male nurse   male librarian
                   female meter reader   male secretary
                   female semi-truck driver   female basketball coach
                   male dental technician   female sport trainer
                   female referee or umpire   male homemaker
                                                etc.

(2) Invite several of these persons to speak to the class about how they became interested in the job, how they started, the advantages and disadvantages of their position. How has their occupation affected their relationships with others? Have students prepare questions ahead of time that they may wish to ask the speaker.

SPECIFIC OBJECTIVE: Learn to analyze the wage structure of occupations and the values implied in such a wage structure.

3. Careers, Occupations, and Wages

when: one class period

what: list of occupations and salaries in 1932 and now

how: (1) Have students examine the list of occupations and note the wages paid in 1932 in comparison to the wages paid now.

OCCUPATIONS THEN AND NOW		
PUBLIC SERVANTS	1932	1980s
Mailman	$1,284	$21,500
Mayor (city of 30,000–50,000)	$2,317	$28,000
Policeman	$1,500	$17,270
PROFESSIONAL JOBS		
Airline Pilot	$8,000	$68,000
Doctor	$3,382	$98,000
Engineer	$2,520	$34,745
Lawyer	$4,218	$43,249
Priest (room, board, car)	$ 831	$ 5,100
Registered Nurse	$ 936	$15,500
OTHER JOBS (entry level)		
Bus Driver	$1,373	$16,000
Typist	$ 624	$11,915

(2) Have students answer the following questions:
(a) Examine the occupations and pay in 1932, then note the pay in the 1980s. Which occupation gained the most in wages and which gained the least over that period of time?
(b) By looking at this list, what would be suggested as the values of the culture that pays these salaries? In other words, what does the culture value? Can you identify a culture's values by the wages paid?
(c) Is there a relationship between years of training (college degrees) and wages paid?
(d) Suppose you had this list of comparative wages in the year 1932. What occupation might you have chosen knowing the comparison in wages between 1932 and the 1980s?

(3) Have students look at the list of wages paid for various
    occupations in the 1980s below.

WAGES 1980s STYLE	
PUBLIC SERVANTS	
University full professor	$43,000
School corporation superintendent	$52,000
Beginning teacher	$12,828
County prosecutor	$44,250
Circuit Court judge	$39,182
County Court judge	$34,307
Fireman (1st class)	$17,270
Garbage collector	$10,000
Librarian (county, MA degree)	$14,465
PROFESSIONAL JOBS	
Railroad engineer	$50,000
Minister	$30,000
Entry Level:	
Licensed mortician	$20,000
Accountant	$18,996
Social Worker	$14,581
Reporter	$11,960
OTHER JOBS (entry level)	
Kitchen helper (McDonald's)	$ 6,968
Gas station attendant	$ 6,968
Bank teller	$ 6,968
Telephone operator	$ 9,942
Stock boy and clerk	$10,088
Auto mechanic	$10,400
Beautician	$11,024
Union carpenter	$19,136
Truck driver	$19,469
Mill worker	$19,552

(4) Have students answer the following questions:
    (a) Of the list of careers above, in which category (pub-
        lic servants, professional jobs, and other jobs)
        would you most likely wish to seek a job?
    (b) Ten years from now, which of the above jobs would you
        wish to be qualified for? What training and degrees
        would you need to qualify for that job?
    (c) Suppose you had an unlimited opportunity to pursue
        training for a job, which of the above jobs would
        you find most attractive?

Alternative: Encourage students to list those occupations
which they would most like to investigate. Ask them to identify the entry pay level, then have them determine what the
pay would be five years later if they remained at the same
job. As a final thought, ask the students to think about
careers which might help them be eligible for jobs in all
three categories. If they thought in terms of preparing in
the three categories they would obviously have a greater
opportunity for employment.

B.   General Objective: To develop skills necessary to <u>process</u> information

SPECIFIC OBJECTIVE: Examine the concept of equal job opportunities through the values expressed in advertised jobs.

4.   <u>Job Hunting</u>[21]

when: three class periods

what: pictures of occupations and personal history card; classified ads

how: (1) Have students collect illustrations of different occupations (cut from magazines and newspapers) and bring them to class. Teacher may have to supplement the selection.
(2) Have students examine pictures and establish an approximate date when minorities (blacks, Mexicans, women) could have expected to be considered for the position. List occupations and dates on the board.
(3) Have students fill out the personal history card. Using the card as a reference, students should identify those occupations they could consider applying for when they graduate from high school.

PERSONAL HISTORY CARD

name _____   age ____ male ___ female ___

street address _____   height _____ weight _____

city   state   zip   area code/phone number

EDUCATION
 schools attended   graduation date   major
_____
_____

SPECIFIC SKILLS: _____
_____

PREVIOUS EXPERIENCE: _____
_____
_____

(4) Select at least ten help wanted ads from the classified section of the newspaper. Make sure the ads have restrictions such as: over 21, previous experience, specific skills. Restrictions can be added to existing ad if necessary.

(5) Using the personal history card, how many of these jobs would the students be eligible for?

(6) Looking at the classified section as a whole, what seems to be a promising occupation to train for? Do the students predict any trends developing in the future?

C. General Objective: To develop the skills to examine <u>values</u> and beliefs

SPECIFIC OBJECTIVE: Learn to examine values and how they relate to future careers.

5. <u>Identifying Interest In and Feelings About Careers</u>

when: one class period

what: occupations chart below

how: Have students complete the chart and then answer the questions that follow.

The following categories and list of occupations are merely suggestive of the items that could be included. Invite the students to consider other classifications and types of jobs, keeping in mind that the jobs the students may, in fact, hold ten years from now may not have yet been classified or named. This is merely to say that students may wish to pick categories rather than specific jobs because of the growth and change in technology.

NOTE: The occupations listed are not mutually exclusive. There may be occupations from two or more categories that fit together. Students are encouraged to add occupations to the list in the space provided.

!CAREERS!

What are your goals, your future career: _____

_____

Instructions: In the <u>left</u> hand column place a plus (+) next to the occupations you find most interesting and a minus (-) next to those you are least interested in. In the <u>right</u> hand columns, indicate your strength of feeling as to which type of work you enjoy by circling the appropriate number(1 = greatly enjoy, 2 = enjoy, 3 = neutral, 4 = dislike, 5 = strongly dislike).

Occupations that require "hands on" activity:

Artist	1	2	3	4	5
Carpenter	1	2	3	4	5
Farmer	1	2	3	4	5
Electrician	1	2	3	4	5
Plumber	1	2	3	4	5
Janitor	1	2	3	4	5
Barber	1	2	3	4	5

____	Tailor	1	2	3	4	5
____	Chef	1	2	3	4	5
____	Typist	1	2	3	4	5
____	Garage mechanic	1	2	3	4	5
____	Bus driver	1	2	3	4	5

Occupations in the service field:

____	Mayor (elected officials)	1	2	3	4	5
____	Fireman	1	2	3	4	5
____	Policeman	1	2	3	4	5
____	Mother	1	2	3	4	5
____	Social Worker	1	2	3	4	5
____	Food service worker	1	2	3	4	5
____	Nurse	1	2	3	4	5

Occupations in technology:

____	Computer programmer	1	2	3	4	5
____	Statistician	1	2	3	4	5
____	Computer salesman	1	2	3	4	5
____	X-ray technician	1	2	3	4	5
____	Production line technician	1	2	3	4	5
____	Bookkeeper	1	2	3	4	5

Professional and licensed occupations:

____	Banker	1	2	3	4	5
____	Architect	1	2	3	4	5
____	Clergyman	1	2	3	4	5
____	College professor	1	2	3	4	5
____	Teacher	1	2	3	4	5
____	Judge	1	2	3	4	5
____	Lawyer	1	2	3	4	5
____	Journalist	1	2	3	4	5
____	Doctor	1	2	3	4	5
____	Dentist	1	2	3	4	5

Questions:
(a) Are the choices marked in future career supported by the strength of feeling marked in enjoyment?
(b) Are there categories the student would wish to add to the careers rating form?
(c) Is it important to be consistent between occupational interests and enjoyment of the type of work?

6. Personal Interests and Career Collage

when: two class periods

what: large size grocery bags, magazines, and newspapers

how: This is a pre-careers activity to encourage students to picture and clarify their interests and future goals--sometimes their goals and interests are compatible and sometimes they are not.

(1) Have students cut large grocery bags so that each student has a large flat side on which to build a collage.

(2) Using pictures and words from magazines and newspapers,

have students construct a collage of the "things" they
are presently interested in doing and learning about and
"things" they want to do in the future--careers.

(3) When students have completed the collages, have each
student examine his/her own collage--the pictures of
things the student is interested in and the pictures of
the career or occupation the student would like to pursue
after graduation. Are the interests and proposed career
consistent? Will the career allow the student to continue to enjoy the interests presently held?

(4) Display collages. They should be a stimulant to discussing inconsistencies between the students' goals and the
students' interests and help clarify the relationship
between what students project as goals and what they
actually do or have as skills.

D.   General Objective: To apply knowledge through active <u>participation</u>

SPECIFIC OBJECTIVE: Be able to explain the uncertainty of the job market
and alternative means of support by participating in a game activity.

7.   <u>The Job Game</u>[22]

when: one class period

what: game board and materials (included)

how: This game can be played individually, by twos, or in small
groups with the members taking turns.

The purpose of the game is to alert students to the uncertainty of the job market and to the possibility of having to
maintain themselves when jobs may be hard to find. The game,
in part, is an examination of alternative means of support.

GAME DIRECTIONS:
This is the Job Game. You advance from First Job to Retirement by
flipping a coin, making the right decision, and following directions
on the game board or on cards that you may draw. When flipping a
coin, advance two spaces for heads, and one for tails. When directed
to choose one of the numbered cards, you must decide "Can You Collect"
before you draw the card, because what you are directed to do will
be different depending on a "yes" or "no" answer. If you get a Good
Times Card, you have what is on the card, but you may also lose the
card under certain conditions. When directed to go back a square,
<u>you do not follow any directions that may be on that square</u>.

Can You Collect? Cards

Good Times Cards

1	YES--Sorry, you're wrong. Lose one space. NO--That's right, but she gets well and you find another job right away.
2	YES--Wrong, you lose one turn. NO--Right, but you are able to find a good job right away.
3	Case is not too clear and when your case is not accepted, you appeal to a referee. Lose one turn while you await decision.
4	YES--You collect unemployment while you train for a new job. Because you were right, take a Good Times Card. NO--You have to take a low paying job, and lose a Good Times Card.
5	YES--Correct. Strike is not your fault, collect insurance for 3 weeks 'til strike is settled. NO-Since you weren't smart enough to file, kids don't get shoes.
6	YES--Sorry about that. This is one instance where you can't collect. NO--Right, every state has certain time limits to fulfill.
7	YES--U.I. was designed to help in cases like this. NO--For failing to collect, lose a Good Times Card.
8	YES--You collect, if you report for employment interviews. NO--Since you didn't try to collect, you can't pay your doctor bills.
9	YES--You can collect benefits depending on how much you are earning in your part-time job. NO--Since you didn't know enough to collect, go in debt.
10	YES--You didn't leave voluntarily and the boss can't show cause for firing. NO--Lose Good Times Card for not realizing your mistake.

Good Times Cards:

A SECOND CAR

A HOUSE

A NEW CAR

AN APARTMENT

A VACATION

MONEY FOR AN EVENING OUT

A NEW SUIT

A DAY AT THE RACE TRACK

The Job Game

Your wife takes a job. Draw a good times card.

A power plant is destroyed and your factory closed for 5 months while it is rebuilt. **CAN YOU COLLECT?** **7**

You work for a month on your first job and they lay you off with half the other help. **CAN YOU COLLECT?** **6**

You have been able to save some money. Draw a good times card.

Plant closes down for retooling. You are laid off for 4 weeks. **CAN YOU COLLECT?** **8**

You advance at the office. Draw a good times card.

DIRECTIONS: Advance by flipping a coin—2 spaces for head and 1 space for tail. If you fall on a numbered square **YOU MUST MAKE A DECISION BEFORE PICKING UP THAT CARD.** If the card directs you to another square **do not follow the directions on the new square** but wait for another toss. If you land on an unnumbered square pick up a GOOD TIMES CARD.

There can be 2 winners: one, the person who reaches retirement first; second, the person with the most GOOD TIMES CARDS.

NOTE: The answers given in this game may not necessarily apply to your state.

Strike in an industry that supplies yours. You are laid off temporarily. **CAN YOU COLLECT?** **5**

Better paying job. Draw a good times card.

When you lost your last job, you were able to find a part time job—but not enough to live on. **CAN YOU COLLECT?** **9**

You are laid off at 64 before you are ready to retire even though the union has an agreement you can stay on—and you want to work. **CAN YOU COLLECT?** **10**

YOU WIN!

Plant closes and moves to another location. You are unemployed. **CAN YOU COLLECT?** **4**

You have a chance to go to college. Advance four squares.

FIRST JOB

Your wife ill. You must quit your job. **CAN YOU COLLECT?** **1**

Job doesn't pay enough so you quit to look for another job. **CAN YOU COLLECT?** **2**

You get a raise so draw a good times card.

The boss doesn't like the way you are doing your job so you quit before he can fire you. **CAN YOU COLLECT?** **3**

SPECIFIC OBJECTIVE: Be able to show, through the use of a decision tree, possible alternative career objectives.

8. A Career-Decision Tree[23]

when: two class periods

what: sample tree and blank tree

how: The decision tree is a means of mapping out possible career objectives and graphically showing the crucial decisions that must be made along the way. The tree can be compared to a road map with a distant city being your destination or career objective. The other towns or cities you must go through to reach your destination represent the crucial decisions you must make to reach your career objective.

Below is a sample tree completed and a blank tree for students to plan on. Notice that the tree branches are major points of decision. At certain points it is possible to move horizontally; however, if a major career change is comtemplated after, say, 1991, considerable backtracking would be required. Whether the ultimate goal is worth this extra time is up to each individual.

Have students fill out their individual career-decision trees. The purpose is to have them realize that continuous planning is necessary to remain in control of one's future.

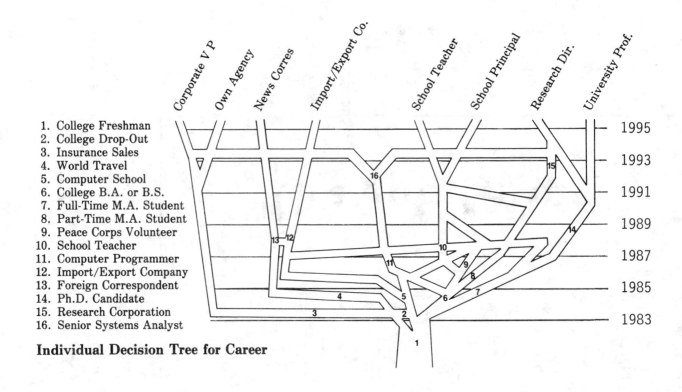

1. College Freshman
2. College Drop-Out
3. Insurance Sales
4. World Travel
5. Computer School
6. College B.A. or B.S.
7. Full-Time M.A. Student
8. Part-Time M.A. Student
9. Peace Corps Volunteer
10. School Teacher
11. Computer Programmer
12. Import/Export Company
13. Foreign Correspondent
14. Ph.D. Candidate
15. Research Corporation
16. Senior Systems Analyst

Individual Decision Tree for Career

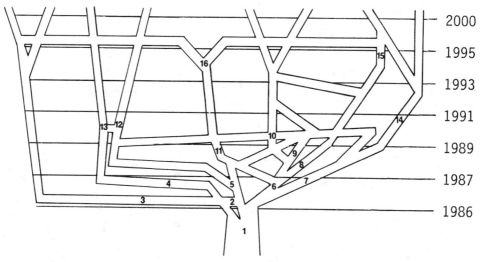

DO YOUR OWN DECISION TREE

for career, lifestyle, personal growth.
Make it your autobiography for the future.

    1.

    2.

    3.

    4.

    5.

    6.

    7.

    8.

    9.

   10.

   11.

   12.

   13.

   14.

   15.

   16.

Notes

[1] Barth, J. L. Advanced social studies education (Washington, DC: University Press of America, 1977), pp. 24-28.

[2] Barth, J. L. Methods of instruction in social studies education (Washington, DC: University Press of America, 1979), pp. 114-115.

[3] Ibid., pp. 110-113.

[4] Shermis, S. S., & Barth, J. L. Cultural foundations of modern American education (Lexington, MA: Ginn and Co., 1981), p. 28.

[5] This activity was first presented as a paper at the "Teaching About the Holocaust in Indiana" pre-convention, 1981 Indiana Council for the Social Studies clinic by Professor S. Samuel Shermis of Purdue University. It has been modified for publication in this text.

[6] Ibid.

[7] Ibid.

[8] This activity appears in the Election unit (Indiana Department of Public Instruction), p. 78, and has been modified for publication in this text.

[9] Ibid., p. 47.

[10] Ibid.

[11] This game was developed by Rod Clemmons, Hayfield Secondary School, Fairfax County, Virginia, and has been revised for publication in this text.

[12] This activity was originally developed in 1980 for "Questions Social Studies Students Ask," a Division of Innovative Education ESPA Title IV-C Research Project of the North Montgomery School Corporation, Linden, Indiana. In particular the author wishes to recognize the contribution of James Spencer and David Horney in the development of this project. The activity has been revised for publication in this book.

[13] Ibid.

[14] Ibid.

[15] Ibid.

[16] Dilling, D. R. Studies in the spirit of seventy-six (Indiana Department of Public Instruction, 1976), p. 67. This activity has been modified for publication in this text.

[17] Ibid., p. 74.

[18] Ibid.

[19]This activity was originally published in Elementary and junior high/middle school social studies curriculum activities and materials (2nd ed.) by J. L. Barth (Washington, DC: University Press of America, 1983), p. 287. It has been revised for publication in this text.

[20]Ibid., p. 139.

[21]Ibid., p. 275.

[22]"The Job Game" was developed as part of a multimedia kit for "Instructional Materials for Teaching About Unemployment Insurance," a federally funded project co-directed by Professor S. Samuel Shermis and the author in 1970.

[23]Studies in the spirit of seventy-six, pp. 78-80. This activity has been modified for publication in this text.

INTEREST FORM

You have just completed the Chapter Senior Problems, Values/Issues, Futures, and Careers. In an effort to have you identify activities and materials that seem most promising to you in this subject area, please fill out the following interest form.

Instructions:

Identify two activities from this chapter. Name the activities and briefly describe why these particular activities are of interest to you.

ACTIVITY 1

ACTIVITY 2

NOTES

NOTES